MASTER TRAINER HANDBOOK*

*Previously titled: *Creative Training Techniques Handbook*

Tips, Tactics, and How-Tos for Delivering Effective Instructor-Led, Participant-Centered Training

Bob Pike, CPLP Fellow, CSP, CPAE Speaker Hall of Fame

HRD Press, Inc. • Amherst • Massachusetts

Copyright © 1989, 1994, 2003, 2015 by Bob Pike

All rights reserved. No part of this publication may be reproduced, stored in a retrieval system, or transmitted, in any form or by any means, electronic, mechanical, photocopying, recording, or otherwise, without the prior written permission of the publisher. Printed in the United States of America. Fourth Edition, 2015.

Published by: HRD Press, Inc.
                22 Amherst Road
                Amherst, MA 01002
                413-253-3488
                800-822-2801 (U.S. and Canada)
                413-253-3490 (fax)
                www.hrdpress.com

ISBN 978-1-61014-402-5

Editorial services by Sally Farnham
Production services by Jean Miller
Cover design by Eileen Klockars

With special thanks to:
Andrea Sisco Pike, Sam MacLeod, and Alan Pranke

Publisher's Note: The first three editions of this handbook used the words "Creative Training Techniques™" in the title. In 2013, Bob sold the assets of his company, The Bob Pike Group, which included the "Creative Training Techniques™", but not any of Bob's books. Therefore, this book, which is a revision of his previous works, carries a new title and Bob now refers to his process as Instructor-Led, Participant-Centered (ILPC).

Master Trainer Handbook

For more than 45 years, Bob Pike and his colleagues have been developing and presenting seminars, workshops, and training programs throughout the world.

Year after year, trainers, consultants, managers, and senior executives have asked:

- "How can we get more out of our training efforts?"
- "Our training is routine—how can we make it exciting?"
- "Results! Help us get the results we need—and fast!"

Bob Pike's Master Class in Instructor-led, Participant-centered Training is a practical, results-guaranteed solution to your training needs. More than 125,000 persons on five continents have attended previous versions of this intensive, results-producing two-day workshop.

Consulting Services

Bob Pike is available for individual consulting, design, and training engagements as well as keynotes. On average, applying our design process to current training materials can reduce delivery time by 25 to 30 percent, while increasing retention and application. You can learn more at www.cttnewsletters.com.

Supplements to this book including free resources, templates, and case studies can be found at www.cttnewsletters.com.

Table of Contents

Foreword	xi
Preface	xiii
Acknowledgments	xv
Chapter 1: Creative Genesis	1
Chapter 2: Presentation Preparation	15
Chapter 3: Learner Motivation	37
Chapter 4: Visual Aids	55
Chapter 5: Group Involvement	81
Chapter 6: Creative Materials	107
Chapter 7: Creating Effective Resource Materials	123
Chapter 8: Presentation Techniques	139
Chapter 9: Customizing Training	163
Chapter 10: Instrumented Learning	177
Chapter 11: Transforming Existing Training Programs	183
Chapter 12: Participant-Centered Techniques for Technical Training	195
Chapter 13: Participant-Centered Techniques for Computer Training	209
Chapter 14: The Myths and Methods of eLearning	217
Chapter 15: Classroom Management Techniques	225
Chapter 16: Closing the Circle	231
Appendix 1	237
Appendix 2	241
Appendix 3	245
Index	249

Foreword

by Elliott Masie, founder of The Masie Center;
author of *The Computer Trainer's Handbook*

Bob Pike has always been on the cutting edge of practical approaches to learning and training. This book continues that leadership, focusing our attention on the need to have complete processes for building and delivering creative training that will increase the productivity of our organizations.

While the book contains many research references, what you'll really find is the nuts and bolts, practical processes and techniques that can help to ensure that you are delivering results to your organization, not simply events.

Too many training organizations today are still emphasizing activities. By applying what you'll find in this fourth edition of *Master Trainer Handbook,* you will be well on your way to focusing on results.

The world of eLearning is a combination of technology and methodology. The technology will get ever better and more robust, month by month. But, the methodology side of the equation is in the hands of working training and learning professionals. This book is designed to give you methodologies that apply directly to the classroom, and at the same time can be effectively adapted to eLearning situations as well.

A couple of years ago, *Training Magazine* conducted a survey of its readers. Interestingly enough, the second edition of this book came up third among the books readers wanted on their book shelves (only Covey's *Seven Habits* and ASTD's *Training and Development Handbook* ranked higher). And when asked who they would like a direct phone line to or help on their training problems, Bob ranked third (only their own CEO and Tom Peters ranked higher).

Bob's interest has always gone beyond training for the sake of training. He has always looked at running the training function as a business, focused on getting results for clients—and that's the approach that you'll see here.

Bob has been a frequent presenter at many of the computer, e-Learning, and LEARN conferences that I've hosted, and the ideas he has shared have always been one of the conference highlights. People leave feeling there are things they can do immediately to make a difference in their training. You will gain the same sense from this book as you read each chapter.

One suggestion—read this book with highlighter, pen, and paper in hand. As you read, make your own list of action ideas and highlight those things in the book that have immediate application for you. I think you'll find that this book makes your top 10 list of books you need at your fingertips as a trainer—and as a performance consultant.

Preface

by Philip Jones, Vice president of Lakewood Media Group,
publishers of *Training Magazine*

A participant in one of Bob Pike's Master Class in Instructor-led, Participant-centered Training workshops once asked on a post-workshop card, "Can you please make some clones of this guy?" His request wasn't unusual—and it's one reason why this book was probably inevitable.

For over four decades, Pike has been one of the most popular and sought-after speakers on the HRD circuit. Bob's Instructor-Led, Participant-Centered methodology (ILPC), a remarkable system of ideas, techniques, strategies, tactics, and tips for anyone who wants to train or give presentations with maximum effectiveness, is why. This book is an expanded and revised fourth edition of the handbook Pike developed for Bob's Master Class participants. It is intended both for ILPC graduates and for those who have never heard of Pike or his system. It recreates the ILPC process in a way that is stimulating, easy to understand, and so practical you will start putting some of Pike's ideas to work *tomorrow*. That's almost guaranteed.

To understand ILPC you need to understand a few things about Bob Pike. After an achievement-filled adolescence followed by a Congressional appointment to the United States Naval Academy, Pike did a surprising about-face and entered the Moody Bible Institute in Chicago. His goal was to be a preacher. Later, after being pastor at a small evangelical church and discovering that preaching couldn't pay the rent, Pike wandered into training—first, as a salesman and trainer for a Denver-based training company and, eventually, as one of the company's top marketing executives, product developers, and presenters.

Over the next decade, Bob Pike's "style" began to take shape. That style combined Pike's instinctive ability to inspire and motivate people (not surprising from a preacher turned salesman), an increasingly sophisticated grasp of adult-learning theories and techniques, and, maybe most important, a deep belief in the inherent abilities of people to control their own destinies and development—in other words, their essential "goodness," a term I don't think Pike would object to. By 1980, when Pike formed his own business, he was on his way to being a "master" trainer. His training activities since then have spanned the HRD gamut, but at the core of Pike's special appeal was what he called ILPC processes. By 1987 after years of presentations before scores of groups, ILPC became a bona fide phenomenon—thanks partly to Pike's indefatigable energy (a former marathon runner, Pike is still on the road giving presentations over one hundred days a year) and mostly to the special appeal of his message.

Bob's ILPC process aims to create a comprehensive conceptual and practical framework for generating learning results through participant discovery and involvement.

It gives trainers the power to unleash the inherent learning potential of adults. By making learning enjoyable, it encourages participants to keep learning long after the training session. By all accounts, it succeeds. With ILPC, training becomes more productive, more satisfying, more fun. Many of the elements of ILPC aren't necessarily original or unique, but few (if any) HRD professionals have Pike's ability to synthesize so many ideas into such an easy-to-follow, common-sensical and, at the same time, insightful set of training tools. Pike dips effortlessly into philosophy, psychology, technology, and other weighty areas to explore the elements of adult-learner perception, motivation, and retention. At the same time, he discusses such seemingly simple topics as seating arrangements, flip charts, overhead transparencies, magic markers, and so on. And, as he shuttles back and forth between concept and practice, the ILPC "process" begins to take shape. Pike includes plenty of techniques to keep the process fresh in your mind and ready when you need it. Thanks to ILPC, no one we can think of, in a field crowded with rivals, has been as successful as Bob Pike in helping people become effective trainers.

How successful? Over 125,000 people internationally have attended a ILPC seminar as of this writing, and hundreds of companies have sponsored ILPC seminars. Walt Disney World, Citibank, IBM, AT&T, Shell, American Express, and others have incorporated Pike's ideas and techniques into their in-house train-the-trainer programs. More than 330,000 copies of this book were sold in the first three editions—making the book you hold in your hands the best-selling train-the-trainer book ever published. *Bob Pike's Master Trainer Newsletter*—a short monthly roundup of training tips, tactics, and ideas founded and edited by Pike, attracted 6,000 subscribers in its first year alone. After 23 years it is still the most widely read newsletter in the field. And when Pike appears before groups of trainers at conferences and professional events, it's virtually always standing room only.

Later in this book, you'll come across this passage: "Our purpose as trainers is not primarily to counsel, interpret, instruct, or in any way lead people to believe that we are to supply the answers to their questions. Instead, we should let the seminar, the instruments, the projects, the case studies, and other materials serve as resources that the participants can draw on to solve their problems and develop appropriate plans of action. The approach I recommend limits lecture and maximizes discovery and participation. Sometimes, it may not seem as if you're needed, but you are—often in ways the participants don't perceive. Ideally, you're the best kind of teacher—a facilitator of insight, change, and growth who teaches that answers come from within. Your personal attitudes and your role modeling will set the tone for your participants. And your seriousness of purpose, your personal planning, and your adherence to the guidelines you establish, along with your interest and enthusiasm for both the content and the participants, will facilitate change and learning for your participants."

Such an approach requires—both for you as a trainer and presenter and for participants—some adjustments from the old teacher-centered way of doing things. Bob Pike's special gift is showing you how to make those adjustments easily and effectively.

Acknowledgments

When I wrote the first edition of this book, I never envisioned a fourth edition. So much has changed in the training and performance field—and yet so much has remained the same. As of the end of 2014, more than 125,000 trainers have been through the Bob Pike Group's two-day ™ seminar.

Although I am no longer a part of the Bob Pike Group (BPG), I must acknowledge the BPG trainers/consultants who continue to do an outstanding job of delivering hundreds of days of public seminars, as well as in-house seminars and consulting. Lynn Solem, one of my original trainers and an inspiration, passed away in 1999 of a brain tumor. We still miss her. Her memory continues to set a high standard for us all. Doug McCallum continues to set a high standard for excellence as the last of my three original trainers. Becky Pike Pluth (my daughter and now CEO of the Bob Pike Group), Rich Meiss, and Priscilla Shumway who have all been with me for fifteen years and longer set wonderful examples for all the other BPG trainers and their international licensees. They have also applied their talents and skills to help increase BPG's ability to meet a wide variety of training and performance challenges that their clients face.

Additional acknowledgments should go to:

- Dave Arch who as senior vice president, along with Sue Ensz, helped enormously in applying our processes to Web-based training. The chapter on eLearning is based largely on their work.

- The support staff at Resources for Organizations, Inc. (ROI), the Bob Pike Group, especially Sandi Dufault who has provided me with more handouts and PowerPoints since joining BPG more than 25 years ago.

- The staff of HRD Press, especially Sam MacCleod, vice president, and Eileen Klockars, art director.

I would be remiss if I did not acknowledge Audrey Roholt, who worked with me for over fifteen years and who passed away in 2014. She was a trusted colleague and friend who did much to advance the organization. There have been a number of true friends who have been rock solid supporters personally and professionally over the years: Elizabeth and Jim Craig, Kate and Jack Larsen, Rich and Barbara Meiss, Peter Jordon, Jim and Naomi Rhode, and most especially Steve Miller. Thank you.

My daughter Rebecca completed her Masters in Adult Learning in 2002. We now have a blended family of twelve adult children. She is the one child who has captured the vision of what training is and can be. She started using our techniques in high school to enhance her learning and later as a classroom teacher. She served as a training consultant to several organizations and worked in training and development for various Target Corporation divisions before joining BPG as a consultant. She then served five years as VP of Training before buying BPG in 2013 and now serves as

CEO. She challenges me constantly to remember what I know and use what I've learned.

And finally my wife, Andrea Sisco Pike: She spent hours and hours helping clean up the scanning from previous editions so I could work on this fourth edition. She has traveled with me as I've worked with clients in Singapore, Malaysia, Australia, Korea, and South America. She is the cultural expert. I value her more than I can say.

Chapter 1:
Creative Genesis

The Origin and Foundation of Instructor-Led, Participant-Centered Process

We have a real problem today. It has been a problem for decades. Our children have been told to learn—but have not been taught how to learn. And much of our education system id focused on learning in order to pass, rather than learning for living. For years I've asked participants in my seminars if they would accept this challenge. We all put our degrees on the table. We each receive a test personalized for us that tests the knowledge we should have because we possess those degrees. If we pass with just 70 percent, we get to keep them. If we fail we lose them. How many will accept the challenge? Only a few of the thousands of participants have been willing to accept the challenge. Even I would not accept this challenge. And I love learning. But much of my education was study hard, take the exam, breathe a sigh of relief—and move on.

But today we live in the information age. In the 1960s, Buckminster Fuller first verbalized the "knowledge doubling" theory. Basically, for several thousand years, knowledge doubled about every 100 years. In the 1960s, Buckminster Fuller estimated that it was every 25 years. Today, Google estimates that depending on what type of knowledge you are talking about, it doubles every 18 to 24 months. The learning is never going to stop.

But participants come to our classrooms with a prior education experience that was not positive and with doubts about their ability to learn. They wonder whether they are going to made to look or feel stupid, whether they will be able to contribute, whether the course material will have any practical value—and this is how they start. As trainers we are behind before we start.

And if we are still using lecture and death by PowerPoint as our principal delivery methods, we are even worse off. I've never seen a participant write on an evaluation form: I wish there was more lecture.

Let me ask you a question: Would you like to be able to:

- listen better?
- read better?
- think better?
- remember better? Or
- learn better?

If you answered, "learn better," you've made an excellent choice. Because if you know how to learn better, you've automatically improved in all of the other areas. This book will help you teach and train more effectively so that you create an amazing environment that helps your participants learn faster, better, and easier. At the same time, you'll gain tools that will help you become a better learner, and if you have children or grandchildren, help them to do the same thing!

The tools, techniques, and strategies in this book are supported by research, but they do not come from research. Rather, throughout my 45-plus–year training career, I would try things. If they seemed to work, I kept using them. If they did not, I stopped. And along the way, I discovered why the ideas worked. Sometimes I discovered it through my own personal reading. I am an informative learner. I love reading. Even more often it was because someone in my class would say, "You make great use of the 'Zeigarnik Effect.'" In the first 10 years of my training career, I had literally hundreds of psychologists come through my training, and many of them added some additional insight into why what I was doing during the training was so effective. I would thank each of them and then go to the university library (yes, today I could Google it, but that was then and this is now!) and look it up in the psychological abstracts. And then, going into the future, I would reference to people in my Train-the-Trainer programs why the various techniques worked.

So from Hermann Ebbinghaus, I got his forgetting curve and was able to show why reviewing key content six times with interval reinforcement was needed to move key learnings from short-term memory to long-term memory.

From Harry Lorayne and Jerry Lucas (authors of the still in print *The Memory Book*) and a variety of other memory experts, I got the seven ways to remember anything, and from that came the concept of windowpaning.

From Steven Halpern, I first learned about the importance of music in enhancing learning. After meeting him at a conference and sitting in on some of his seminars, I got his book, *Tuning the Human Instrument*. His 25-plus years of research at the time helped me enhance my participant's learning environment tremendously. Later, both he and Daniel Kobialka would actually present at our annual conference. It was an honor.

What has been true for me is that I care about research if it helps me to improve my results as I design and deliver a variety of learning experiences. Throughout this book, you'll find research factoids, and in one of the appendices, you'll find my top-20 books on why my instructor-led, participant-centered approach works.

My techniques are instructor-led, participant-centered training concepts. Training, as much as possible, should be a do-it-yourself project for the participants involved. But I didn't realize that when I began my career in 1969 selling and delivering sales-training and management-development programs. I was, if I may say so, an effective presenter. Twice a week, I would conduct seminars, and I always received among the highest ratings of any of the presenters, even those with significantly more experience. At just 22, I felt I had arrived as a trainer; in retrospect, I see that I was essentially an effective presenter or speaker. When you're the only one who knows anything about a particular subject and you're giving presentations that last a couple of hours or even a whole day, being an effective presenter is important. But it doesn't necessarily mean you know how to deliver training.

The purpose of any training program is to deliver results. People must be more effective after the training than they were before. What do they now know that they didn't before? What can they now do that they couldn't do before? How have their feelings and attitudes changed and/or improved as a result of the training? If change hasn't taken place that benefits the individual and the organization, I'm not really sure that training has been delivered.

Three years after my career began, I had developed a variety of training programs for internal use that ranged in length from two hours to three weeks. I learned to break people into groups and to give them hands-on opportunities to apply the content being covered. Yet I continued to rely on a lecture format.

That changed in 1973 when I traveled to Minneapolis to evaluate a seminar I was considering adding to my business. Called Adventures in Attitudes, it was a 30-hour course in human relations, communications, problem solving, interpersonal skills, and self-management. The first day, 30 of us gathered in a room and were seated in groups of five. The instructor made a few brief introductory remarks and then passed out written materials for each group to discuss. After each group summarized its discussions, we moved on to the next activity. When it was time for a lecture, the instructor would play an audiotape. By noon, I was still waiting for him to say something so I could evaluate the quality of the program. I was still waiting at the end of the first day.

The second day continued in much the same vein. I kept waiting. I finally decided that, if the time and money I had invested were going to be worth something, it was going to be because of me. I wasn't going to get it from the instructor.

Finally, on the third day, it hit me like a ton of bricks: I realized I could recall almost all our discussions and activities because I was involved. I had made some significant discoveries and decisions—and I had truly learned—because I had truly participated.

I consider that experience to be my first, and most significant, contact with training that is based on discovery, participation, and involvement. I returned to Denver, and, in the last four months of 1973, I did 10 percent of the company's volume. In 1974, I moved from Denver to Minneapolis and became vice president of Personal Dynamics. Over the next six years, enrollments in the Adventures in Attitudes program grew from 4,000 per year to over 80,000 per year! Today, over 40 years later, I have clients that continue to use the program to make a difference in their organizations.

In 1980, I decided to go out on my own. I started by developing a course on team building and conflict management, and I found the principles of learner-discovery, participation, and involvement worked there. Next, I designed and delivered a program on problem solving and decision making, and the techniques based on those principles worked there, too.

In 1981, I conducted a three-hour seminar on the techniques themselves for a local chapter of the American Society for Training and Development (ASTD). I reasoned that, if I was designing do-it-yourself training, trainers I worked with should also be applying the principles as a do-it-yourself project. That's what the seminar was all about, and it was an unqualified success.

I presented these ideas to a national audience for the first time in 1982 at the ASTD national conference. Three hundred people crowded into a room designed for 160, and more than 100 others were turned away. At every ASTD conference since then, in more than 100 ASTD (now ATD, the Association for Talent Development) chapters, at more than four dozen ASTD regional conferences, a host of international conferences on five continents, at every conference *Training* magazine has sponsored since 1980, I've presented the concept, and the response has been overwhelmingly positive. Furthermore, the concept seems to be global: audiences representing more than 50 countries have been excited about the ideas when I've presented them at conferences in Europe, Japan, Australia, Korea, Malaysia, Indonesia, Singapore, China, Egypt, South Africa, South America, and the Middle East.

For almost 20 years, we've been working with school systems like Cypress-Fairbanks outside of Houston, Texas, and Los Angeles Unified School System in Los Angeles, California, to empower classroom teachers and staff to apply the IL-PC processes in the classroom as well as in staff development. The results have been significant and measurable. You will find some of the results of the research that has been done in Appendix 3 of this book.

As soon as people learned about my IL-PC approach to learning (remember, this is the mid-1970s), they asked where they could get more information on the subject, but I didn't know where to direct them. I had read and researched, but the most I could find were snippets here and there. So I wrote a manual on the subject that has formed the foundation for this book, which is a greatly revised and expanded version. Since 1981, over 125,000 trainers and educators have been through a one-day or longer version of learning about my IL-PC process. I hope that, by the time you finish this book, my Instructor-Led, Participant-Centered approach will seem as eminently practical and applicable to you as they have proved to be for me.

What Is Bob Pike's Instructor-Led, Participant-Centered Process (IL-PC)?

Let's start by identifying what it is not. It is not a miscellaneous collection of tips and techniques. Rather, it is a system that combines an understanding of how people learn best with processes that accelerate learning, retention, and application. It is a system that emphasizes getting results that count in the real world. It is also a system that is dynamic. While the foundation principles remain the same, we constantly incorporate new ideas based on the latest research to continue to make what we do effective as well as efficient. Finally, it is a system that most often is instructor led, but remains participant centered. The focus is always on what will help people learn best.

Some Foundation Principles

A lot of different threads run through my techniques. I've devised what I call "Pike's Laws of Adult Learning." These, along with an aphorism from Confucius, are the foundation principles underlying my techniques and this book.

Law 1. Adults are babies with big bodies. Recall the kinds of learning activities we did as small children. In kindergarten, we colored, drew, played games, modeled with clay, finger painted, etc.—all hands-on activities. Children with very little experience learn through experience.

When we reached first, second, and third grades, we lined up in rows and we were talked at. Rarely were we encouraged, or even permitted, to be involved in the learning process. The more experience we had, the less that experience was used. As adults, we bring a lot of experience to our training programs. We want to acknowledge, honor, and celebrate that experience. If, as children with very little experience, we could discover and learn, how much more as adults can we discover and learn.

Law 2. People don't argue with their own data. If I say something is true, you might say to yourself, "He's got to believe it; he's teaching it." But if you say it, for you it's true. For example, through research we might identify 15 characteristics of an effective leader. But rather than presenting them, I might choose to have small groups discuss the most effective leaders they've ever known and identify the characteristics that made those leaders effective. Normally, the

groups will come up with 80 percent of the characteristics. It's easy for the instructor to fill in the other 20 percent. In addition, I find the group much more willing to accept my suggestions for that remaining 20 percent than if I try to present all of them.

That's why I also have participants compile action idea lists in my seminars. I ask participants to look for ideas, concepts, and techniques for which they see an immediate use back on their jobs. From time to time, I'll ask volunteers to share the ideas they've picked up. It reinforces the value of the training and demonstrates, again, that people don't argue with their own data. Whether it's a technical course, management course, sales course, math, or English—the concept works. People look for the things they can use in their everyday lives.

Law 3. Learning is directly proportional to the amount of fun you have. Now I'm not necessarily referring to jokes or pointless games or entertainment. I'm referring to the sheer joy of learning that can come from involvement and participation—from realizing that you can use your own energy to learn and enjoy learning because you're gaining information, tools, techniques, etc., that can benefit you. These acquisitions are going to help you do your job and live your life faster, better, easier, and they're going to help you solve problems.

We live in the age of entertainment. When I was growing up in Chicago in the early 1950s, there were only a couple of television channels, both of them black and white. People watched one channel all evening long because there were no other options. Today it's different. Many of us have cable television or satellite, along with remote control units. We turn on the TV and say, "You've got six seconds to grab my attention, or I'm gone." We then flip through over 100 channels, look at each other, and say, "There's nothing on." Years ago, we happily watched one channel all night long, but today there's nothing on! We have the same attitude toward on-demand movies; we look through hundreds of titles, and declare, "There's nothing good available." And if we do end up paying to view a movie, we will quickly turn it off if it turns out to be not worth watching.

Few of us have the entertainment skills of Jerry Seinfeld, Jimmy Fallon, Jimmy Kimmel, or Tina Fey. Few of us are able to keep the riveted attention of an audience for hours. Fortunately, we don't have to. We can use the energy, involvement, and participation of our audience to put into their personal learning experiences the excitement they vicariously get from some of their entertainment activities.

Humor itself, the kind that produces genuine, heartfelt laughter, can enhance the learning that takes place. One only has to read Norman Cousins's *Anatomy of an Illness* to realize that humor can aid enormously in reducing stress and anxiety, allowing people to relax and be more open to the learning process. That kind of humor should make a point and not simply provide amusement. Used judiciously, it should enhance the learning process and enable participants to derive greater benefit.

Law 4. Learning has not taken place until behavior has changed. In training, it's not what you know but what you do with what you know that counts. That's why skill practice is so important in our training sessions; if we want people to do things differently, we must provide them with many opportunities to be comfortable accepting new ideas in a nonthreatening environment. It's one thing to know something intellectually; it's quite another to have the emotional conviction that comes from personal experience.

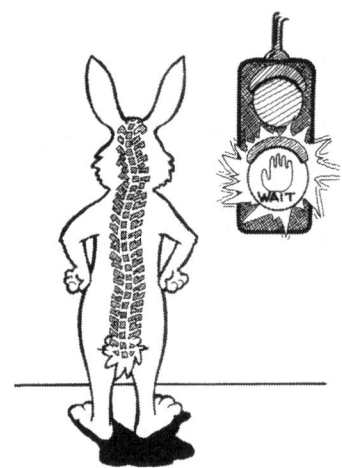

C. S. Lewis, the English philosopher, said, "A man with an experience is never at the mercy of a man with an argument." Today, he probably would have said "person," but his point would be the same: Give people success experiences in using our information and techniques in whatever learning environment we have available so that we increase the likelihood of on-the-job application.

Law 5. Fu Yu, Wu Yu, Wzu Tu Yu. Roughly translated this means: Momma's having it or Papa's having it ain't like baby having it. If I can do something, so what?

That's like Momma's having it. The fact that you, as one of my participants, can do something, so what? That's like Papa's having it. It's when you can pass on what you've learned to someone else that I, as a trainer, know I've really done my job.

This law may seem silly, but in my seminars and in this book, I am using that silliness to make a serious point: It does not matter what I can do or what I can teach you to do. Ultimately what matters is what I can teach you to teach others to do. This is one confirmation of your competence—when you can pass on what you know to someone else.

In his book, *The Empathic Communicator*, William Howell identifies various levels of competence. They are stages we all go through in the learning process. Howell identifies four fundamental stages, and I'd like to add a fifth.

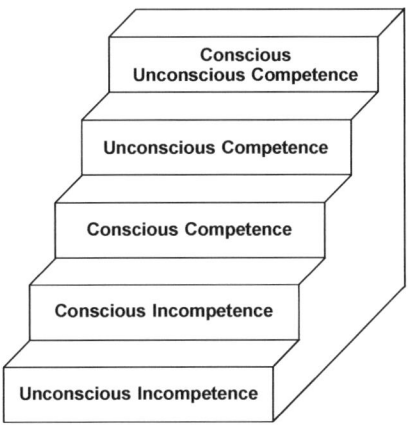

Howell's model starts at the bottom of a stairway with Level 1 Unconscious Incompetence: We're not competent, but we don't know it. Most of us, until the age of 16 or so, were unconsciously incompetent in terms of our ability to drive a car. We thought it would be a breeze to drive because our parents did it so effortlessly. How wrong we were! I'll never forget my first time behind the wheel. I put the key in the ignition, depressed the clutch, gave the car some gas, put the car in reverse, and let up on the clutch. The car shuddered to a halt. In an instant, I moved to Level 2—Conscious Incompetence. I was incompetent, and now I knew it.

After a lot of practice, I arrived at Level 3—Conscious Competence. I now could drive the car, but I was always tense about my abilities—or lack of them. It was difficult to relax. Finally I arrived at Level 4—Unconscious Competence. I no longer had to think about everything that driving a car involved because the act had become automatic.

The level I'd like to add is, Level 5—Conscious Unconscious Competence. Not only are we competent and can run on autopilot, so to speak, but we also can verbalize to others the how-to's of how we're able to do what we do. Many of us can arrive quite readily at Level 4, but it's far more difficult to reach Level 5. For example, I seem to have the knack of using natural humor in my presentations. I don't tell jokes, but the real-life illustrations I use and the way I "play" off participant comments bring laughter. I haven't, however, arrived at the point where I can explain that part of what I do to someone else. I'm still at Level 4 in this department.

In some of our training, Level 4 may be just fine. That is, enabling people to transfer what they know to someone else without our continually needing to be the focal point of the learning process is certain to be one training target in the future. Considerable training (and retraining) will be needed, but there won't be enough "professionals" to do it. So creating awareness of Level 5 and allowing some practice at reaching that level in class will be crucial.

According to students of mine in China, a protégé of Confucius back in 451 B.C. made a sage observation that still applies today: "What I hear, I forget; what I see, I remember; but what I *do* (emphasis mine) I understand." And isn't that the purpose of training? Not simply to have participants hear nor even necessarily to remember but to apply, to do—and to do with understanding. Change based upon action and understanding invariably is change for the better.

– Protégé of Confucius, 451 B.C.

So much for "Pike's Laws of Adult Learning." There are also several other premises that the Instructor-Led, Participant-Centered process is based on:

1. Training is a process, not an event. It begins long before participants either gather (or sign on) for training and continues until we see the knowledge, skills, and attitudes being applied in their everyday lives. This means that we start creating a climate where learning can take place. We first start identifying needs and gaining manager buy-in for the training that will be developed and implemented. It continues by creating participant-centered opportunities for learning to take place. It includes post-training strategies for ensuring that participants have the opportunity and support to practice the skills and apply the knowledge in their real-world settings.

2. The purpose of training is to deliver results. The primary reason for making training available is that we want to improve performance. Why do we want to improve performance? We believe that improving performance will help move the organization from where it is to where it wants to be. However, lack of performance does not always indicate that there is a need for training. Why? Because of premise number three.

3. When performance is the question, training is not always the answer! It should actually be the sixth answer! There are at least five areas to consider before looking at training as the solution. This is best illustrated by looking at my Performance Solutions Cube. It has three sides to it.

Step 2: Determine level of organization (WHO)

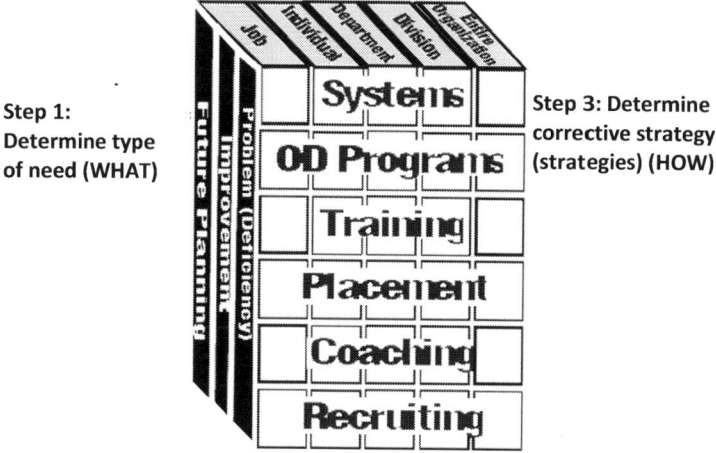

Bob Pike's Performance Solution Cube

The first side, **Step 1: Determine the type of need (WHAT),** identifies three possible reasons we may need to examine performance:

1. Problem or deficiency: There is a gap between low and high performers. What are high performers doing that low performers are not? What are low performers doing that high performers are not?

2. Opportunity for improvement: Things are fine, but there is always an opportunity to move everyone to the next level. For example, at The Bob Pike Group, all of our trainers and consultants average well above 4.7 on a 5.0 scale. Yet each of us is constantly looking for ways to be just a bit better in the work that we do.

3. Future planning: A new product is being released, a new plant is coming on line, new government regulations are taking effect—each of these might indicate a need for training before the fact so that there is no slowdown in performance when the changes take place.

The second side contains **Step 2—Determine the level of the organization that is impacted by Step 1 (WHO).** Given your response to Step 1 (what), you identify the level of the organization that is impacted. Problems or deficiencies may be isolated to the individual or job level, whereas future planning, such as a plant opening may require a shift by the entire organization. Select the level of the organization impacted by the type of need. You will notice that the individual comes before the job in this hierarchy. This is because many individuals have multiple jobs or roles in today's organizations.

The third side contains **Step 3—Determine the corrective strategy (HOW).** There are six other options for performance improvement to consider before selecting training as the option:

1. **Is there a systems problem?** Train people all that you want to, but if they don't have the needed systems and resources to perform, performance will not improve. (Let's say you're a call center, shift A completes 3,000 calls while shift B completes only 2,000.) At first glance, you might assume that shift B needs training—after all, there is a performance gap. But on looking at the situation more closely you discover that shift B can only complete calls during four hours of their shift due to the time zones their customers are in. The additional four hours are spent in researching unresolved internal issues uncovered by shift A. You also discover that one of the compression, archiving, and data back-up functions takes place during shift B, resulting in the loss of availability of the computers needed for calls. So, shift B's performance in calling is a systems issue, not a training issue. It may be that shift A is the shift that needs some additional training.

2. **Is there an organization development problem?** This means we need to look at policies and procedures. It may well be that there are policies in place that punish people for performance—or reward people for performance that we'd rather not have. For example, Chris is a housekeeper and finishes the 12 rooms assigned on the seventh floor by noon. The supervisor checks the rooms and says, "Great job! Jan on the fourth floor is a little behind. Take two of Jan's rooms." This scenario repeats itself for several days—sometimes with Jan, sometimes with other housekeepers. Within thirty days, we notice it takes Chris until quitting time to finish the original 12 assigned rooms. Does Chris need training to improve performance? Not at all. Chris is being punished for performing since there is no additional incentive for cleaning more rooms. Moreover, the other housekeepers are being rewarded for underperforming since Chris has been picking up the slack. While housekeepers other than Chris might benefit from training, the major need is to revise policies so that people like Chris have an incentive to do more than just the MDR (minimum daily requirement).

3. **Are we recruiting the right people?** Are your recruiting efforts targeted to attract employees who start out with the basic competencies to do the job? If an organization has not clearly defined the requirements of the job and its performance standards, it may hire people who do not possess the skills necessary to meet the demands of the job. About 10 years ago in New York City, a fast food chain offered basic literacy classes to potential counter clerk recruits due to the lack of applicants with skills to do the job. This is a solution to a recruitment challenge. It wasn't that they couldn't do the entry-level job, but without basic math skills, they couldn't open, close, or order inventory, and they'd never be qualified to become an assistant manager.

4. **Is placement an issue?** Is the wrong person in the job? Have you properly explored your employees' behavioral tendencies? Are people-oriented employees in people-intensive jobs? Are your more cautious, task-oriented people in high-detail, analytical jobs? People are all motivated...just by different things. Discover whether challenges and results, social recognition and people, harmony and the status quo and teamwork, or analytical attention to detail and perfection turn them on. Match people's natural tendencies to your job's critical competencies for optimum productivity and satisfaction.

5. **Is coaching needed?** Do you need a 10-day class or 10 minutes of coaching? Sometimes, employees may just need a few questions answered or have a skill demonstrated to them. When I wrote the first edition of this handbook in 1986, I was using a word processing package called WordStar on a KayPro II portable computer (it was called portable because it weighed only 45 pounds!). I lugged it through airports for six months writing the book.

   One day, I was in my office editing a chapter. I added some text and it caused some of the words to run off the screen (there was no word wrap yet!). So I moved the cursor over and added a hard return and forced the words to the next line. This made that line too long so I repeated the process. As I was doing this, my assistant came in and looked at what I was doing. After a minute, she asked what I was doing and I told her. She then said, "Why don't you do this?" She pressed the control key and the letter Q and instantly the paragraph reformatted itself! I was amazed and asked her what she had done. She told me that she had used the reformat command. I never knew there was a reformat command! I became instantly more productive. I would never have taken a one-day class to learn just that, but I was grateful for some coaching.

   However, managers may not know how to coach. If they have never had a manager model coaching skills for them, they may not identify coaching as a vital solution. Often times, on-the-job coaching is a better return on an investment than a longer learning session. Coaching provides the employee with enough information to be able to move ahead on the current project or assignment.

6. **Is there a training need?** Use the AWA process to help you confirm this:

   a. Are employees **A**ble to? Do they have the physical and mental capacity to perform the function?

   b. Are employees **W**illing to? Geary Rummler, coauthor of *Improving Performance* says, "Pit an eager, willing employee against a bad system and the system will win every time." Does the system reward people for performing? Does it reward people for *not* performing?

   c. Are employees **A**llowed to? Are managers and supervisors creating an environment that encourages them to perform?

This Performance Solutions Cube should become second nature to you as you carry out your responsibilities as a trainer. Constantly screen the training requests that come your way to ensure that you're really providing training that will make a tangible difference for the individual and the organization.

These are the foundations of my ILPC process. It gives you an idea of what the ILPC process is—and where it came from. Here are the top five questions people ask as they are exposed to these ideas for the first time. By answering these concerns, you might be more open to applying the ideas.

Question 1. Doesn't using these ideas take more time than lecture? Our time is too short as it is!

Answer: While lecture may seem to be a faster way to cover content, it doesn't guarantee that people are going to be able to use what they've heard. I like what Sue Ensz, one of our trainers said, "Just because I've said it, doesn't mean you've learned it!" Training is about learning for living, rather than simply learning to pass. Involving people enables them to internalize ideas and skills—and increases their ability to transfer the skills and knowledge back to their jobs. Having said that, it's also true that involvement can actually be faster than lecture. Lecture often assumes that people know nothing. By using involvement, we can tap past experiences and perhaps avoid content chunks that the participants have already mastered. This reduces training time. We have also designed interactive learning activities that actually helped participant's master skills in 20 to 30 percent less time than traditional classroom methods. The lesson here is: never assume!

Question 2. Isn't the IL-PC process just a bunch of games and tricks?

Answer: No! Absolutely not. Everything about the IL-PC process has always been focused on helping people get better results. If we use a game, it's because it's the best way for people to learn that particular concept. There is always a purpose and a point to everything that we do. Every step in the process is focused on you increasing retention, reducing training time, increasing application on the job, etc. In short, the focus is on getting results.

Question 3. Don't you lose control when you allow people to participate?

Answer: I believe that I'm in greater control of learning taking place when I turn control over to the small groups that we use and spread the accountability for learning among the participants themselves. The only thing lecture ensures is that I'm talking and participants are not. It doesn't guarantee that participants are hearing, understanding, applying, or anything else. I have no guarantee that when I'm talking participants' minds are focused on what I'm saying. Behind those eyes that may be looking at me may be a brain that is focused a million miles and a hundred years away. On the other hand, when a group of four or five participants has a task to accomplish, it's pretty difficult for any one of them to daydream and not do their part.

Question 4. Aren't participants likely to get a lot of misinformation if much of the work is done by small groups with no instructor listening in?

Answer: Not at all. Part of the IL-PC process is identifying participants who may have expertise that can help other participants learn more quickly and who can be used as mentors and coaches. We are also careful to provide participants with resources and references that can enable them to double-check their own thinking as they go along. Also, groups compare answers, findings, etc., so that other groups serve as a check and balance. Finally, we are always asking people to verbalize knowledge and demonstrate skills so that it is clear that they have mastered the right techniques and retained the correct knowledge that are needed.

Question 5. What are some of the characteristics of the IL-PC process?

Answer: Here are some of the most significant characteristics of the IL-PC process:

1. It is instructor led, but participant centered. This means that most of the responsibility for learning is on the participants. As a result, they tend to help one another in a collaborative way, rather than feeling a need to compete. As they teach and coach one another, they anchor the content more firmly for themselves.

2. It can be used to achieve objectives in all four domains of learning: cognitive, the acquisition of knowledge; affective, dealing with emotions and attitudes; psychomotor, the acquisition of motor skills (and other observable behaviors); and the newest domain of learning, interpersonal skills, how we relate to other people.

3. It provides for variety. There is no one best method. We have more than 154 alternatives to lecture that can be selected and used to help any given group learn better. This also keeps the instructor energized since the instructor can teach the content not just in one way time after time, but with different methods that keep the instructor from burning out.

4. It provides for content to be revisited in a variety of ways. Since revisiting key content is critical to building long-term memory, it's important to enable participants to revisit content and yet not feel as though they are going over the same thing again and again, which can seem boring.

Research Factoid

> *"Learning is increased when teaching is presented in a manner that assists students in organizing, storing, and retrieving knowledge."*
>
> – Ellis, E. S., & Worthington, L. A. (1994)

5. It honors the experience of the participants. Often people know much more than we give them credit for. Allowing people to share their insights and experiences provides real-world validation for the concepts being presented in class. It also causes participants to be much more open to new content when they are honored for what they already know, rather than treated as if they know very little—especially compared to the instructor.

6. It uses small groups of five to seven people (and sometimes even fewer!) to foster participation, build confidence, create accountability, etc.

7. It emphasizes real-life application. Since the purpose is to help people achieve results, attention is constantly being focused on how and why content can be applied in the real world.

8. Action planning is built in to the process. Throughout any training program designed using the ILPC process, participants are constantly reflecting, both individually and collectively, on what they've learned and how they've applied it. Leaving a program with an action plan is critical to real-world transfer and application after the program is over.

In the following chapters, you'll be exposed to a system that will provide a recipe for instructional success. You'll also be going through a cafeteria line of techniques that can help you make your training instructor led but participant centered immediately—even without time to redesign existing courses. Let me suggest that you create your own action idea list as you proceed. Just as you don't pick up all the food on the cafeteria line, neither should you try to pick up and apply every idea I offer here. Instead, look for those you can use now. Then return to the book when you're ready for "second helpings."

Chapter 2:
Presentation Preparation

How to Get Rave Reviews and Results Before You Open Your Mouth

I believe that 80 percent of being creative and being able to involve people in a presentation depends on adequate preparation. Granted, some presenters like to take their expertise and simply shoot from the hip; experience tells them they can hit the target often enough to do the job. Most others, though, realize that preparation is the real key to an outstanding training program. They are the ones who accept the six Ps of an effective presentation: Proper Preparation and Practice Prevent Poor Performance.

Proper
reparation and
ractice
revent
oor
erformance

Preparation assures them that they'll be able to deliver what the client needs. And that's your goal too—to design and deliver training that gets results. Systematic preparation increases both the ease and the likelihood of successful training.

Eight Steps to Effective Instructional Systems Design

Step 1: List the Needs, both General and Specific

The first question I ask regarding this step is: Who says these are needs? In my experience, training should be designed for three groups of people, two of which may never show up in the classroom: senders, sendees, and payers.

Designing training for only one person (e.g., the participant or sendee) is a little like trying to sit on a three-legged stool that has only one leg. You can do it, but it's not very comfortable. Anyone who has ever spent time on a farm knows that milking stools have three legs. Why? Because a three-legged stool will provide a solid base to sit on when you're milking—even if the ground is uneven. Contrast that to restaurants you've been to that have tables with four legs that you're constantly trying to stabilize by sliding pieces of folded paper, matchbook covers, etc., under one or more legs. It doesn't take much for them to be unstable!

Design for 3 Different People

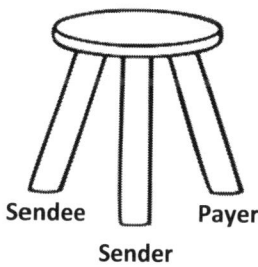

Sendee — Payer
Sender

[15]

The first group that training should be designed for is the senders—the managers or supervisors who are sending people to a particular training program. What are these people's needs and expectations? What is it going to take to make these people eager to support the training program? Obviously, we want their support, but if we don't consider them as we're developing the program, we may not have it.

Second, we need to design for the sendees, the actual participants. Most of the time, we're pretty good at focusing on these individuals.

Finally, we need to design for the payers, those who provide the budget. What return do they expect for their training dollar?

As we draw up a list of needs that must be met in this training program, we also have to ask: How important is it that we meet all of them? To answer this question, we should keep two things in mind. First, our needs assessment must be complete and thorough, and, second, we must have buy-in from the three groups whose support we need.

In order to encourage that buy-in, keep in mind two important baseline rules:

1. Get input from one level up and one level down when doing any needs assessment. For example, if you're designing training for supervisors, ask both the supervisors' managers for input and the supervisors' employees for input. The training target group may not clearly see its own needs.

2. Use nonrepetitive redundant measures. This means we must assess the needs in at least two different ways. If, for example, you're designing a training program for salespeople, you survey the salespeople, who might say, "Our problems concern closing and time management." The managers of those salespeople would agree: "Our salespeople seem to have problems with closing and with time management." If you don't choose to talk with the involved customers about the needs of these salespeople, you would stop at this point and conclude, "We understand the needs because the managers and the salespeople have identified them." You've used one measure—the interview method—and you've found that the two groups have the same perception. Now, let's say that you've used another measure. You've spent a day observing high-performance and low-performance salespeople and noted that both groups used their time in exactly the same way.

The only difference between high- and low-performing salespeople, then, is their approach to closing.

Nonrepetitive redundant measures provide two different methods for looking at the same information. Nonrepetitive means that the measure does not repeat itself. Redundant refers to the fact that it measures the same thing. In this example, the primary focus of your training would be on the issue that has been identified—closing. Because both the salespeople and their supervisors also have a perceived, or psychological, need for time management, you might also provide some material on this subject, but your primary focus would be on closing.

Participant support and ownership are imperative in order for the IL-PC process to succeed. And achieving the total involvement of trainees must be considered in completing the first step of the instructional systems design process. The more buy-in we have, the more likely we are to get the results we want.

One strategy we have found useful is the formation of an advisory committee to review the program during its development. This committee generally consists of people whose support is key to the program's implementation and on-the-job follow-up. Committee members might be managers, subject-matter experts, performers—in other words, a representative cross-section of the senders, the sendees, and the payers. You also want to consider people who will enhance the credibility of the program as it is being designed and eventually introduced.

We are looking for two things from an advisory committee: input and influence.

- input because some of the members may be experts on the subject matter, may have a history with the organization, or may possess other valuable information

- influence because of the respect that these members have in the organization that can loan credibility to our programs

Step 2: Assess Your Audience

Research Factoid

> *"Students learn more efficiently when the teacher organizes the lesson in such a way that it relates to the background knowledge of the student."*
>
> — Schuck, R. F. (1985)
>
> *"Competent teachers consider whether students possess the specific background knowledge that is required in learning new information."*
>
> — Fogarty, J. L., Wang, M. C., & Creek, R. (1983)

Learn all you can about your participants in terms of the following factors:

- **Knowledge**—How much knowledge and experience will participants bring to a program? Remember the adage: Never underestimate the intelligence of your listeners; never overestimate their need for information. For example, you may take for granted that most business people are familiar with the concept of equipment depreciation, but don't expect them to know which depreciation formula necessarily applies to their organization or to various kinds of equipment.

   You can also identify what level of knowledge your participants have and at what level they need to be:

Levels of Knowledge

They can recognize things when they see them.	There is some degree of recall; if they need something, they can find it.	They can apply the knowledge and use the skills.	They can transfer the concepts and skills to others.

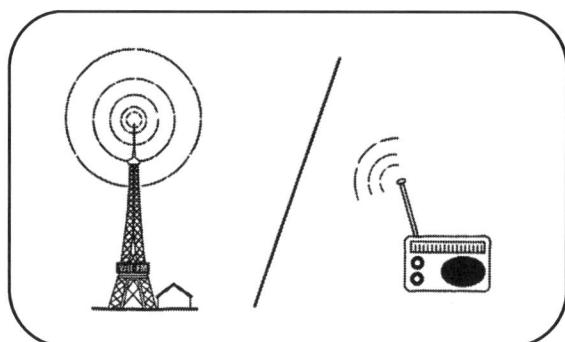

- **Interest**—The success of your presentation is 50 percent assured if your audience's interest is working for you from the beginning. Every single person in the audience is going to be tuned in to radio station WII-FM; they are all going to be asking themselves, "What's in it for me? How will it help me do my job faster, better, easier? What losses am I going to avoid? What benefits am I going to gain?" Each of the three key groups we mentioned earlier—senders, sendees, and payers—will be tuned to this radio station. What is the payoff if they support or are involved in this training?

Levels of Interest

They are sent and don't want to be there. They'd rather be almost anyplace else. Attendance is a punishment.	They view attendance as a way to escape work. It's better to be in class than at work.	They view attendance as an opportunity to have a good time and meet new people.	They are there to gain new skills and knowledge.

Planning for the Learner is easy. Planning for the other three types is challenging—and also critical to a successful learning environment for everyone who is there. In *Dealing with Difficult Participants*, which I co-authored with Dave Arch, nearly half the book deals with preventative strategies that come straight from participant-centered instruction. By following the recommendations that we are making in this book, you will have resolved most, if not all, the conflicts that arise when you have difficult participants in your sessions.

Once we've considered their level of interest coming into the program, we have to look at what can we do at the beginning of the program to stimulate that interest even further? How can we develop in them a sense of anticipation for a pay-off?

One other point to remember here is that people don't argue with their own data. If somebody says something is true, it is true—for that person.

One way to open a training program is to ask people to brainstorm responses to two questions:

1. What kinds of problems do people have because they don't _____ (fill in the blank with the topic of your training program, e.g., solve problems effectively, delegate effectively, follow safety procedures, know how to handle objections and put-offs, understand or use reference manuals, etc.)?

2. What happens when you and I do_____ (fill in the blank with the same answers provided to the first question, e.g., solve problems effectively, delegate effectively, follow safety procedures, know how to handle objections and put-offs, understand or use reference manuals, etc.)?

You can then ask the group for their responses to these questions and post them. Or you can have participants discuss their responses to the two questions in small groups. If I have more than 15 people, I generally split them and have half my audience discuss the first question and half discuss the second one. Then I'll ask two volunteers to work at flip charts and have a leader from one group discuss the first question: "What kinds of problems do people have because they don't...?" I'll move from group to group and take single responses. The volunteer at one flip chart posts the first response, the second response goes on the second flip chart, and we alternate back and forth. When I've exhausted the responses to the first question, we post them and proceed to the second question: What happens when you and I do...

This simple exercise produces a list of benefits to attain and losses to avoid. Notice that the first question is couched in the third person. It doesn't ask, "What kinds of problems have you had because you don't...?" Now, everyone in the group may be terrible at delegating or problem solving or whatever, but it's not my purpose, in terms of generating interest, to point out their weaknesses or to have them admit them to one another. By giving me a list of problems they've observed that other people have, they also may be admitting their own problems, but they are doing so in a subtle, nonthreatening way.

By the same token, the second question requires positive answers. Of course, the participants may, in fact, be mediocre delegators and problem solvers, but they don't have to admit it. They may be terrible supervisors, but they've seen good supervision, just as they've no doubt seen good delegation and problem solving. We can use the experience of the entire group to draw up a list of very positive reasons why it would be useful to focus on our topic. From their own data, they've spelled out several reasons why it will be valuable to pay attention to the contents of the program.

- **Language**—Make sure you understand the level of linguistic sophistication of your participants. Don't use jargon.

Research Factoid

> *"McCormick's (1979) study of effective teachers suggested that effective teachers (a) more often adapted instruction for students, (b) used ability-...appropriate vocabulary for students, (c) adjusted questioning levels to the ability level of their students, and (d) made their presentations at an appropriate level of difficulty for students."*
>
> – Ellis, E. S., & Worthington, L. A. (1994), p. 31

Levels of Language

We're talking down to our participants. In other words, we're too basic for the audience.	We're on the same wavelength as our participants.	We're using "insider" language that creates barriers to learning. Nothing loses an audience faster than language it doesn't understand. If in doubt, spell it out. If it's important to use technical terms, define those terms.

    A number of years ago, I designed a training program that dealt with various financial concepts. In the program was a section that described the importance of having a will. As you perhaps know, a person who dies without a will is considered to have died intestate. Many people, however, are not familiar with this word, but they are also unlikely to admit that they don't know its meaning. Consider the likely response if you were to ask participants in a training program, "How many of you do not know what *intestate* means?" Silence? But how about the more positive, "How many of you know what *intestate* means? Good. Would you define it for us?" Chances are, someone will be able to define the word, so that you, the trainer, can proceed with your presentation.

    But, you also face the possibility that no one knows or that someone will guess incorrectly, and you will have to tell that person he or she is wrong. The best strategy is to define an unfamiliar term immediately after using it. For example, "It's important to understand the consequences of dying intestate—of dying without a will."

    The language problem can be more complex when several disciplines are represented by participants in your training program. For example, the chemical terms used to describe an air pollution problem and the symbols that represent these terms may be part of the scientist's or engineer's everyday vocabulary. If, however, managers from manufacturing are also in attendance, they might have difficulty recalling scientific terms.

In another example, if you're talking economics, the terms may be familiar to an executive, who has acquired this knowledge either through education or on the job. But they might mystify a supervisor or front-line person unless they are explained.

- **Influence**—What kind of influence does each participant have back in their workplace? What kind of support are they likely to need if they are going to successfully apply the knowledge and skills that they've been learning in your training program? Generally speaking, the lower the person is in the organization, the more support that is needed to ensure the transfer of the skills and knowledge back on the job.

Levels of Influence

This means that support systems need to be put in place to ensure that participants have the time and resources to practice the new skills and apply the new knowledge they've learned.	This means that minimal support is required. This person can put his or her own support in place. However, putting that support in place and creating accountability is just as important for this person since people have multiple responsibilities and the class may apply only to a small part of their responsibilities.

Also ask yourself, who are the decision makers in this group? What are their problems and personal interests? What can you tell them to make their tasks easier? How can you challenge them? How can you build them in as partners in the program? Does your message have the potential of threatening their influence and prestige?

All these questions are important to consider, because we want to build in the expertise of any experts in the program. But one caveat, one warning, here: Do not accept, at face value, someone's personal identification of expertise. Just because someone considers himself or herself an expert doesn't necessarily mean it is so. One consideration, before we run our first program, would be to have the advisory group enlighten us about the experience level of the people in the group. You might also ask those who are sending people to this program for their perceptions of the experience and expertise the individuals in this group will bring.

We also may want to have participants in the group complete an effectiveness grid to assess their expertise. I frequently use an effectiveness grid myself. In one program I conducted, I wanted to gauge the computer literacy of the participants, so I gave each one a computer-literacy grid and asked everyone to rate themselves on their knowledge of computers. This computer-literacy grid, shown on page 121, was designed for managers who were going to participate in a computer literacy program; its purpose was to familiarize them with computers that were going to be available for their use and that were going to be used extensively in the future by the people who reported to them.

On our grid, we asked them to rate their own computer literacy. If, for example, they felt they knew everything there is to know about computer software, they would rate themselves 100. On the other hand, if they thought that a utility was the gas or electric company that served their homes, they'd probably want to rate themselves 1, because when we're talking computers, that's not what a utility is.

As people were completing the grid, I went around the room to see how they were scoring themselves. If somebody was scoring himself or herself extremely high, it might have meant—and let me emphasize *might*—that this person had a lot of computer experience and/or expertise. To find out just how skilled in computers a high scorer really was, I would kneel down next to him or her and, without making it obvious to everybody in the room, say something like, "It seems you've had a lot of experience in this area and I'd like to be able to tap into that. I wonder if you would be willing to do some of the demonstrations that are part of this program in front of the group. Also, when we break into work groups, would you consider not being in a group but working with me instead to check on the other groups?"

Now, one of two things is going to be true here. If the person really is an expert, I'm likely to get a response like, "Sure, no problem. I'd be happy to help." If he or she isn't an expert, however, I'll hear something like, "Well, I really came here just to be a participant." Either way, I've gotten some worthwhile information. First, if the person is an expert, I've helped build his or her experience into the program. In the case of those who just think they're experts, I've taken some steps that will help minimize disruption and the exchange of misinformation; if they really want to be involved and verbalize what they know, they'll carefully consider the possibility of being asked to "perform" before the entire group.

Occasionally, I will encounter somebody with an ego that just won't quit. Even though this person has very little or no experience at all, he or she will say, "Sure, no problem" to my request for assistance. But just because I've asked somebody to come up and do a demonstration or be prepared to help work with groups rather than be part of them doesn't mean I'm going to encourage an obviously inexperienced person to do that. I don't want to put people in situations where they're going to fail.

To those people who have volunteered to share their expertise, I say, "There will be times, I'm sure, when questions will come up, and I'd like you to help answer them. So when someone in the group asks a question that seems relevant to your expertise, I'll look over at you. If you nod, I'll know that it's a question you can handle."

Never yet has an inexperienced person made eye contact with me when a question was being asked by someone in the group. That tells me that, if these individuals aren't willing or able to respond to questions the group might ask, then I certainly don't want them to come up in front of the group and be embarrassed.

Some other items to consider are:

- **Number of people attending:** What is the size of the group? How many people you have will dictate the amount of equipment you need, the amount of space you need, and so on.

- **Location:** What kinds of facilities do you have for the training program? Are they ideal or less than ideal? Are the chairs comfortable or uncomfortable? Are you able to rearrange the room from time to time just for variety?

- **Time of day the program is going to be offered:** Generally speaking, people are fresher in the morning, if that's their normal time to start work, than they are in the afternoon. If your program is scheduled for the afternoon, you'll need more involvement and participation to keep people focused and alert.

All these should be considered before we even begin to design the program.

Step 3: Decide Your Aim

To determine your aims, or goals, ask yourself, "As a result of this training, what do I want people to know, feel, and do?" Psychologists have identified four domains of learning. The cognitive domain deals with knowledge. The affective domain deals with feelings and emotions. The psychomotor domain deals with skills. And the interpersonal domain deals with behaviors. As trainers, your aim will be to affect one or more of these know, feel, do, relate areas.

You can narrow your focus by asking yourself these questions. What do I want participants to know that they didn't know before? How do I want them to feel? Do I want them to have a more positive attitude toward the subject, to be excited about implementing the subject, to feel self-confident about their ability to perform? What do I want them to be able to do that they haven't done before? How do I want them to be able to relate to people in ways they haven't before? How are the results of this training going to be measured and evaluated? Do people have to perform at a particular skill level? How are the payers and senders going to measure success?

Insider's Tip

> One technique that I use is creating a group mind-map. This is a process that is outlined in Chapter 9. We put up three or four sheets of flip chart paper with the central topic in the center and the people who know the topic well—my subject matter experts—will begin creating a mind-map of all the content that we're thinking of covering in a particular training program or all of the things that people need to know about a specific subject.
>
> As that mind-map is developed, it gives us a visual representation of the subject and, because it's more visual than a traditional outline, it allows us to see gaps—what is not there. When we look at a traditional outline, we have a tendency to evaluate what is there. It is much more difficult to see what is missing. The mind-map allows us to see the holes that might be in the content. It also allows us to sequence the material by looking at the material as a whole and then looking at the various orders in which we might sequence the material.

To answer these tough questions, you must thoroughly research your topic: collect more information than you plan to use, over prepare, and then boil it down. How many times have you seen presenters run out of content because their audience was better informed than they had anticipated? Or hit bottom before getting to the depth of content that their participants needed?

How much do you already know about your topic, and how much does your audience need to know? You'll have a research gap to fill if your audience needs to know more than you already know. Which of your ideas needs more support than you have provided, and where can you find that support efficiently? Don't scrape the bottom of the barrel. There's nothing worse than having an hour left and nothing to say. It's better to leave participants feeling that more could be said. In other words, it's better to run out of time before you run out of material.

Here are some quick research tips:

1. What articles on the topic have appeared in trade or industry publications in the past 12 to 24 months?

2. What articles have appeared in business or popular publications in the past 12 to 24 months?

3. What books have been published on the subject in the past year?

4. What topics appear again and again on industry conference programs?

Using these tips can help you become more aware of the trends and the needs that may exist in your industry or organization.

Step 4: Plan Your Approach

Research Factoid

> *"The use of novelty and surprise help generate student interest in the topic of the lesson. Introducing a lesson topic in an unusual or unexpected manner can enhance student interest and motivation."*
>
> – DeCecco, J. P. (1968)

How are you going to get favorable attention? We've already touched on one way—asking questions, such as "What kinds of problems have you observed?" To introduce the program, consider answering these questions that the participants may ask: "What's in it for me? How will I be able to do my job faster, better, easier? What benefits can I gain? What losses can I avoid?"

It's important to be aware of the difference between an opener for a program and an icebreaker. People are going to remember what we do first, best. It's important, therefore, that what we do really fits the program. One mistake trainers tend to make is to mistake an icebreaker for an opening. An icebreaker may get people acquainted, but it may not be relevant to the program content. Here are my six tests for an effective opening—the first three are fundamental—raising the BAR. The second three dig a little deeper.

1. **B**reak preoccupation? People may be physically present in a room, but not mentally present. They could be preoccupied by other things—work left undone at the job, an argument they had at home that morning, a frustrating traffic delay on the way to the seminar, or maybe just wondering whether or

not this content is going to be useful—at least useful enough to justify being away from the job. We need to break through that preoccupation and get people focused on the class and not on external concerns. The key to breaking preoccupation is involvement. It is easy to ignore an instructor. It is much more difficult to tune out a group of peers that you are a part of and that have a task to accomplish.

2. **A**llow networking? Does my opening help people become comfortable with one another? When tension goes up, retention goes down. People may be sitting there concerned about whether or not they fit in, whether they know as much as other people in the room, whether or not they're really going to be able to contribute. The longer a class, the more important it is to help people get comfortable with one another.

3. **R**elevant to the program? Can people see the logical tie-in between the opening that I'm doing and the content of the course? This is critical, especially for the people in your class who are practical learners. Too many instructors have done an icebreaker and been asked, "What's the point as related to our content?" When the instructor says, "I thought it was important to get acquainted," participants frequently feel that they could have been fifteen minutes late and missed nothing of relevance to their job. And, they'd be right. With a little thought, we can create an opening that has relevance and gives the participants the feeling that every minute is going to be useful.

Research Factoid

> *"Learning requires focused attention, and awareness of the importance of what is to be learned."*
>
> — Angelo, T. A. (1993), p. 5

4. Does it maintain or enhance self-esteem? I believe that one of the purposes of training is for people to leave impressed with themselves, not intimidated by the instructor—excited about what they now know that they didn't know before, excited about what they can now do that they couldn't do before and with greater confidence in themselves than before. We can begin that process of building confidence right in the opening of our program by making people feel good about themselves and the fact that they're there. Often I hear trainers complaining that they don't have much participation in their classes. Maybe it's because the participants don't believe they bring anything worthwhile to the party. The opening is the perfect moment to reinforce what they do bring to the party. By way of example, if I were teaching a course on the XYZ Company's approach to customer service, I would quickly realize that my participants don't know my content yet. However, they have had experiences with both good and bad customer service. So in my opening, I would want them to be sharing those experiences they bring to the party that relate to customer service. This reinforces their confidence that they have something

to contribute. I'm building the foundation for stronger participation throughout my program.

5. Is it fun for both the trainer and the participants? The fun factor may not always be important, but having some fun at the beginning of the program can help people realize that this is not going to be another boring lecture-educational experience, but in fact they're going to learn things and at the same time be able to have some fun. I believe that it must first be fun or enjoyable for the trainer. In other words, work hard to insert an activity in your opening that you enjoy doing. Typically, such an opener is in your comfort zone. It is a low-risk activity for you. You can lead it with confidence. Participants will sense this, feel secure, and participate more fully compared to an activity that you are unsure of. When the trainer hesitantly says, "Would anyone like to go to the wall and make some posters?" be assured no one will want to go to the wall.

6. Is their curiosity aroused? Curiosity can be a very powerful motivator. We've used many different openers in a variety of training programs. The key is that each of them needs to meet the test of effective openers that we've given here.

Finally, decide what transition you're going to use as you proceed from the introduction to the main content. Here's a good place to identify and clarify the group's goals. One way almost all trainers could significantly improve the impact of their training would be to strengthen the beginning and end of their presentation. From the participant's perspective, the beginning must gain their interest and create a sense of anticipation for what lies ahead.

Step 5: Plan Your Lesson Development

Whenever I design a training program, I make a brief outline, because I don't want to be tied to my notes. Sometimes, trainers are so tied to their format that, if they can't follow it exactly as planned, they can't deliver the content. How many times have you heard a presenter say, "My computer's down. I have no PowerPoint. There's not going to be a class." Or "The DVD doesn't work, so I can't play the video I brought. There's not going to be a class."

In one of my college speech classes, I learned this little rhyme:

> *The room was hushed, the speaker mute.*
> *He'd left his speech in his other suit.*

If we are masters of our content before we begin to deliver, we won't suffer this humiliating fate.

Too many instructors are lost if the LCD projector bulb burns out and they cannot use PowerPoint—or if the DVD player is broken and they cannot show a video. We have all been in classes where we did not dare to ask a question because if the instructor lost his or her place in their notes, they would be lost.

Within my base outline, I first must consider my manner of presentation. The longer the presentation, the more variety and changes of pace I need.

Tony Buzan in his book, *Use Both Sides of Your Brain*, says that his research indicates that the average adult can listen with. understanding for 90 minutes, but can only listen with retention for 20 minutes. That means that we need a distinct change-up or change of pace every 20 minutes. Based on Buzan's information, I developed the 90/20/8 rule: no module we teach ever runs more than 90 minutes, the pace is changed at least every 20 minutes, and we try to find a way to involve people in the content every 8 minutes. (For webinars, it is the 90/20/4 rule, which I explain in chapter 16—The Virtual Trainer.)

Second, I consider learner participation and response. Remember, my goal is to tap people's experiences and to have the program be instructor led but participant centered. How will I get and keep participants involved? The methods of instruction in Chapter 5 will provide ideas that you can apply to get your participants more involved.

Research Factoid

> *"Research has suggested that effective teachers spend 15% less time on management and organization tasks, and 50% more time on interactive activities."*
>
> – Ellis, E. S., & Worthington, L. A. (1994), p. 18

Third, I decide how I will review or revisit previous content, which I'll need to reinforce constantly. In the 1880s, Hermann Ebbinghaus discovered that if people are exposed to an idea one time in 30 days, they retain less than 10 percent. One hundred years later, Albert Mehrabian presented some fascinating information in his book *Silent Messages*. In his research, he found that if people were exposed to an idea one time, at the end of 30 days they retained less than 10 percent (the same findings as Ebbinghaus's). But if they were exposed to an idea six times, with interval reinforcement, at the end of 30 days, they retained more than 90 percent. Interval reinforcement means that the idea was presented once and then reviewed perhaps 10 minutes later, an hour later, a day later, three days later, a week later, two weeks later, three weeks later. In other words, there were intervals between each review.

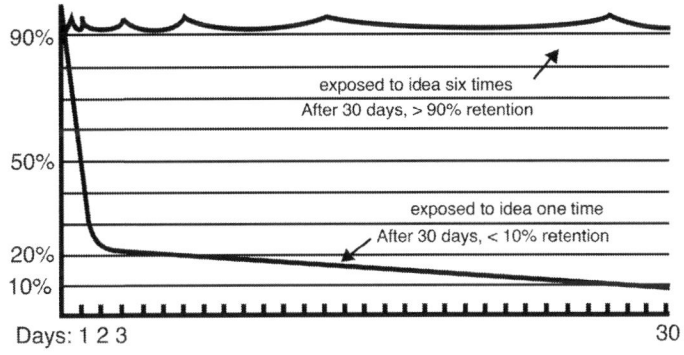

THE KEY IS INTERVAL REINFORCEMENT

The Ebbinghaus Curve of Forgetting

Finally, I determine how to vary my transitions from point to point. The importance of this step lies in "Pike's First Law of Adult Learning": Adults are babies with big bodies. Think for a moment about the kinds of activities children pursue in preschool and kindergarten. They paint, play with blocks, color, play games, tell and listen to stories—all kinds of hands-on involvement carried out in a room conducive to participation. As they advance to first, second, and third grades, children tend to be lined up in rows and talked at. And the more they grow and mature, the less they involve themselves actively in the learning process. The older they get, and the more experiences they acquire, the less they get to use them. Hence, my conclusion that adults are babies with big bodies.

Just as young children can learn well through direct experience, so can adults, particularly when they're allowed to use their shared life experiences. Remember what Confucius protégé said? "What I hear, I forget; what I see, I remember; but what I do I understand." If there is a way to get involvement, I want to use it, because the focus of training is to help people get results, not simply to cover content. I haven't done my job if I've only covered content. What counts is the application that participants can make once the program is over.

Step 6: Plan Your Lesson Application

Remember that all of our participants are tuned to two radio stations, one we've already given: WII-FM—What's In It For Me? How will this help me do my job faster, better, easier? What are the benefits that I'll gain? What are the losses I'll avoid?

Research Factoid

> "Student achievement rises when teachers ask questions that require students to apply, synthesize, and evaluate information in addition to simply recalling facts."
>
> – Berliner, D. C., (1984)

The second radio station they've tuned to is MMFI-AM: Make Me Feel Important About Myself. I believe that one of the purposes of training is for participants to leave impressed with themselves, not intimidated with the instructor—excited about what they now know, excited about what they can now do, and with greater feelings of confidence in both what they've learned and what they can now accomplish.

The application step is the step that helps reinforce both what's in it for them and their own personal feelings of accomplishment. Helping them apply what they've learned is an important key to helping participants both know and feel that they've really accomplished something.

People are looking for practical and personal solutions for answers to the question "How do I use this?" To help them find the answers, I use what I call an action idea list in many of my programs. I repeatedly ask people to keep track of useful ideas that they can apply back on the job. From time to time, the group reviews the list, sharing key action ideas and adding to each other's lists. This is a natural way to build in lesson application.

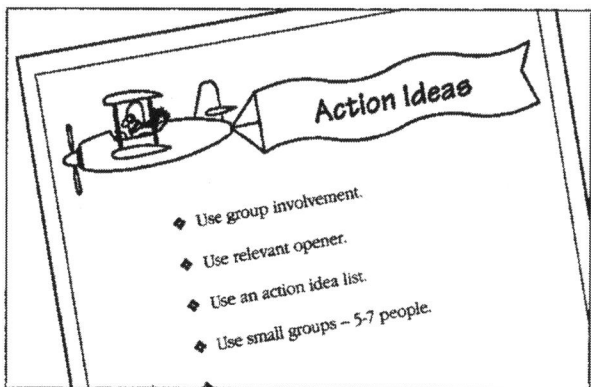

Remember, people don't argue with their own data. If I say something, I'm not objective because I'm teaching the material. But if they say it, their own experience validates it.

Step 7: Plan a Carry-Over Activity

If you are doing multiple sessions, plan an activity that will encourage participants to decide how they can use what they have learned. How will they report back their progress and problems? Ask them to take three minutes to answer these questions: What is the most important thing I have learned? And what am I going to do about it?

Step 8: Gather the Materials and Prepare the Room

I am sure you remember Murphy's Law: Whatever can go wrong, will. But are you familiar with O'Toole's Corollary, which states that Murphy was an optimist?

Here you are, ready to launch a two-week training program, and you want to make positive initial contact with your group. You want to get participants excited and involved by creating a sense of anticipation. You turn the switch on the overhead projector to project a visual. But the light bulb is burned out, and there's no spare. You go over to the flip chart and turn to a clean sheet, only to find that there's no more paper. Or there's plenty of paper but the first two or three markers you try to use have dried out. (By the way, that's another corollary to Murphy's Law: All markers run dry at the same time!)

You haven't even opened your mouth yet, but you can sense the kind of anticipation your participants now feel about the next two weeks—and it has nothing to do with your content. So, gather your materials and prepare the room before you launch your program.

My goal is always to be set up and ready to go 15 minutes before any participants arrive. There are two good reasons for this time limit:

- First, I can take care of any glitch before participants arrive. If handouts don't show up or visual equipment breaks down, I can arrange alternative delivery methods.

- The second, and perhaps more important, reason is that I like to interact with participants for 15 minutes before a class begins. This demonstrates my belief that the participants are as important as the content.

Getting acquainted with participants helps them feel comfortable with you and vice versa. It also provides you, the trainer, with further insights into the group and helps you gauge their readiness to learn, their interest, their reasons for attending, and their level of experience. It lets you address questions and concerns they may have. And it helps you relax and move naturally into the program itself.

How We Set Our Rooms

The physical environment that you do your presentation in can have a great deal of impact on your program. Here are just a few of the things to take note of on the room diagram below that we use for our Train-the-Trainer workshops. First, notice that the screen is set at a diagonal for the LCD projector in the corner of the room to maximize everybody being able to see it. The bottom of the screen is placed approximately 42 inches above the floor level and we always get a minimum of a 10-foot ceiling height in order to make sure that we can project the visuals high enough for everybody to see.

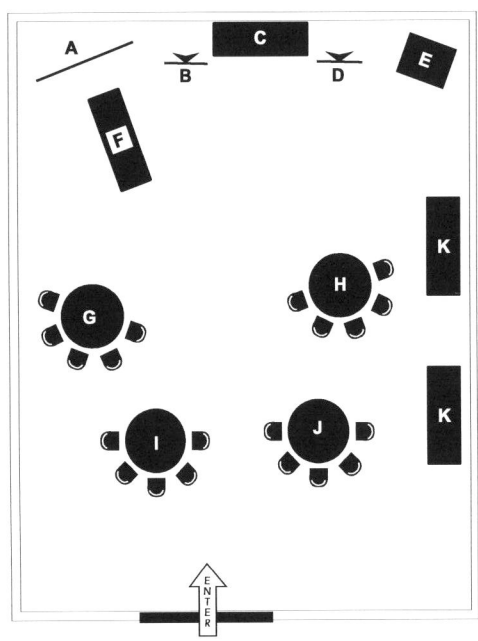

Layout:

A   6' x 6' screen with keystone bar

B, D   Flip charts

C   6' skirted table

E   Display table

F   LCD Projector

G, H, I, J   72" diameter round tables

K   Two 6' skirted tables

Room:

Minimum 10' ceilings

No columns or other obstructions

Notice that the participants are seated at half rounds that immediately make them feel part of a group. Also, we try to minimize the rounds to five to seven people. We always put fewer chairs than we think we're going to need, and stack extra chairs. It is always better to be adding chairs once the tables are filled the way you want them to be than to have more chairs than you need and to have some tables with too few participants.

We also allow plenty of table space for putting materials that people are either going to pick up themselves or that you are going to be distributing later. People enter from the rear of the room so that any latecomers are not a distraction in the way that they would be if they were entering from either the side of the room or the front of the room.

For flip charts, we use graph paper that has light blue 1-inch squares on them. It makes it easier to create lines, charts, and also to print on an even line across the pad.

Power Tips on Preparation

Because we want results from training, our focus is on instructor-led, participant-centered learning. This means that my goal is to find ways for participants to discover, for themselves, the knowledge, skills, and attitudes that they need to succeed. This means that I maximize participant involvement and minimize lecture. This does not mean that I eliminate lecture, however. It does mean that I first seek alternatives and then, when necessary, prepare lecturettes to cover content that would be difficult to learn or know in other ways. With this in mind, you'll find these tips for preparing lecturettes helpful.

Memorizing also makes it difficult to refer easily to any "new" material, such as something said by a previous speaker or by the person who introduced you. If you are distracted by what goes on around you (such as a loud sneeze in the audience, a door slamming, a waiter dropping a tray, etc.), there is a good chance you will falter and forget what comes next if you're a slave to memory.

Express Your Ideas Clearly and Concisely

Concentrate on communicating worthwhile ideas in order to help others, not to make an outstanding personal impression. Polished words and fancy phrases are no substitute for a good idea sincerely and simply expressed. As Aristotle said, "Think as the wise men do, but speak as the common people do."

Build the Outline

In preparing any talk, first *limit* your topic to one specific idea. Second, *select* specific material suited to that limited purpose. Third, *arrange* your material, illustrations, examples, facts, and statistics in a coherent order.

A skeleton outline based on such abstract words as "introduction," "body," and "conclusion" won't help you much. Instead, use phrases like "take hold," "transmit," and "drive home." Start with a word picture or a story that is relevant to your dominant purpose that takes hold of your listeners' attention. After transmitting your idea and the specific incidents, illustrations, or other evidence to back it up, you're ready to drive home your point with an effective conclusion. This might be a brief summary of your idea, a quotation, a call for action, or even a poem. It should highlight your talk and nail your point with intensity.

Use the KFD Principles to Identify Learner Response

We covered the know-feel-do principle in the Eight Steps to Effective Instructional Systems Design. Now let's explore these three domains more thoroughly. First, we must ask ourselves, "What new information or content do the participants need to know?" This addresses the cognitive aspect of your training presentation.

Second, we should ask, "How do we want them to feel?" Do we want them to feel motivated, inspired, energetic, sad, angry? How do we want them to react to the presentation? Do we want them to feel challenged to use these new insights? Do we want them to feel dissatisfied with present behaviors and present procedures? Do we want them to feel confident that they can use their new skills or knowledge?

Finally, we should ask, "What do we want people to do? What actions do we want them to take?" Since learning doesn't take place until behavior has changed, we want participants to convert ideas into action.

Use Information Overload to Ensure You Are Prepared

The third step to effective design and delivery suggests that you'll want to gather more information than you'll be able to use. It is much easier to boil down too much information than it is to expand or puff up minimal information. This preparation step will depend on your group members, their experience level, and their backgrounds. Much of the information you gather may be simplistic or fundamental to some groups, but new and necessary to others. To find out what information your attendees need to know as well as what topics are of concern to them, consider doing a content analysis:

1. Collect the past 12 months of several publications devoted to the concerns of your target group, the group for whom you're preparing a presentation or training program.

2. Starting with the most current issues, list the relevant topics covered and the amount of print or space devoted to each. Then compare this with the amount of coverage these topics received 12 months ago.

   Exclude feature articles from this initial analysis. You may want to share information from feature articles with trainees, but don't use them to analyze whether or not specific topics may enhance your program.

3. Once you've completed the current month's issues and compared them with those of 12 months ago, analyze the remaining issues of your publications (magazines and/or newspapers). As you list your topics, also list the amount of space devoted to each. You may find that something that had merited only a few inches of space four months ago has 12 or 18 inches devoted to it today. You also may notice that a hot topic 10 or 11 months ago is getting much less coverage now.

   Issues that receive the most recent attention probably will provide the greatest stimulus for attendees at your presentation. This quantitative part of your content analysis will give you broad topics.

4. To do a qualitative analysis, read the material about the most relevant topics and pinpoint those that are most helpful. Be consistent in your review. You can't simply use one or two publications or use only two or three months' worth of publications. Review as many as you can over a period of 12 months.

Another way you can gather information is to create a system of files on training topics that you are going to present. For example, if you are developing a program or a presentation on IL-PC, start an IL-PC file, clip out pertinent articles you come across, and put them in that file. When you're ready to design the program, you can review that file.

Note the titles of books and page references you'll want to refer to on 3" × 5" cards and insert them into the file, too.

Remember as you're researching, you can find all kinds of ways to help participants discover the information. Think of lecture as the last resort. I never saw anyone write on an evaluation form, "I wish there was more lecture."

Use the AIDA Formula in Developing Your Presentation

AIDA is an acronym based on the names of the four major steps into which a presentation or segment of a training program can be divided: attention, interest, desire, action. (Music lovers will also recognize it as the name of a famous opera by Verdi.)

Attention

At the beginning of any presentation, you must get the attention of the group. One of the most obvious ways is to ask a question. Members of your audience may be preoccupied with their own conversations; when you solicit an answer to a question, you break through that preoccupation and gain their attention.

If for example, you were running a program on decision making, you might ask a group of managers, "What kinds of problems do some managers have because they don't make decisions effectively?" Or, to begin a program on budgeting, you might ask, "What kinds of problems do people encounter when they don't handle money well?" As your participants begin responding, the side conversations will stop. You can then record participant responses on a flip chart.

There are three advantages to this particular technique:

1. You break through preoccupation and gain favorable attention.

2. You immediately involve your audience.

3. The question you ask begins to build a case for why your topic, or this particular part of the training program, is important. As people give their answers, they're acknowledging that a particular problem exists, and, as the list grows longer, some people in your group can identify with aspects of that problem. You're not only gaining attention; you're also demonstrating why the particular topic you're presenting is relevant.

Interest

In the interest step is where you begin to answer the question "What's in it for me?" Every person to whom we will ever make a presentation is tuned to radio station WII-FM—What's In It For Me? As we gather the information we want to present and as we recognize that there are things we want our audience to know, feel, and do as a result of our presentation, we also have to determine how each participant will benefit from knowing what we want them to know, feeling what we want them to feel, and doing what we want them to do.

Desire

In the desire step, we begin to share the content, the practical how-to's, that we suggested were forthcoming in the attention and interest steps.

Here's where we offer the means toward the end results. How can I solve the problem, close more sales, make more effective decisions, appraise performance more effectively, train more creatively? These questions are explored in the desire step.

Action

This wrap-up step is based on your asking the group, "What actions are you going to take? What did you learn, and how are you going to put your learning into practice?" Ideally, their feedback will indicate to you that training has provided a new, more effective way to do something and that they're willing to give it a try.

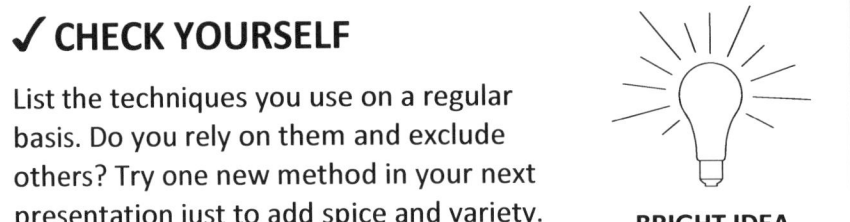

✓ **CHECK YOURSELF**

List the techniques you use on a regular basis. Do you rely on them and exclude others? Try one new method in your next presentation just to add spice and variety.

BRIGHT IDEA

Determining the Manner and Method of Presentation: Involvement Techniques and Content Application

In making presentations, we can use a wide variety of techniques. As you prepare your program, consider the following possibilities, most of which eventually will be described in greater detail. Here, we simply want to give a sampling of the kinds of methods and involvement techniques available to you (see list in Chapter 5).

There are at least two or three effective ways to make any point we want to convey. Take a look at your own methods of presenting. List the techniques you use on a fairly regular basis. Do you find yourself relying on the same ones to the exclusion of many others? If this is the case, you might want to consider adopting other presentation techniques and methods to put variety, creativity, spontaneity, and impact into your training.

Application or Carry-Over Activities

The final part of our preparation is to spend some time thinking how we're going to help people put into practice the things they've learned. One way is to introduce activities that help people decide how they will apply their new knowledge. One of the simplest such activities is to ask the participants, "What have you learned? How are you going to put it into practice?"

Chapter 3:
Learner Motivation

Making Sure the Audience Keeps Learning after You Are Finished Teaching

Have you ever faced a group of less-than-eager participants, people who didn't necessarily want to be there?" In every audience of trainers I've presented to, more than 90 percent of the hands go up when I ask that question. My response is: "That means you've been in training longer than a week!"

Most of our classes and meetings, whether one-on-one or small groups, are attended by people who don't want to be there. Sometimes it's because of pressures on the job, and sometimes they can't see the relationship between themselves and the content being covered. So how can we motivate these people?

Research Factoid

> *"Motivation to learn is alterable; it can be positively or negatively affected by the task, the environment, the teacher, and the learner."*
>
> – Angelo, T. A. (1993), p. 7

Basic Principles of Motivation

Learning tends to be effective to the extent that the student is properly motivated. And what is motivation? Basically, it's what incites a person to action. Motive/action: Motivation is a motive for acting, a reason for doing what we do. And almost all of us can justify or explain our actions.

Three Basic Principles of Motivation

There are three basic principles of motivation:

1. You cannot motivate other people.

2. All people are motivated.

    You might say, "Hey, wait! I know some people who are late two mornings a week and sick the other three days. You mean to tell me they're motivated?" My response would be, "Absolutely! They're more motivated to be sick and late and absent than they are to be on time and effective."

    Almost all of us have reasons, which are valid for us, for why we do what we do. So all people are motivated. Maybe not the way you and I think they ought to be, but they are motivated.

3. People do things for their reasons, not your reasons.

This gets back to the fact that people are tuned to the radio station WII-FM: What's In It for Me? People have *their* reasons for doing things. Principle Number One states that you cannot motivate other people. True enough—but you can create a climate or an environment in which a person is self-motivated.

This underscores what we talked about in the previous chapter about getting people's attention and answering for them: "What's in it for me? How will I benefit if I learn this information, if I feel these feelings, if I take the action that's suggested here?"

The question I must have uppermost in my mind as I approach a training program is: What's the payoff—for the participant, for the participant's boss, and for the person who's paying for the training? It's important that not only you and I clearly see the benefits of training but that these individuals do as well.

Over and over again, as I've observed trainers, I see the basic principles of motivation violated. It's almost as if they wanted to kill the motivation in their adult learners. Over time, I've identified five key ways to squelch motivation.

Five Ways to Squelch Motivation

1. **Have Little Personal Contact.**

Research Factoid

> *"Interaction between teachers and learners is one of the most powerful factors in promoting learning; interactions among learners is another."*
>
> — Angelo, T. A. (1993), p. 7

Be the last one there, the first one to leave, and make it clear that lunch and coffee breaks belong to you. You may have to teach content, but you certainly don't have to relate to anyone.

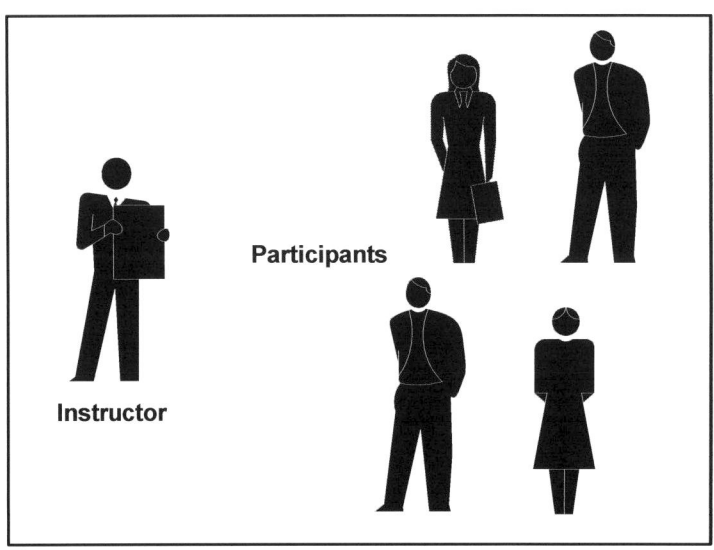

When I lived in Colorado, I led a series of human-relations and communications seminars that were given in 10 three-hour sessions. Not only was I conducting the courses, I also was responsible for marketing them. It wasn't too long before I was leading three-hour seminars on Monday, Tuesday, and Thursday nights, on Wednesday and Friday mornings, and one weekend a month.

Needless to say, this plus the marketing gave me a rather full schedule. So I thought it would really be helpful if someone else could lead some of these seminars. After completing one particular course, a participant who had an MBA and who was executive director of a very large volunteer organization in Denver came up to me and said, "If you're interested in having someone in our group be a seminar leader, I'd sure like to learn how to do it!"

I was excited about this opportunity. So I asked my mother, who was my receptionist at the time, if she could help out on Tuesday nights—opening the seminar room, greeting people as they came in, putting on the coffee, and so on. Then Tim, the new leader, would come and conduct the sessions.

The sessions ran from 7:00 to 10:00. My mother would be there around 6:30, put the coffee on, get the name tags out, and greet people as they came in. At 6:59 on the button, Tim would show up. He would run the seminar exactly the way it was supposed to be run. Then, at 10:01, he was the first one out the door. My mom, however, would stay around while people talked—sometimes to her, sometimes to one another—and finally she would lock up the training facility around 10:30 and go home.

Tim wasn't able to lead the seventh session, so I came in to run the class. By the time the coffee break was over, 75 percent of the students had asked me why my mother wasn't teaching the course! Now, my mother hadn't gone to college, and she had no experience in the subjects under discussion, but she had made a more positive impression on the group's participants than Tim had. Why? Because she had demonstrated that she cared about them personally.

If you want to squelch motivation, show up just in time to make your presentation, leave immediately after, and make sure you stay unavailable during breaks.

2. **Get Participants in a Passive Mood and Keep Them There.** This means, for example, that you don't allow any questions. When the participants come back from lunch, start out by showing a video. Ensure that the video is black and white, 20 years old, and an hour long. If any equipment is demonstrated, make sure that it's obvious that the equipment is obsolete. Raise the room temperature 10 degrees, and make sure you don't have any water available. Speak in a monotone. Avoid eye contact. All these things will put people in a passive mood and keep them there.

In our seminars, we even take this one step further. Rather than have the trainer go from table to table distributing materials and thus signaling to the participants that they should just sit there and let the trainer serve them, we have a volunteer from each table come to the front and get enough materials for their table. Never do for your participants what they can do for themselves.

3. **Assume the Class Will Apply What Is Taught.** Don't bother with specific examples. Remember, these people are adults, so you don't have to draw pictures for them. Just give them straight content. You can cover more in less time if you don't bother with illustrations. After all, it's your responsibility simply to present. It's their responsibility as adults to apply what you present. Forget about the fact that often people remember examples and illustrations better than other content and that, in fact, this can be one of the strong keys to memory. (Of course I am being facetious with these comments!)

   On the other hand, don't make all the applications for them. Many times I find it more effective to deliver the content and stop just this side of making application. However, then I have them discuss applications in their small groups. However, remember to give them adequate time to process and apply the content being delivered. We know from experience that they won't be going home at night and spending time making those applications. We must give them time in class.

4. **Be Quick to Criticize.** Remember the management adage that "criticism should be delivered in public; praise, if any, given in private." If somebody asks a dumb question, say so. If somebody misses something, point it out with a tactful comment such as, "You know, you just asked a question that I answered not more than three minutes ago. Perhaps one of the other participants was more alert than you."

   One way to avoid even the temptation to criticize is to make sure that you don't hand out knowledge questions for discussion at the table. I try to have most of my small group discussions around application questions. When someone is sharing how they plan to use the content back on the job, the potential for criticizing is minimized. Seldom will there be a right or wrong answer.

5. **Make Participants Feel Stupid for Asking Questions in Class.** Having a safe learning environment is essential to keeping the tension low enough in a training room for content retention to occur. When we make someone feel stupid for asking a question, we sabotage the safety of the learning environment. That's why in many of our seminars, we will use group-generated questions where an entire small group lists a couple of questions they wish addressed or we use a question board where participants can post their questions anonymously through the use of self-sticking notes either at a break or at lunch.

   A couple of years ago, I attended a presentation made by a guest speaker to about 40 training professionals. What I witnessed illustrates a number of points I've been making and will continue to make throughout this book.

   The speaker began by saying, "I don't really know why I'm here because I don't do any training. However, the people who invited me seem to think I've got something to say, so I guess I'll go ahead and say it. I could have been better prepared, but I thought this presentation was next week. I didn't know until I got a phone call reminding me yesterday that it was actually today."

With that, he picked up a piece of chalk, which was supposed to fool us into thinking he might actually use a visual aid. After about 45 minutes, he asked, "Do you believe that if you change attitudes, you will change behavior, or that if you change behavior, you will change attitudes?"

He paused and looked at the group for a response. No one said anything for about 20 or 30 seconds. So I raised my hand, and he asked, "Do you want to give it a try?"

I said, "I believe that if you change attitudes, you will change behavior; but that if you change behavior, you will sometimes change attitudes."

He replied, "Do you still believe that? All the literature indicates..." and he went on in that fashion.

My immediate thought was, "All what literature?" I considered myself fairly well-read on the subject, and I thought there were points to be made on both sides of the issue.

He continued his presentation. "One time," he said, "we did some research for an insurance company that was bothered by a particular problem. When they hired a new life insurance agent, that agent's sales performance would increase for about 18 months, but then it would drop and level off. The client wanted to find out what happened at 18 months, almost consistently across all agents, that caused the drop in sales performance.

"We evaluated all kinds of things, considered all kinds of options, and examined all the possibilities. Yet we found only one significant thing happening at 18 months."

The speaker asked the audience, "And what do you think that was?" He waited for a response.

Finally, I raised my hand, and he acknowledged me by saying, "You want to try again?" I said, "They ran out of relatives?"

He glared at me and snapped, "That's wrong. Anybody else want to try?" Nobody did.

I didn't attempt to answer any other questions during his presentation. And, as a matter of fact, no one else would answer any either.

At the end of his presentation, the speaker got a polite round of applause. He went up to the president of the group and gloated, "I really had some doubts about doing this presentation, but it was obviously well-received. I'd like to come back." And on that note, he left.

About 35 of the 40 people went to a nearby bar and grill, where the real learning took place. "Did you hear when he said that?" Did you see when he did that?" Only then did the participants dare ask questions and involve themselves in the experience.

Think back to the five ways to squelch motivation, and you'll see how effectively the speaker in my example employed them all.

1) Have little personal contact: he was the last one there and the first to leave.

2) Get people in a passive mood and keep them there: he asked two questions in nearly two hours, not exactly what you'd call involvement.

3) Assume they'll apply the information, so skip the examples: he did have one good illustration—about the insurance agents, which I'll return to—but it was the only one in a lengthy presentation.

4) Be quick to criticize: he was great at that.

5) Make participants feel stupid for asking questions: he not only made us feel stupid for asking questions, he made us feel stupid for trying to answer them.

True, this unskilled presenter did use specific examples, yet he was certainly critical. For example, when he asked the question, "What do you think caused performance to drop?" he squelched my answer about running out of relatives. He might have said something like, "You know that's a really good guess. It wasn't the cause, but it is a really good guess. Does someone else have a guess?" That more tactful approach would have encouraged further responses.

He did use one good illustration, though, and I'd like to discuss it further. When his organization did research for the insurance company, it found that, for the first 18 months, the new agent would go to a prospective customer's home and ask questions like: "How long have you lived here? What is your mortgage? What are the payments? How many children do you have? What are your educational plans for your children?" After about 45 minutes of asking questions, the agent would say, "By using your answers to my questions, I can formulate certain plans and strategies that can help you achieve your financial goals."

After asking the same questions over and over again for 18 months, each agent became an expert. He or she could look at a customer's home and conclude, "They've lived here 4.6 years, the mortgage is $286,900, and the payments are $669.50. They have 2.6 kids, and 1.6 are going to go to college." In 10 minutes, the agent could tell the customer what he or she needed. And once the agents stopped asking and started telling, their sales results dropped.

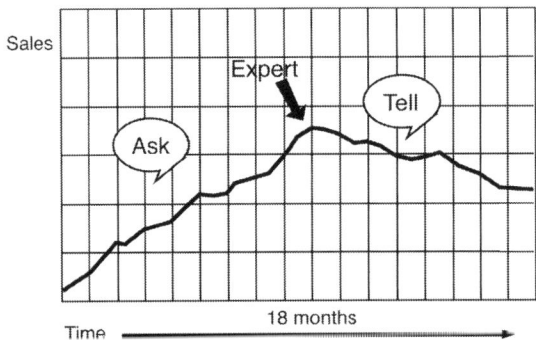

Learner Motivation

How many times do we as trainers tell our participants things that they could have discovered for themselves—if only we had asked? Remember, people don't argue with their own data. If they think something is true, then for them it is true. But if you say it's true, it may be suspect. After all, you've got to believe it; you're the instructor!

Furthermore, nobody likes experts. We want to knock them off their pedestals. Let's say, for example, that your 10-year-old daughter comes running home from school one day and says, "Look, Mom! Look, Dad! Can you solve this equation for 'X'?" You stare blankly at the problem and finally confess, "No, I can't." When she says, in a superior tone, "Well, I can!" your response might be something like, "Great. But is your room clean? Have you taken the garbage out yet? What about the book report that was due last week?" Why does your child's know-it-all attitude annoy you? Because no one likes it when someone—even your child, of whom you're very proud—says, in effect, "I know something you don't. But if you're lucky, I may share the information with you, stupid!"

Yet imagine that the same daughter came running in and said, "Look, Mom! Look, Dad! Look what I learned to do today. I can solve this equation by multiplying the top by 4 to get 36, and then I multiply the bottom by 3. Next, I subtract..."

Our likely response to this child's enthusiasm and desire to share new learning is: "Chip off the old block! Have some cookies and some milk. Honey, come here and look at this! Let's save this for Gramma!"

The basic difference between these two scenarios is simply this: "Let me share with you what I've been learning" instead of "I know something you don't."

Just as we can kill motivation in our participants, we can also create an environment where they motivate themselves. Over time, I've identified 11 ways we can create that environment.

How to Motivate Adults

1. **Create a Need.** Remember that people are constantly asking themselves: "What's in it for me?" Since they're all tuned to that radio station WII-FM, make sure you spend some time at the beginning of every presentation talking about what's in it for them.

- Why do they need this information?
- How will they benefit from it?
- How can they make use of it in a practical, real way?

2. **Develop a Sense of Personal Responsibility.** Remember the basic principle of motivation: You cannot motivate other people; you can only create a climate or an environment in which they can motivate themselves. Each individual is responsible for the learning, but it is your responsibility to create the best possible climate in which that learning can take place.

An effective way to do this is to give participants an opportunity at the beginning of the class to indicate

- what expectations they have (once you've provided the parameters of the class);
- what outcomes they expect; and
- what they're willing to do to achieve those results.

You can also distribute partial handouts that participants must complete themselves in order for the material to be useful. You can make the group responsible for various learning activities. And you can make participants responsible for the simple mechanics of the class, such as returning from breaks on time.

Participant-Centered = Results

BOB PIKE'S MASTER CLASS

Motivation

Motivation

Basic Principle:

Learning tends to be effective to the extent that the student is properly motivated.

Basic Definition:

Motivation is that within a person that incites that person to action.

Five Ways to Squelch Motivation

1. Have little _____.
2. Get participants in a _____ and keep them there.
3. _____ the class will apply what is taught — don't bother with examples.
4. Be alert to _____.
5. Make them _____ for asking questions in class.

3. **Create and Maintain Interest.** One effective way to do this is to encourage question asking throughout. Questions generate interest; questions create alertness. There is only one thing we are more conditioned to answer than a question—and that's the telephone!

   Another way you can create and maintain interest is to use variety. You don't need to rely exclusively on games or role plays. You can use the various techniques and methods discussed in Chapter 4. For example, you can use charts, discussion, lectures, films, posters, projects, and case studies. Mix and match a variety of techniques in order to grab your participants' attention and engage them in the learning experience.

   Another involvement technique is to give people handouts for them to complete. Two examples are handouts with partial PowerPoints on which they fill in key words and partial outlines that they complete as the session proceeds. This activity keeps participants involved in the learning process and also gives them something of value that they can refer to in the future.

   This simple device also allows you to cover more material in less time. A well-prepared handout indicates in a nonverbal way that you're thoroughly and thoughtfully prepared for the presentation. It tells your participants that you cared enough about this presentation to prepare superior supplemental materials.

4. **Structure Experiences to Apply Content to Life.** In most of the presentations you make and the training you do, people want to know: "How will this work for me?" and "Will this really help me make better decisions, solve more problems, make more sales, etc.?"

   They want practical applications. Sure, theory is important, but people must see how that theory can be put into practice so that their jobs can be done faster, easier, and better, and their lives and work can be more interesting.

5. **Give Praise, Recognition, Encouragement, and Approval.** William James, a Harvard psychologist, said that the greatest need of every human being is the need for appreciation. Most of us are like dry sponges waiting for a drop of appreciation. People are very quick to point out when we've done something wrong; they're slow to acknowledge that we've done something right. When we finally do something that is so absolutely right, we can hardly believe we've done it; we wait for somebody to acknowledge our accomplishment. And we wait and wait and wait. Finally, we grab someone and explain in full color and vivid detail this absolutely right thing we've done. And we're likely to hear something like, "Well, it's about time" or "Isn't that your job?" or "Isn't that what you're paid for?"

   We, as trainers, must recognize that need for appreciation in the classroom. One good way to do this is by repeating comments that people may make. For example, someone might approach you during a break and comment about something that was said during the session. As you begin the next segment of your presentation, you could use this brief exchange in a positive way: "Fran made an interesting comment during the break, one that certainly applies to the things we've been exploring in this program. I think it bears repeating."

What has been accomplished by employing this simple technique?

- You gave recognition.
- You not only encouraged Fran but you encouraged the rest of the group to become more involved.
- You certainly demonstrated by your approval that you want feedback and comments.

Remember that recognition should flow like a river—or rather a **RIVR**. It should be:

> **R**andom
> **I**ntermittent
> **V**ariable
> **R**einforcement

Random says that it's unpredictable at times. Intermittent says that it's not all the time. Variable says it's not the same. Yet when you apply these three principles, the reinforcement is incredible.

When I was at the U.S. Naval Academy as a plebe, I was returning to Bancroft Hall from class one day. As I entered the seventh wing, I noticed a candy wrapper lying near a vending machine. Almost without thought I picked it up, threw it away, and then started running up the stairwell. Suddenly I heard, "Halt, Plebe." I stopped immediately, came to attention, and sounded off, "Midshipman Fourth Class Pike, sir." The first class midshipman asked if the paper I picked up was mine. I said, "No sir." He then asked if someone had told me to pick it up. I replied, "No sir." He then asked why I had picked up the paper and threw it in the trash can. I replied, "Because it didn't belong there, sir." He asked for my company number and dismissed me. Several days later, I was called into my company officer's office. The midshipman had written a letter of commendation stating that with all the responsibilities placed on plebes in their first year it was refreshing to see a plebe doing something because it ought to be done, not because of an order.

Here's the point of the story. Ten years later, I'm at Disneyland for the first time. As I walk up Main Street, I see a piece of paper. Before I could reach over to pick it up, a young man in white shirt and pants swept it up and took it away. In an instant, Disneyland became the cleanest place on earth for me. Thousands of times since that letter I've picked up wrappers and thrown them away. Never once was I hoping for another letter (and for the record, I've never received one!), but each time I do, I remember how good it felt the time I did. Remember to practice RIVR in your classes.

6. **Foster Wholesome Competition.** Wholesome competition enables people to measure themselves with themselves. Success is what I am, compared with what I can be. It is me compared with me and you compared with you. It lets them say,

"I don't compete with you; I compete with myself." And ask, "Where am I right now, and how can I improve myself?"

Research Factoid

> *"Teachers who present the information in a dynamic manner and who display a genuine interest in what they are teaching have a positive effect upon student achievement."*
>
> – Larkins, A. G., McKinney, C. W., & Gilmore, A. C. (1984)

7. **Get Excited Yourself.** You certainly can't expect people to get more excited about your program or content or presentation than you are. So let people see your own genuine enthusiasm for your topic. This does not mean that you have to come running from the back of the room and leap across three tables!

    There are at least two ways to do this, no matter what your personal style. First, be available. Being available to participants at least 15 minutes before the class starts shows our interest, enthusiasm, and excitement for the subject and for the participants themselves.

    Second, make eye contact. People who are not confident in their subject or are disinterested in it have a tendency to never look at their participants. They have mastered what I call the "soft glaze." They either focus about 12 inches above everybody's head or are constantly looking at their notes. But the one thing they don't do is make eye contact. Here are three quick tips for making great eye contact:

    1) Look at one eye only. If you try to look at both eyes, you only focus on the bridge of the nose. Focusing on one eye gives great intensity.

    2) Make eye contact for three to five seconds only. Longer than that and it starts to get uncomfortable. Shorter than that and people aren't sure you've looked at them.

    3) Make random eye contact with participants. You're not a camera sweeping the room back and forth. Look at someone up front, then someone to one side, then someone at the back of the room—you get the idea!

8. **Establish Long-Range Objectives.** Adults like to see the big picture, then they can focus on the individual pieces. Help people realize how they can benefit—in the long run—as they increase their level of confidence in the areas you're discussing, presenting, and training them in. Here is where adults differ from children. You can give a child a task, and the child simply goes to work and does it. The task doesn't necessarily need to relate to anything. But adults like to see the big picture; then they can concentrate on the individual pieces.

9. **See the Value of Internal Motives.** You, as a trainer, may have organizational objectives; however, individual, or internal, desires and objectives may be far

more motivational to program participants. Recognize and encourage these more personal motives.

I've seen people who came to management training just because they thought it would help them get a promotion. You might say that that is a lousy reason—and I'd agree. However, it is better than no reason at all!

10. **Intensify Interpersonal Relationships.** Give people in the class the opportunity to meet and connect with one another and also make yourself available to them. That means being there early, staying late, and making yourself available during the breaks, lunches, and social times.

    Connecting with your participants on a one-on-one basis can be extremely valuable, but helping them connect with one another on a one-on-one basis can be even more valuable.

    After the training is over, it may be very difficult for you to stay in touch and be available. After all, tomorrow or next week you'll be working with a different group and it will be difficult to be available to this group. But if we connect them with one another so that they are comfortable enough in calling one another after the class, then we've expanded their network, their relationships, and the support that they have available to make sure that they can implement the content of your training program.

11. **Give Them a Choice.** For example, develop two or three case studies, and give participants a choice of which one to examine in depth. Or design three carry-over activities and ask them to do one of the three.

    All of us like to feel we have control of our lives. When we can make choices, we feel we have that control.

    It's virtually impossible for you to develop a single exercise, project, case study, or activity that's exciting to every single person to whom you present it. By providing two, three, or even four activities and letting participants choose among them, you give them an opportunity to select something that creates a more personal motivational environment.

    Control is one commodity that participants tend to give over to the trainer at the beginning of the class. There is no other way for the training to proceed. The unwise trainer takes the control they have voluntarily given and proceeds to lord it over the class—showing at every opportunity that he/she the trainer is in control. The wise trainer figures out how to give control back to the participants as quickly and completely as possible. The giving of choices is one of the primary methods of getting this done.

    Of course what the participants might not first understand is that in the giving of choices there is the implicit understanding that personal responsibility is not far behind. For those of us who desire participants to take personal responsibility for their own learning, the giving of choices is essential.

It's a peak experience to have in our programs eager, willing people who are there because they want to be, not because they have to be. We are not always so fortunate to have that learning environment created for us. But, by focusing on the preceding guidelines, we can improve the way we create an environment that produces better results from the training we deliver.

Learning Preferences

In the early 1990s, Inscape Publishing (now part of Wiley) asked me to help validate an instrument that they developed. Called the Personal Learning Insights Profile (PLIP), it is a valuable resource that I have used ever since. We have now profiled more than 75,000 people in 25 countries and used it in many of our seminars to help trainers design and deliver training that appeals to all learning preferences. The three learning preferences that the profile looks at are specific structure versus general structure, informative learner versus practical learner, and participative learner versus reflective learner.

Let's look at each of the three. The first scale specific structure versus general structure provides a measure of how the participants like their learning structured. Specific structure basically says that I'd like all of the I's dotted and all of the T's crossed. For example: what you want me to learn, when do you want me to learn by, how will I know I've learned, what are the resources that I have available to learn, etc. General structure says that I will be responsible for organizing my own learning: tell me what you want to learn and I'll figure out how to acquire the knowledge and skills.

On this scale, when we look at all of our participants from a variety of walks of life and economic backgrounds and levels of education, we have almost a normal curve of distribution 50 percent prefer specific structure and 50 percent general structure. So when we look at designing for the classroom or online, we look at choices. For example, we might design a case study. Those with a preference for specific structure love it: A case study—I know exactly how to do that. But we don't design one case— we will design two or three or four and say to the participant, "Look these over and then choose one that you're going to work on." Participants who like general structure say I love this because I've been given a choice, not an assignment.

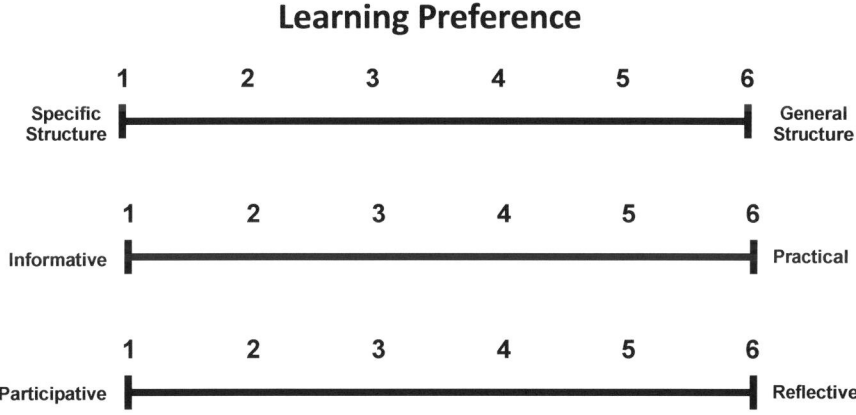

When we look at the second scale, informative versus practical, we again use an almost 50-50 normal curve of distribution—that is, 50 percent of the people we profiled are extremely practical learners—if I can't use this immediately, why are you teaching me? The other 50 percent are informative learners: they love input. They love data, so when we design any program, we basically gather all the information and then divide it into three content chunks:

- "Need to know," that is the core content.
- "Nice to know," that is great value-added content.
- "Where to go," that is references and resources for participants to use later.

Typically in our workbooks, the need-to-know sections are printed on white paper, and 80 percent plus of the workshop time is spent on need-to-know content. The nice-to-know sections are most often printed on a lavender-colored paper, and about 5 to 10 percent of the time in the workshop may focus on this content. The where-to-go section is printed on yellow—we look it up in the yellow pages. This section is referred to, but we spend very little time on it. So from the perspective of learning preferences, practical learners of the courses that we design are engaged because they see that immediate and practical value of everything they are spending time on. However, the informative learners also like the course structure because we provide lots of additional information—lots of additional resources that appeal to their informative bent.

The final scale, participative learner versus reflective learner, is where we see the biggest skew. Over 75 percent of the people that we have profiled profile as participative learners—that is I've learned better with other people. So all of our courses are designed to allow people to interact in a variety of ways. The primary group that they interact in is typically a group of five to seven. But we also have participants choosing one or two learning bodies that they will interact with periodically, and we use a large variety of temporary groups to allow people to connect with, network with, and learn from one another throughout the course.

The biggest thing that we need to understand in the design and delivery of training is that anytime we get a group of people together, virtually all of the learning preferences will be present. We need to design and deliver in a way that appeals to each of the learning preferences. And that's what our instructor-led, participant-centered approach allows for and encourages.

Teaching Across Cultures and Generations

There has been quite a bit of research conducted on generational differences. Some of the research is directed at the generational differences in learning. The challenge in applying the research is two-fold. First, almost all of the research is based on U.S. and European populations. The second is that you seldom have a class made up of only one generation. So the labels used in identifying generations fits with western culture and history. The Traditionalists, Baby Boomers, Generation X, and Millennials work in the United States and Europe because the things that shaped each generation are the same: World War I, the Great Depression, World War II, the postwar economic boom, the technology explosions, etc. But different things at different times shape generations in Africa, the Middle East, China, India, etc. So from a design and delivery standpoint, generational differences don't always apply.

What I have found, however, is that there are teaching strategies that I can use that work regardless of the generations and regardless of the cultures that I work in. Building these into your training will help to ensure that both the design and delivery of your training will appeal regardless of the age groups that are present and regardless of the culture that you may be working in. Here are 11 strategies:

1. **Give choices.** There is no generation or culture that likes assignments. Especially as adults, we like to be in control, and we're in control when we're given a choice. As an example, for activities, I'm going to use group leaders, but I will give you a method for choosing your own leader. There will be four case studies, but you will choose the one that you work on. Your group will create a poster, but what goes on the poster will be your choice.

2. **Use variety.** Any teaching method, no matter how good, loses its impact when it is used over and over again. So if you look at the flow of any of the courses I design, you'll notice that over the course of three days, people may brainstorm five different times, but not five times in a row. There may be a small group discussion, followed by a short lecture, followed by a paired share, followed by the small group creating a chart at the wall, etc.

3. **Be optimistic.** It is my responsibility as a trainer to be positive about the course, the content, the potential of the participants, etc. As Bette Miller sang in the song "Wind Beneath My Wings," I am supposed to be the wind beneath my participants' wings—they are not supposed to be the wind beneath my wings. I am supposed to lift them up—not expecting them to lift me up.

4. **Rotate group roles.** The most frequent role used in my programs is that of the group leader. So I want to be sure that every time there is a project or an activity that needs a leader that the role rotates.

   We are focused on primarily using groups of five to seven people, so I want to constantly reinforce that this is your group, not one particular person's group. And I use choosing the group leader as a way to energize the group. One time it may be that the group leader is the person with the most siblings, another time the fewest siblings, still another time the most children, the largest high school graduating class, traveled the farthest distance to attend this course, longest time with the company, shortest time with the company—you get the idea. So networking goes on and we are always rotating the role of the group leader.

5. **Provide practical experiences.** I always want to be sure that my participants have an opportunity during the class to apply what they're learning so that they are making the practical and immediately usable connection between the class and what's going to happen when they get back on the job. Several examples come to mind. In one course, I use a window pane to teach the seven ways to remember anything. This models the concept of windowpaning as a memory technique. Then I follow that with giving participants

time to reflect on their own content and creating a windowpane based on their content.

6. **Encourage participation.** Not everybody enjoys having to perform in front of an entire class, so I'm going to structure activities that are done in a small group of five to seven, or done with a learning buddy, etc. This makes it easier for people to participate, and it gets everybody participating—not just one or two—with everybody else looking on.

   As an example, in one course, I show a customer service video, and I ask participants to pair off. They then decide as pairs to be either Ps or Ms. Ps stands for policy and procedure. M stands for mistake. As they watch the video, each pair has one of the two focuses: the customer service mistakes that were made or what is it that exists within the company's policies or procedures that allows it to happen. After they watch the video, all of the M pairs gather together to combine their ideas. At the same time, all of the P pairs that focused on what it was about company policies or procedures that allowed it to happen gather and share their ideas. Once those discussions are finished, everyone returns to their original small group and a final debrief takes place: Ms debrief to the Ps and vice versa. This maximizes the participation of everybody, not just one or two.

7. **Provide recognition offline.** There are a few people who would like to be recognized in front of a group, but far more often, people prefer a personal comment or private remark from the instructor rather than recognition from the instructor in front of the entire group.

8. **Hold people accountable.** The biggest thing that I do to make this one work is by having participants set their own standards and norms for both themselves and me at the beginning of the course. Once they've set the standards and norms, I simply make a point of revisiting them once or twice a day to have them determine how well they're doing living up to the standards and norms that they've committed to and how well I'm doing living up to the standards and norms that I've committed to. If either of us is less than a 7 on the 7-point scale, I ask what we need to do more of or less of to see the scores improve.

9. **Create networking opportunities.** The most powerful benefits of attending any training program are the new connections and relationships that we build during the program. Most people hate that I build in opportunities constantly throughout the course for people to meet others whom they haven't met to accomplish a small task or goal. By the end of the course, participants meet, connect with, spend time with, and learn about every single person in the room and probably develop deep connections with three or four. This is valuable during the course and becomes far more valuable after the course because now they have a support group that can help them apply what they've learned but can also be valuable in their job role as their career moves on.

10. **Allow for individual work.** People need reflection time. If they don't get a chance to think about how to personally apply what they're learning during the course, they don't get a chance to think about how they're going to use

what they've learned after the course. They need to develop a plan of action while the course is going on, because chances are they won't have the opportunity to do so when they get back on the job. So I provide people with an action idea page and provide three or four times a day when people can reflect and make personally apply what they've been learning.

11. **Enforce personal responsibility.** In the final analysis, as teachers and trainers, you and I can teach anybody anything. We can create a climate or environment where learning takes place, but people have to be responsible for their own learning.

Chapter 4:
Visual Aids

How to Keep Their Attention When You Absolutely Have to Talk

Why Visual Aids?

Research has proven that it's possible to learn much more in a given period of time when visual aids are properly used. Studies at the University of Wisconsin have shown an improvement of up to 200 percent when vocabulary was taught using visual aids. Studies at Harvard and Columbia show between a 14 to 38 percent improvement in retention through the use of audio visuals. And studies done at the University of Pennsylvania's Wharton School and at the University of Minnesota demonstrate clearly that the time required to present a concept was reduced up to 40 percent and the prospect of a favorable decision was greatly improved when visuals were used to augment a verbal presentation. Barriers of language, time, and space can be minimized by using appropriate audio visuals.

Visual aids generally can be divided into two categories: projected and nonprojected. Projected visual aids include computer graphics (like PowerPoint), video recordings, and desktop visualizers (such as WolfVision). Nonprojected visuals include pictures, posters, flip charts, flannel graphs, models, object lessons, simulators, maps, audio recordings, bulletin boards, chalkboards, and whiteboards.

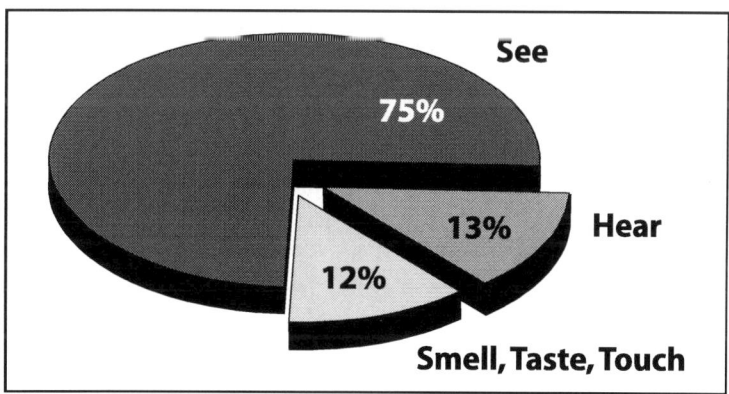

In his book *Presentations Plus*, David A. Peoples, a consulting instructor for IBM, says that 75 percent of what people know came to them visually, 13 percent through hearing, and a total of 12 percent through smell, touch, and taste. A picture, he says, is three times more effective than words alone, and words and pictures together are six times more effective than words alone.

Research Factoid

> *"Studies show that presentation graphics can reduce teaching time by as much as 28%."*
>
> – Mucciolo, Tom & Mucciolo, Ric, (1994)

Clearly, there are some significant reasons for carefully designing and using visual aids. The ten most obvious reasons are these:

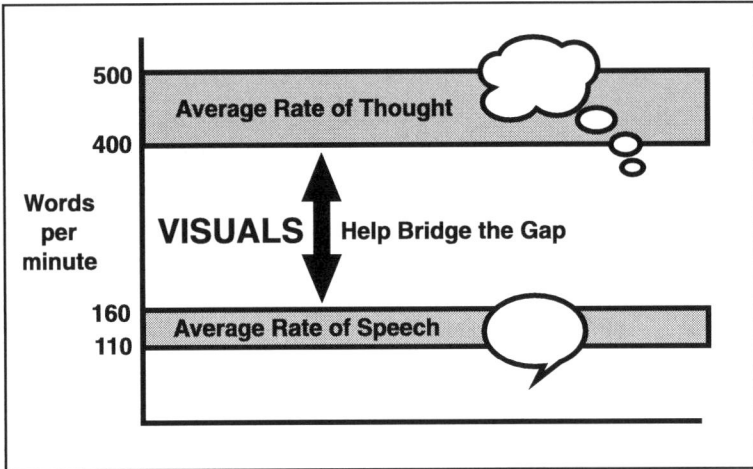

1. **To Attract and Maintain Attention.** The average individual speaks about 110 to 160 words per minute, but he or she thinks at a rate of 1,000 to 1,500 words per minute. Giving people visual stimulation can help keep them tied to the presentation rather than allowing their minds to wander elsewhere.

2. **To Reinforce Main Ideas.** We tend to put much more emphasis on what we see than on what we hear. If you don't believe that, recall the last time you saw a presentation where a visual was projected for which you did not have a handout. Wasn't there a tendency for you and for many of those around you to copy the information hurriedly before the visual was taken away? Yet how often do we hang onto the words of a presenter so attentively that we feel the need to write down everything that's said?

3. **To Illustrate and Support the Spoken Word.** The Chinese proverb says that a picture is worth a thousand words. But let's make that: A *well-chosen* picture or visual is worth a thousand words.

4. **To Minimize Misunderstanding.** Visuals can give meaning to words not clearly understood. Assume for a moment that you're going to visit a friend whose home you've never been to before. How would you like to get directions? Would you prefer simply to hear the instructions? Would you like the instructions written down? Or would you like a map? The importance of visuals becomes readily apparent. Think about the last time you went to a shopping center or a mall and

studied the building directory. How much easier is it to locate yourself and your destination when you see on the map the little red dot that says "You are here" and identifies the stores you want to visit.

5. **To Increase Retention.** Here's the Chinese Proverb again: "What I hear, I forget; what I see, I remember; what I do, I understand." We have to remember something in order to be able to use it.

6. **To Add a Touch of Realism.** It may not be possible to have all the props, support materials, etc., that we would like in the classroom, but visuals can bring a welcome piece of the real world into an academic setting.

7. **To Save Both Time and Money.** Audio visuals can help us communicate more clearly and quickly so that participants understand the content we are trying to communicate.

8. **To Aid in Organizing Your Thoughts.** Audio visuals can help us clarify our thinking and provide a logical path for communication.

9. **To Ensure Covering Key Points.** Not only do visuals give us a path to follow, they also ensure that we do not omit key points and that we cover them in the proper sequence.

10. **To Build Your Confidence.** Knowing that you don't have to rely entirely on your memory for every facet of your presentation and knowing that your visuals are a "road map" that can guide you, they can help you deliver your presentation with more confidence.

Projected Visuals

Films/Videos

Film has gone the way of the dinosaur in most of the world. Yet these tips apply equally to videos.

Videos give you the advantage of showing motion, which is important for certain kinds of learning (for example, showing the steps involved in operating a machine). A video also can capture an event that you want to present as an illustration in a training program (for example, a sample interaction between a manager and an employee or a customer and a clerk).

If you're going to use a video, choose it carefully and be sure to preview it. As you do, ask yourself these questions:

- Does it fit your needs?
- Will your audience perceive it as relevant?
- Is the language familiar and consistent with what your participants know, or does it require them to learn new terminology?
- Does it have direct application?

- Does the video come with listening guides, application activities, etc., that can help you integrate it into your learning process, or will you need to create these yourself?

A video is not simply an opportunity for a change of pace. It can and should be a significant learning activity that requires application. You don't want your participants tuning out when you turn on the projector. Pay careful attention to how you will introduce the video. Are there particular things you want your participants to look for? Perhaps it would be useful to break your participants into groups with each group looking for certain things; after the video, you can fully involve all your participants in a discussion of the various elements each group was looking for. Do you want to show the video in its entirety, or would it be useful to view parts of the video and then break away for discussion, application, etc., before going on to the rest of the movie?

For smaller groups, your playback system may consist of a flat screen LCD panel rather than a video projector. The rule of thumb I use is to have one diagonal inch of viewing screen for each participant. So, if I were running a training program with 25 participants, a 32- to 36-inch monitor would serve my purposes. Once I get beyond 75 people or so, it becomes more effective to use a video projector. But, again, costs can be a constraint. A 32- to 36-inch monitor can be purchased for as little as $300. A DVD player can be purchased for as little as $75 (and you may be able to run some videos right from your laptop embedded in your PowerPoint presentation). But a good LCD projector with at least a 1,200-lumen lamp can run between $800 and $1,200. How often you're going to use the equipment can significantly affect the kind of investment you might be prepared to make. If you're going to use this medium infrequently and with large groups, it might be best to rent the LCD projector. Rental fees, depending upon your geographical location, can range anywhere from $75 a day to $400+ per day.

Videos can also be used "real time" in the classroom. This can be especially useful if participants are doing a skill practice, such as giving a presentation or practicing a performance appraisal, closing a sale, or handling a customer complaint.

I like the model given to me by Bernie Birnbrauer and Lynn Tyson; we served together as faculty for an education forum for IBM's technical educators that was offered for graduate credit at Vanderbilt University. Rather than video recording in front of the entire group of 35 to 40 participants, Bernie and Lynn formed work groups of approximately six participants and video recorded within these groups. Subgroups, or triads, were formed in each of the work groups. The process goes something like this (updated for today's camera and equipment):

1. A short presentation is given in front of the group of six, with five group members observing the presenter. The video recording is done with digital cameras using SD cards. Each participant has their own card, which is inserted in the camera when they are being video recorded. Since each person has his or her own SD card, all of their presentations are on the same medium and can be kept afterward for personal review and use. (I might add that presenters feel more secure when they know that the only permanent record of their presentation is in their own possession!)

2. During the presentation, each group member fills out a feedback sheet to give to the presenter later.

3. After the presentation, participants meet in their subgroups.

4. In the subgroups, each participant cycles through three roles: mentor, student, and observer. Let's say, for example, that the three participants are Chris, Jan, and Lee. In the first round, Chris serves as mentor, Jan serves as student, and Lee as the observer. All three watch Jan's video recording. Chris, as a mentor, has a checklist of things to look for, and Lee has a mentor's checklist, too. After watching the video recording (which can be done on a laptop, since most laptops have SD card slots), Jan, as the student, has the first opportunity to debrief and identify the strengths and weaknesses of the presentation. After Jan's debriefing, Chris (as the mentor) would provide further feedback on the strengths and weaknesses of the presentation. Finally, Lee, as the observer, wraps up the process, giving feedback to Chris on how effectively Chris coached, or counseled, Jan. The three individuals would then rotate their roles, according to the following chart, until each had an opportunity to be mentor, student, and observer.

Round 1	Chris	Jan	Lee
Round 2	Lee	Chris	Jan
Round 3	Jan	Lee	Chris

A fourth member can be added to the group. The rotation would then look like this:

Round 1	Chris	Jan	Tim	Lee
Round 2	Lee	Chris	Jan	Tim
Round 3	Tim	Lee	Chris	Jan
Round 4	Jan	Tim	Lee	Chris

This method offers a number of advantages. First, it maximizes group participation. Each person gets an opportunity to practice the skill and receive feedback. Second, it enables the group to review and reinforce significant concepts several times without becoming bored. Even though each participant is going to view a number of presentations the process stays fresh. In one case, a participant looks at the presentation through the eyes of someone who must provide feedback to the presenter; in another case, the participant assumes the role of an observer, looking not only for items to comment on but also considering the feedback from this altered position.

Another advantage is that the feedback is balanced. If I'm the mentor, I know that I'll be receiving feedback about my effectiveness as coach or counselor. This knowledge helps me follow the "Goldilocks approach" to coaching and counseling: not too hot, not too cold, just right or not too hard, not too soft, just right. Most of us, at one time or another, have received "Pollyanna" feedback, where we were praised so much we could hardly believe it was really justified. Perhaps each of us also has experienced the opposite, where someone comes down on us like a ton of bricks, and we wonder if criticism that severe was really justified either. As you may have already deduced, this model also works great for role plays too.

The drawback to the method just described is that it may not be cost effective. It does require a digital video camera, which can cost anywhere from $250 up, depending on quality, for each group of six. It requires a laptop for each group of six or, preferably, for each group of three—but in many cases participants have their own and these can be used. If each person has a smartphone—even these cameras can be used—then connected to a laptop for playback. Just make sure that whatever you use you make sure that your sound recording is of good quality.

Video also can be used to create in-house presentations that can be used in much the same way as films. But before you make major video purchases, be sure you're going to use the equipment often enough and effectively enough to justify the expenditures. One of our clients, for whom we conduct a five-day Train-the-Trainer program once a year, thought the video feedback method was appropriate, but they realized they would only use the equipment this intensively once a year. They had two cameras, DVD players, and 36-inch LCD flat screens in-house and discovered, through a little creative research, that they could rent LCD flat screens inexpensively for the week and that several course participants had camcorders they could borrow. Thus, they were spared considerable expense.

Another option to consider is conducting your training in a hotel that has DVD players in the individual rooms. I conducted one four-day train-the-trainer session in an Embassy Suite because each DVD player connected to the LCD flat screen in the sitting area of their sleeping rooms. That enabled the participants to use the sitting areas as breakout rooms that saved us the expenses of renting DVD players and of providing additional breakout rooms.

You also might consider renting or borrowing the equipment before making a final purchase decision. Determine how frequently the equipment will be utilized and whether or not it will give you the results you desire. You may decide that, if you're going to use the equipment extensively and get the most out of it, you would have to invest either in outside experts (that is, video consultants) or add an internal staff that has the expertise to operate the equipment and to script and edit video.

And frankly today, I'd consider getting small tripods for participants to use with their smartphones, upload the videos to a private YouTube Channel, and then watch the playback on a laptop, tablet, or iPad.

Computer Graphics/PowerPoint

Computer graphics are used extensively in business presentations as well as in the training room in a variety of ways. They can be developed and displayed on most LCD flat screen panels. Programs such as PowerPoint and Keynote allow you to create visuals that can be displayed on a computer monitor in a sequence. Individual images are still called "slides" for those of us that remember the days when we used 35mm slide decks for training! But far beyond the old slide decks, they offer the additional advantage of providing video-like effects, such as wipes, dissolves, and fades. They also can provide animation.

Computer graphics can be output from the computer into other types of presentation media—most often we create narrated videos of PowerPoint presentations offering participants a chance to revisit content any time they want when posted online. However, as you will see in the chapter on the use of handouts, we encourage the utilization of partial handouts (where participants need to fill in information as the session progresses). Consequently, if you should choose to use the feature of printing your slides as your handout, at the very least please go into your slides and remove words and replace them with blanks (to fill in) prior to printing your slides. This will encourage your participants to stay with you as opposed to moving ahead in the presentation. They can output into color transparencies, using either a color plotter or a color printer. (Some of you reading this will not even understand what an overhead transparency is, but in some parts of the world, they are still used extensively—so I still make occasional reference to them.)

Depending on the programs you have, your computer graphics also can be incorporated into videos. Programs like Camtasia make these relatively easy. Assuming that you already have a computer (and what trainer doesn't these days!), you may discover that the use of computer graphics is not as expensive or as difficult to incorporate as you thought. The software necessary to create computer graphics can run from as little as zero dollars—for graphics packages that can be picked up as freeware or shareware from places like CNET—to very complete packages in the $495-and-up range. If you want to add graphics to your visuals and also have the option of using them in your handouts, you should certainly explore this area.

Opaque Projector/Elmo/Platform Projector/Video Copy Stand

With opaque projectors, you can project solid materials, such as drawings, magazine photographs, etc., without turning them into overhead transparencies. It's a good process to use if you have to display and discuss intricate diagrams. It can also be effective in projecting material from which you would like to make charts; you can trace this material onto flip-chart paper and then keep it for later use. The use of such a projector (oftentimes referred to as an Elmo or Platform Projector or WolfVision) allows the trainer to hand draw spontaneous illustrations that can be seen by a large group. Think of it as an electronic easel chart. It also allows the display of solid objects—like a computer circuit board—and then explode the view so that very small parts of the circuit are easily seen by the audience.

Non-projected Visuals

Pictures

Pictures can be effective visual aids, particularly in such presentations as orientation programs—where you want to provide an overall view of a company and its various divisions and components. If you're describing new machinery, equipment, products, etc., large pictures mounted on foam board (which then can be placed on permanent display) are very effective.

Posters

Almost every training program lends itself to some key concepts that can be captured on a poster board. Posters can be particularly effective for presentations that you're giving several times. Guidelines for the use of other permanent visual aids apply here as well. Posters can be used effectively in conjunction with other visual aids.

I also use posters when I introduce what I call the Funnel Concept. The poster shows a funnel with the word "unknown" above it. Beneath the unknown we have a number of prospects. Those prospects tend to filter through the funnel. To the right of the funnel are the words "prospecting," "appointments," "presentations," "enrollments," and "referrals." There are holes in this funnel, indicating that some prospects are eliminated at the prospecting stage—that is, they never become an appointment. Others are cancelled at the appointment stage—that is, the appointment cancels and you never make a presentation, etc. Some prospects come out the bottom of the funnel as sales. Again, after I explain the concept, the poster remains on display in front of the group.

As another example, in one seminar I do, I introduce what I call the Sales Success, or PAPER Cycle, which consists of these key points:

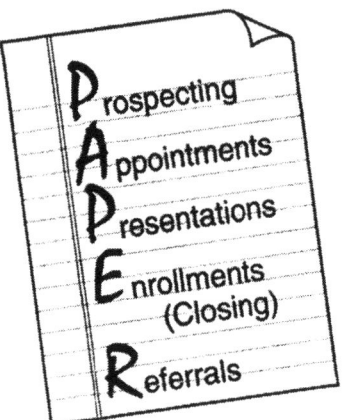

I had a sign painter depict the following cycle, in five different colors, on foam board. When I first present the concept in the seminar, I use PowerPoint slides to relate the points and build the cycle with an arrow going clockwise from "prospecting." I continue to add arrows around the circle until I reach "referrals," which points back to the first step, "prospecting." After we have discussed the basic concept using PowerPoint slides, I reveal the permanent poster to the audience so that they can refer to it for the rest of the seminar.

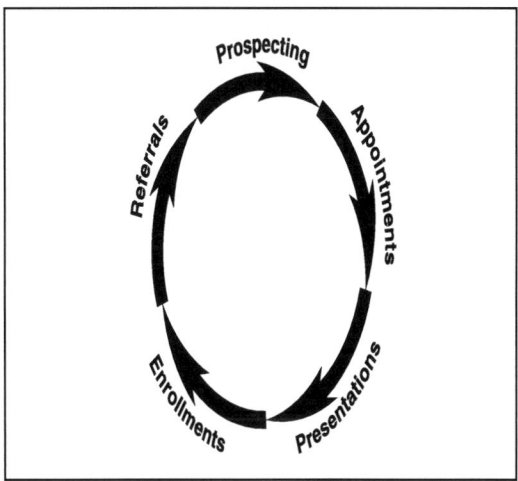

Chalkboards and Whiteboards

The whiteboard is the modern-day version of the chalkboard, and each can be effective in communicating information to participants. Markers come in a wide variety of colors, which makes writing stand out on a whiteboard. Many whiteboards are magnetized, so items can be affixed to them with magnets.

If you are presenting basic concepts with a magnetic whiteboard, print key words on show cards with magnetic strips attached. Then, simply place the signs on the magnetic board wherever you want them. I frequently use this technique in seminars when we're building on concepts. As each idea is presented, it's placed on the magnetic board so that participants can see how the concepts relate to one another.

Flip Charts

Flip charts are widely used—and misused—in the training process. They can be used effectively to create real-time visuals (that is, they're drawn as the presentation takes place), or they can be developed in advance.

Basically, flip charts from the front of the room are suitable only if your group is relatively small, 15 to 20 people at the most. People sitting in the back of a larger group have trouble seeing flip charts. However, having small groups create and post flip charts can be used with almost any size group.

We have already discussed the preparation of PowerPoint; many of the same rules apply to flip charts.

Here are some simple tips that can increase the effectiveness of a flip chart:

1. If you have basic points to make, pencil them in lightly on your various sheets of chart paper before the presentation. Then you can use your markers to write in the words so everybody can see them. In a sense, your chart paper becomes a very large set of notes or an outline.

2. Prepare some of your charts in advance, and simply overlay them with two or three sheets of paper to keep them from being prematurely visible.

3. Prepare some of your charts in advance, and cover the basic points with cut strips of paper. Then, as you get to each point in your presentation, you can simply remove the paper strip you've taped over that particular point on the chart.

4. Use a variety of colors beyond the basic black, red, and blue that we so often see. Consider not using these common colors at all. Try bright colors that people aren't used to seeing. For example, I use water-based markers, manufactured by Sanford, called Mr. Sketch, in such colors as teal, forest green, and purple—colors that are easily seen and just a bit unusual.

5. Leave the bottom third of your flip-chart sheets blank. This will allow people in the back to see your entire page, and, as you post flip charts on the wall, it leaves space to go back and add more information.

6. Brighten the chart's visual appeal. You can do this by underlining or boxing key words. Use color, graphic designs, and geometric shapes to add visual interest to your chart.

7. Use flip-chart pages to record information. For example, during a brainstorming session, write key words that reflect each contributor's ideas. Better still, have two or three participants record on flip charts ideas as they come up. This allows you to maintain control of the group, clarify ideas, etc., while someone else does the writing. Give participants who will be recording material two different-colored markers, and ask them to alternate colors as the ideas are presented.

Remember the Four Ts of flip charts:

1. Turn to the flip chart as you address information on it and stand to the side as you're discussing the information.

2. Touch the information that you're talking about. You may have three or four items listed on the flip chart. Touch the particular item that you are talking about or use a movable keynote that you can place next to the item under discussion and then move it as you move to another item.

3. Tear off the flip chart when you have finished using it. Don't simply flip it over to the back. If the ideas have value, tear it off.

4. Tape it to the wall so that that information can serve as an ongoing reminder of content. This is one distinct value the flip chart has over other types of visual aids.

Flannel Graphs/Flannel Boards

Flannel graphs or boards, in their original form, probably remind at least some people of Sunday school lessons; as the teacher told a Bible story, he or she placed on a piece of flannel board cloth cut-outs representing various characters. Today, we still see flannel boards used; as the presentation unfolds, additional elements are placed on the flannel board. The greatest strength of the flannel board is found in its great portability and the fact that in building the elements of the presentation on the board, the group finds itself focused on the unfolding diagram.

Updated versions of this method use Velcro™ or "hook 'n loop" to accomplish the same thing. Velcro™ has tiny little "hooks" that cause it to easily stick to flannel, yet with a slight tug can be removed.

Models

Models can be effective hands-on visual aids. These might be miniature representations of something too large to be brought into the classroom. Most models are static representations of real objects. They can range from miniatures of cars, pumps, and other machines to houses and skyscrapers, complete with removable cutaways to show key parts of the exterior. While most models are small representations of the real thing, some can be larger. For example, Saudia Airlines has a larger-than-life instrument panel for a Boeing 747 jet. Used to train pilots, it is five times larger than the actual panel on the plane. Operating exactly like the real thing, it allows each member of a class of 20 to see clearly. The trainer can use a model for demonstration, and participants can practice new skills on a model.

Sometimes a model is an actual piece of equipment. Make sure your models are realistic. A friend of mine once participated in a training program that taught mechanics to break down and repair a transmission. The models used in the classroom were elegantly designed, with various parts color coded. By the end of the training program, the participants could readily disassemble and assemble the transmission. They could identify the parts not only by location and function but also by color. Unfortunately, when they went on to the actual shop floor, they had to look at the transmission from underneath, not from on top as they had been able to do in the training room. And, obviously, none of the transmissions they attempted to repair were color coded. They would have learned more by working on real, greasy transmissions that they could have seen from all angles than they learned by working on pristine classroom models!

Simulators

Simulators are mock-ups of the real thing. They can be as simple as a counter with a cash register that simulates a store environment or as complex as a replica of a 747 cockpit that costs millions of dollars and duplicates (through the use of interactive video, videodisk technology, and highly complex and sophisticated electro-mechanical systems) exactly what it is like to fly a 747 jet. Simulators effectively bring into the classroom realistic imitations of things that are otherwise unavailable.

Objects

Tangible objects can be used to teach a lesson. For example, I've used children's puzzles to help demonstrate competition versus collaboration. I've used potatoes and straws to demonstrate the need to follow through. I've used cookies to help participants recall the fun of learning that most of us experienced in kindergarten, where a favorite activity was our cookies-and-milk break.

What Makes a Good Visual?

As you prepare your presentation, ask these seven questions to determine the effectiveness of every visual aid you use.

1. **Is the visual clear?** Is it obvious, at a glance, what the visual you are using is trying to communicate?

2. **Is it readable?** Can people actually *see* the information, or is the material so complex or the printing so tiny that it is not visible to most of your audience?

3. **Does the visual communicate a single idea?** Is your audience able to focus on one key point, as you expand on your visual, or are their thoughts cluttered because more than one idea is presented?

4. **Is it relevant?** Does the audience know why you are using the visual? Does it make a point that fits in with the presentation?

5. **Is the visual interesting?** Does it help focus and keep the audience's attention?

6. **Is it simple?** Is it easy for the audience to relate to the visual, or is it so busy, so detailed, so cluttered with graphics, so colorful, so full of various typefaces that it is difficult to focus on?

7. **Is it accurate?** Does it clearly portray what it is meant to portray? For example, the diagram below illustrates two visuals that convey the same information. The first one shows the bar chart truncated, so that the difference between the two bars does not seem significant. The second visual clearly shows the difference between the two bars. Some will argue that you need to save space and that it's not proportional, etc. But if we're going to be accurate, the audience must see at a glance the vast difference in the two bars.

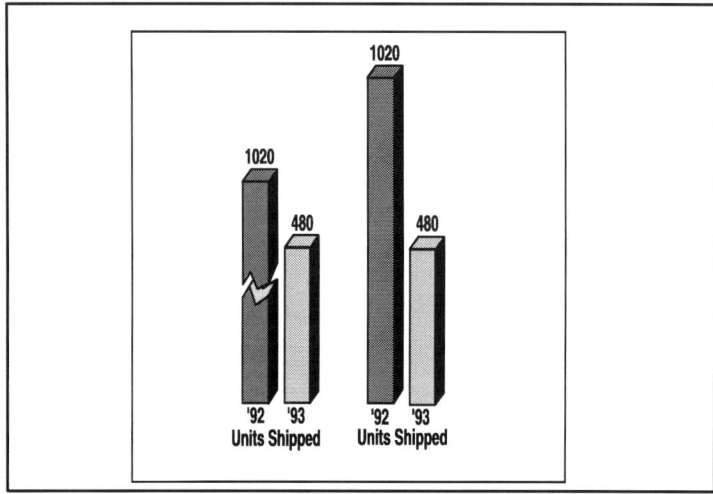

Preparing the Room and Equipment

Projected Visuals

Whenever you're going to use projected visuals, you must carefully plan, in advance, where to locate your projector. The point is simple: Make sure each person in the audience can see every visual you use.

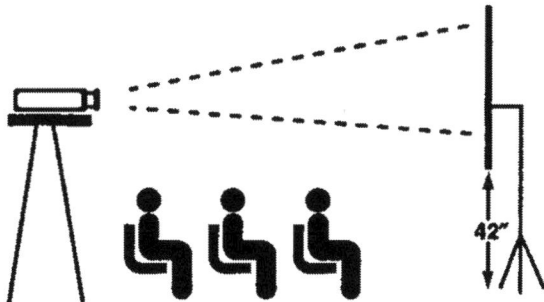

1. Each person should be able to see the screen easily. The bottom of the screen should be at least 42 inches off the floor. This height is higher than the tops of the heads of 95 percent of your seated audience.

2. For best visibility, place the screen in a corner and angle it toward the center of the room. This is particularly true for overhead and opaque projectors, but it applies to other visual projectors as well. You don't want a large, blank screen to be the center of attention when you're not using a projected visual. If you choose to write on certain visuals, this placement allows you to do so while facing your audience and not blocking their view.

Here are some suggested room arrangements that can facilitate visibility.

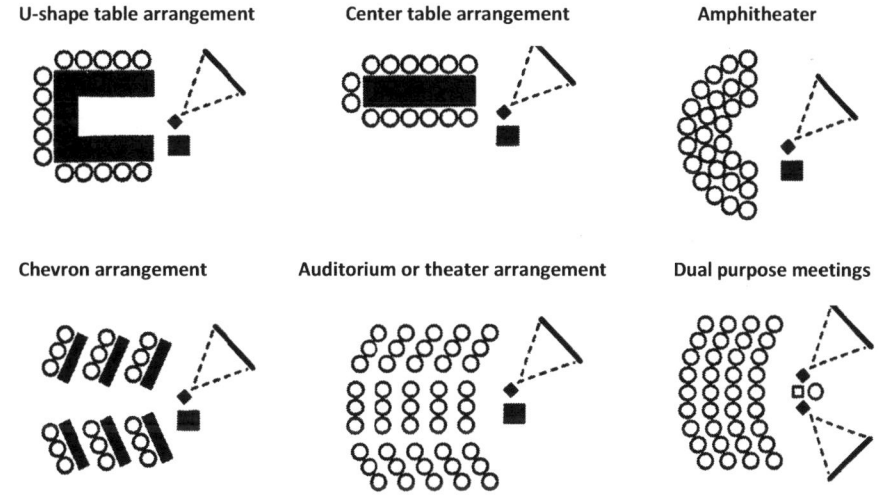

You will notice the chevron is similar to classroom style, but it permits participants to see one another. The auditorium and dual projector arrangements feature seating in an arc for the same purpose.

3. Your projector should not obstruct your audience's view of the screen. If you are using an LCD projector, place it on a stand so that the audience has an unobstructed view of the entire visual. Special lenses are available that permit you to place the projector all the way at the back of the room on a high stand (typically 54 inches high) and project over the heads of your seated participants.

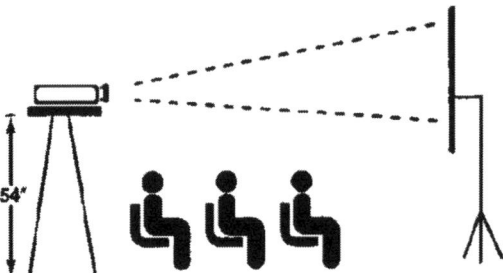

4. Avoid image distortion or "keystoning" by having the projector beam meet the center of the screen at a 90 degree angle. Most LCD projectors have a keystone correction feature built in, but you can also adjust the screen.

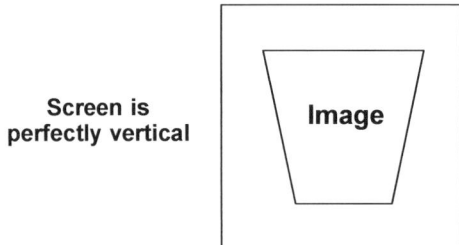

Keystoning occurs when the projector is placed low, in order to keep it out of the audience's line of vision. It is caused by the difference between the distances that bottom and top rays of light have to travel between the focus and the screen. The farther the ray of light has to travel, the wider the image. You can avoid this effect by tilting the screen forward at the top or backward at the bottom so that the distances traveled by the various rays are about the same at all points on the screen.

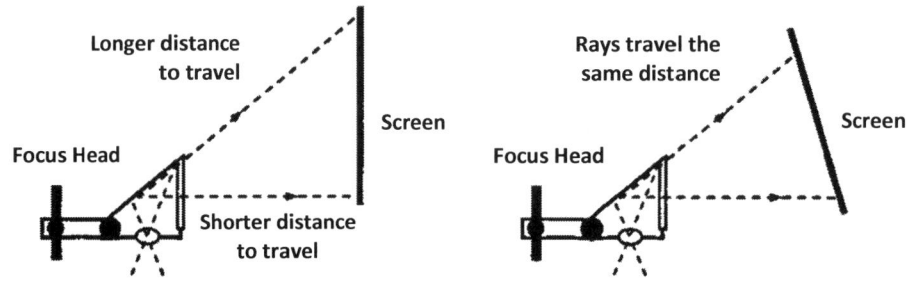

5. Whenever possible, use a matte surface screen for greatest image visibility and seating breadth. Beaded (or lenticular) screens reflect more light to viewers in the center of the room, but the image dulls and drops off when viewed from the sides of the room. A beaded screen is fine if you have a long, narrow room, but a matte screen will serve you best in most situations.

6. To select the right screen size and seating arrangements, remember the 2 x 6 rule:

    - The distance from the screen to the first row of seats should equal twice the width of the screen (2w).

    - The distance from the screen to the last row of seats should equal six times the width of the screen (6w).

    - No row of seats should be wider than its distance to the screen.

7. The projected image should fill the screen completely. If your screen is adjustable from top to bottom, raise the bottom of the screen in order to frame the image you're projecting.

8. Always carry extra accessories. An extension cord, three-pronged plug adapter, masking tape, spare projector bulbs: The availability of these "spares" may mean the difference between showing the visual portion of your presentation and not being able to.

9. Know the room you're going to use. Know the location of light switches, electrical outlets, and heating and air-conditioning controls, and know how to use them. Which light switch do you use in order to darken the room partially? Can you turn off the lights in the area immediately in front of your screen?

10. Know the location of the telephone and the name and number of the individual you can contact in case of an equipment emergency.

11. Set up and check out your equipment in advance. Check the screen for keystoning. Test and focus the projector. If you're using sound, check the levels. If you're using an overhead projector, clean the glass stage of the projector with a soft cloth and water or lens cleaner. Tape any cords to the floor. Know how to change your projector lamp if necessary.

12. Check your visuals. Make sure that they're numbered, right side up, in the proper sequence, and clean and ready to use.

13. Make sure the air vent on your projector is clear. If it's blocked, the lamp will overheat and burn out sooner.

14. Check your projector and screen placement by drawing sight lines at the top and bottom of the screen both for the audience (being careful to allow the sight line to extend over the heads of people seated in the front rows) and for the projector itself.

15. Clean the lens of the projector.

16. For larger rooms, consider a high-intensity projector that will project lots of light over a large distance to a large screen.

17. Short focal-length lenses can be used to produce a large image on a screen from a short projection distance. This is useful for viewing large, impressive images in a shallow, wide room.

18. Long focal-length lenses can be used to produce small images or in places where long projection distances are required for relatively small images.

19. To facilitate viewing, seat people in a fan-shaped area of about 70 degrees with the center perpendicular to the screen.

Picking a Room

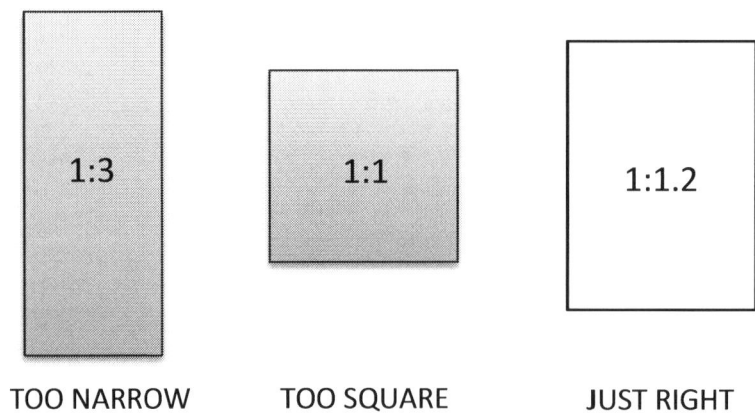

Whenever possible, hold your meeting in a room appropriate to the size of your group. If, however, you have a choice between a room that's a little too small and one that's a little too large, select the latter. There are ways to make a too-large room look smaller and cozier, but there's nothing you can do about overcrowding. The ideal room ratio is 1 foot of width to 1.2 feet of length. For most meetings, 12 to 20 square feet should be allowed per person.

Know the room layout so that you can determine the best placement of people. You'll want to arrange it so that your audience has enough room and your equipment is protected from being knocked around.

Seating

Be sure the chairs are comfortable; uncomfortable chairs can decrease your audience's attention span. Whenever possible, get chairs with armrests. Do you have enough chairs and tables for the number of participants you're expecting? Are the exits to the room clear once the room setup is complete?

Make sure that your meeting room has the exit at the rear of the room to minimize the distractions due to latecomers. Always set 10 percent fewer chairs than you think you're going to need, but have extras at the back of the room. It is much more energizing to be adding chairs than to start a session with too many chairs.

Screen Viewing

Avoid or minimize any obstructing posts or columns that interfere with visibility either of the speaker or the group members. Everybody should be able to see clearly when seated.

Insider's Tip

> Avoid placing an aisle in the center of your audience. The center offers the best seating for viewing, so place the aisle to either side.

Lighting

Make sure the room is well-lit but not so bright that the lights distract your listeners with glare. The room should be dark enough for projection yet light enough for note-taking. Check to see if the lights can be dimmed or switched independently. If not, can the lightbulbs immediately in front of your screen be removed in order to darken the area around the screen? Use lights with dimming systems if possible. Check and label all light switches, and assign a person to turn lights on and off on cue. Light sources that create flicker can cause distraction and discomfort.

Power

Are electrical outlets adequate and conveniently located? How much extension cord will you need to bring power to your equipment? You should know if the current is AC or DC. Will it run your equipment? If you haven't brought an adapter with you, you may have problems with two or three pronged plugs that don't match up to the outlets. How much electricity will your meeting require? Overloading the line running to your meeting room will bring your class to a halt. Check to see if outlets are switched and fused separately from the room lights and if spare fuses and standby circuit breakers are ready. An electrical outlet should be located near the head table to permit plugging in any equipment used by the speaker.

Acoustics

Bouncing sound waves get on the nerves of speakers and listeners, so check acoustics by clapping your hands together slowly. A brittle, ringing echo indicates poor acoustics. If you have this problem, you can reduce the bouncing sound waves by draping walls with fabric, placing carpeting on floors, or, if possible, finishing floors and ceiling with acoustic tiles.

Be sure that sound carries to all parts of the room. "Dead spots" can occur and can distract people from your message by making it difficult for them to hear. Make sure, also, that there is no interference from noisy mechanical equipment (e.g., projectors) placed too close to participants. Check to be sure that no loud sounds from outside the room will distract your class.

13 Things You Need to Know Before Preparing Your Next Visual

1. **Limit your work area on the original to a maximum of 8 x 10 inches.** This will ensure that, once your visual is prepared, you will have room to create and project it without having the framing block part of the visual. Reducing the area you actually use by 15 percent will ensure that all of the key information will be visible, even if you have problems in various media.

2. **Limit each visual to one idea.** If the topic you're covering is more complex, you might want to use builds in your PowerPoint slides to progressively present a complex issue.

3. **Choose your words carefully.** Most visuals use too many words. Excessive wording or too-elaborate diagrams on a single visual not only compete with you, they become more and more difficult for the audience to read. **Remember the six-by-six rule**: No more than six lines per transparency and no more than six words on a line. When creating visuals, try to think in "bullets." Use active words and short phrases.

4. **Use appropriate type sizes.**

   - Use at least 24-point type or more on visuals. Even better is 36-point.
   - Use bold, simple typefaces.
   - Avoid ornate styles for maximum readability.
   - Vary the type size in order to illustrate the relative importance of information.
   - Use the same type style for each series of visuals.
   - Type that is 24-point will be readable by a person with normal eyesight at a distance equal to 5 times the projected image: 5' screen = 25'; 6' screen = 30'

1/4 inch	30'	40'	50'	60'	90'
3/8 inch	45'	60'	75'	90'	135'
1/2 inch	60'	80'	100'	120'	180'

The point size for ¼-inch letters varies based on the font. For example:

Times Roman is 20 point
Book Antigua is 20 point
Arial is 18 point
Bookman Old Style is 21 point
Impact is 18 point

- Each typeface is different. The point size of type is not always uniform. Seventy-two points equals approximately 1 inch. However, printers are measuring the type slug—from the top of the capital letter to the bottom of descenders—such as a lower-case "g". When producing visuals, we measure only the size of the capital letter—or CAP. A capital letter that is ¼-inch high is roughly equal to 20-point type. You can see by the examples above that readability is determined by the size, complexity, and "openness" of the type font.

The font size minimum for video is 3/8 inch, rather than a 1/4 inch. This is because of the 60 line-per-second scan rate used in video and the size of the pixel (or **PIC**ture **EL**ement). This determines the resolution of the screen. Former video guidelines require 1/2 inch or 36-point type for readability. The increased resolution of television monitors has reduced this to 3/8 inch. Readability guidelines for ***eLearning or Computer-Based Training (CBT) and video are the same!*** Even though the resolution on computer monitors are greater, the screen images used in CBT are often smaller to save bandwidth and allow images to load faster. Images often occupy only a portion of the screen.

To compensate for the smaller image size, larger text and bolder, simpler images are needed.

Also, elaborate and colorful graphics take longer to load—so, simplicity has merit... ***It's also easier on the viewer's eye.***

Here are some minimum type sizes for television receivers.

	18-inch	20-inch	26-inch	30-inch	36-inch
	DISTANCE TO SCREEN				
3/8-inch	15 feet	17 feet	22 feet	25 feet	30 feet
3/4-inch	25 feet	30 feet	38 feet	45 feet	55 feet
1 inch	32 feet	40 feet	48 feet	55 feet	70 feet

White space is an important feature for overheads and 35mm transparencies. It is essential for video images and those broadcast to television receivers. In this instance, a "safe area" consisting of outside margins of 15 percent of the image size is allowed to ensure that nothing gets lost in the margins. Where computer monitors display the video image from edge to edge, television receivers do ***not*** display the whole image. Parts are always lost!

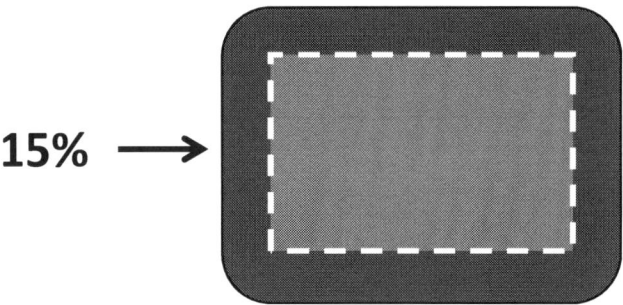

5. **Use upper- and lower-case letters.** Lower-case letters are generally more legible than upper case. Occasionally, use only upper case for contrast or for headings. Using all caps makes text harder to read and eliminates your ability to use all caps when you want to emphasize a word.

   Vary the length of words and provide ample spacing between the letters, between the words, and between the lines of type. A good guideline: between each line of type, leave a space equal to the height of an upper-case letter of the size and style you are using.

   > **USING ALL CAPS INCREASES READING DIFFICULTY AND ELIMINATES USING ALL CAPS WITH SINGLE WORDS FOR EMPHASIS.**

   > **Using upper- and lower-case letters INCREASES readability and allows the use of ALL CAPS for emphasis.**

6. **Be visual.** Most visuals in use today are still pictures of words. However, the mind thinks in pictures. If you hear the word "house," you don't think "h-o-u-s-e"—you see your house or a dream house. Use illustrations, cartoons, graphs, maps, and charts whenever possible, instead of relying exclusively on words or numbers.

7. **Use colored backgrounds on visuals to provide contrast for improved readability and increased interest.**

8. **Position your material on the upper part of your visual.** When you project it, your audience can view it readily since it will be on the top part of the screen.

9. **Avoid using both horizontal and vertical formats (also referred to as landscape and portrait modes).** Many experts suggest using horizontal visuals exclusively for maximum visibility. You can keep the visual higher on the screen in the horizontal or landscape mode.

10. **Use—but don't overuse—color.** A maximum of two to three colors per transparency or slide should be sufficient. More than that will make it difficult for the eye to focus on the important parts of the visual. Color can be used effectively to:

    - point out important words;
    - highlight important sentences;
    - identify;
    - emphasize;
    - influence psychologically; and
    - improve readability characteristics.

    Color can be a powerful communicator—used properly. Have you ever seen a visual where every line was a different color? It makes it very difficult to read and focus. Here are some powerful uses of color:

    - Use color to identify topics in a presentation.
    - Use color to identify products, regions, budget items, or any other topic that can be broken into categories.
    - Use color in pie charts and bar charts. Following through the entire presentation using the same colors from each segment when discussing that topic helps to maintain emphasis and identification.

    Black text on a yellow background appears larger and is more readable than any other color combination.

    Visuals with a light background and dark type project better in a room with partial lighting (for example, using overhead transparencies in a classroom, or using a computer projection system in a conference room that is not totally dark, or using any LCD panel on an overhead projector anywhere).

    Also, be aware of the way different combinations of color work:

    - Where text that had been presented earlier is grayed-out, it becomes almost indistinguishable on some backgrounds.
    - Reversed images (i.e., white or light colors on a dark background) can be very striking in a totally darkened room. But in partially lighted rooms, they can appear faded out and very hard to read.

11. **Avoid vertical lettering.** A quick look at these two visuals shows the importance of this suggestion. Vertical lettering may look fancy, but it's very difficult to read.

12. **Use a maximum of two type styles on any single visual.** Any more than two causes the type styles to compete with the information being presented.

13. **If you are using non-sequential items in a visual, don't number the items.** Use checkmarks, bullets, boxes, arrows, etc.

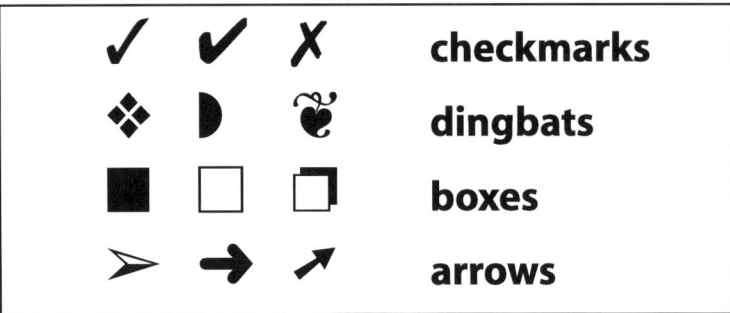

Insider's Tip

> Clip art available online, on CDs, and in books such as those available from Dover can be a great source of copyright-free illustrations, giving you inexpensive ready-made professional art.

A High-Impact Graphic Technique

Windowpaning

We've already stated that the mind thinks in pictures. Pictures can also be used to help people retain ideas much more quickly and with much more permanency. Back in the 1950s, AT&T did research in setting up local phone numbers. As you may know, in the United States, phone numbers are seven digits, grouped in three digits first, followed by four digits separated by a hyphen. This is known as chunking. Based on research, they found that a person could retain in short-term memory seven bits of information plus or minus two. This is one reason that for years the local phone numbering system of the United States used seven digits.

Many of us have had the experience of listening to a voice mail, getting a ten-digit number to call back, and having to listen again because we did not write it down—and we can't remember the ten-digit number. Why? Because short-term memory is on seven digits, plus or minus two. Ten digits pushed the number out of short-term memory and it was not stored in long-term memory for recall. The mind thinks in pictures, so if we take the AT&T idea, it says that we can create an array of pictures of help people remember. This is a technique we call "windowpaning."

For example, look at the windowpanes that we've given here. It's a two-by-six matrix illustrating issues that training directors must consider. The first windowpane has a picture of a computer, representing the fact that training directors of today are concerned about the technology explosion and how they keep people up-to-date with it. The pair of ballerina slippers in second windowpane indicate that training directors are concerned with balancing needs of the individual with the needs of the organization. The book turning into a CD in the third windowpane represents the concern the training directors have for the information explosion. Knowledge is doubling about every 18 months—how will they keep up with people's need for information. The fourth windowpane has a person inside prison with the universal "do not" sign, representing the training directors' concern for retaining good employees without having them feel as if they're in prison. In the fifth windowpane, the egg cracking open with the star coming out of it represents the training directors' concern for finding, hatching, and growing their superstars—the people who can react with the dynamic and rapid change that the organization will experience. And finally, the sixth windowpane represents the training directors' concern with having to downsize when it's needed, and yet be balanced in paying attention to the concerns of the individuals and the communities affected.

Six windowpanes with six critical pieces of information are much easier to retain because it's easier to recall the pictures than a traditional list such as you find below. Here are the six greatest concerns for training directors of the 1990s based on an ASTD study published in January of 1991. As I write this in the fall of 2014 my clients tell me the concerns are still uppermost on their minds.

1. The technology explosion.
2. The need to balance the needs of the individual with the needs of the organization.
3. The information explosion and the fact that information is doubling every 18 months.
4. How do we find, hatch, and grow our superstars who can react to the dynamic change that's going to be happening in the organization?
5. How do we retain good employees without having them feel as if they're in prison?
6. How do we downsize when it's necessary, and yet balance the needs of the individuals and communities who are going to be affected?

It is much simpler for people to recall the pictures that trigger the concepts than to memorize the words or somehow be able to recall the words that represent the concept itself. So whenever you're creating visuals, remember that graphics aid retention. If you've got a series of points, consider using the windowpane to display them graphically. This gives people not only a picture, but also a physical location that the picture is placed in. It also means that if you've got a series of steps to be followed, it makes it much easier to become aware of which step might have been missed.

 ## Keys for Windowpaning

- No more than nine boxes.
- Use simple hand-sketched line drawings.
- Allow people to fill in theirs as you do yours (aids retention)
- Add a key phrase at the bottom of each box.
- Consider letting people create their own window panes.

Summary

Remember, visuals are instruments used in presenting a message, but they are not the message itself. Select your visual materials with care, aiming for simplicity and choosing the easiest and most effective transmission system. Familiarize yourself with the equipment you will use. A few minutes spent with the instruction manuals can save you embarrassment and ensure a smooth-running presentation.

Rehearse your presentation in advance! Review your visuals with your narration. Try to anticipate questions that might arise. You'll be rewarded for the time and effort you invest with greater self-confidence and poise. And your audience will experience a more effective presentation.

You may never have given a presentation before, but, with the help of good visuals and with conscientious rehearsal, you can begin to rank as a skilled presenter. Obviously, properly selected and presented visual aids can add significantly to the power and impact of your presentation. Remembering the six key P's—Proper Preparation and Practice Prevent Poor Performance—will help you achieve the results you want.

Chapter 5:
Group Involvement

There's More to Teaching Than Talking to Them

Basics for Group Involvement

Group involvement is scary to a lot of trainers—especially those with backgrounds strongly oriented toward lecture. One argument given is that time is too short to allow participation; there's too much content to cover. But the question is: Is our job as instructors simply to cover the material—or to empower our participants to perform better back on the job? I think it's to empower participants to perform better back on the job.

Research Factoid

> *"Active learning is more effective than passive learning. But activity, in and of itself, doesn't result in higher learning. Active learning occurs when students invest physical and mental energies in activities that help them make what they are learning meaningful, and when they are aware of that meaning making."*
>
> — Angelo, (1993), p. 5

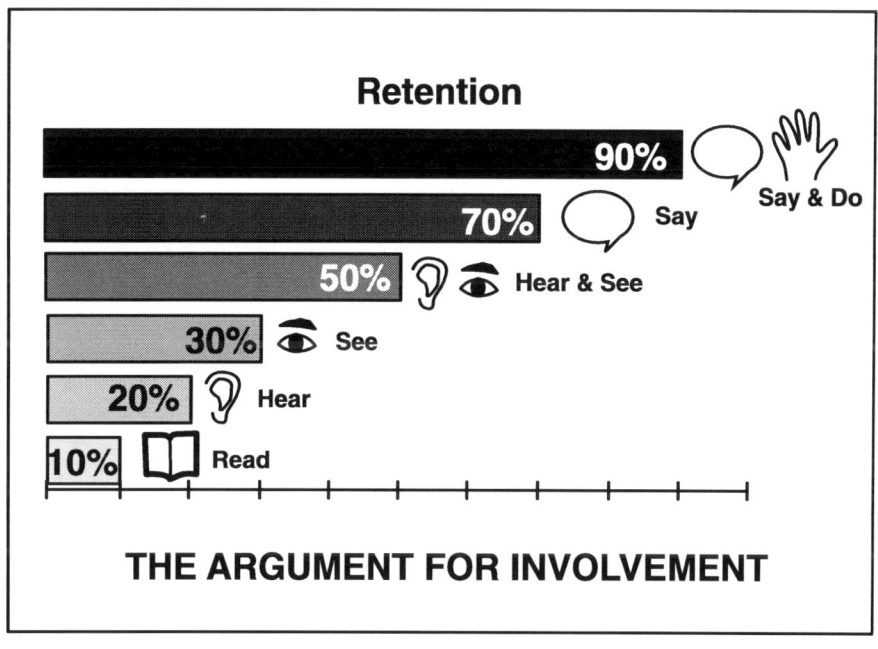

One of my Laws of Adult Learning is that people don't argue with their own data. If I say something, I've got to believe it; after all, I'm teaching it. But if a participant says something, he or she will accept and believe it more fervently.

If we want people to apply what they've learned when they're back on the job, they've got to do two things: buy in to the concepts or skills we've introduced and retain them. Involvement is the key to both buy-in and retention.

Some trainers argue against involvement because they fear it reduces their control. To them, lecture appears to give them more control over their participants. My experience is different. Properly used, participation requires much less effort on the part of the instructor because the learners can manage and control themselves—and they will—given the proper structure and opportunity.

Over the years, I have learned to use an approach to group involvement that I call instructor led and participant centered. It focuses as many of the learning activities as possible on the participants themselves. Sure, it requires some thought and creativity, but it can be a powerful learning tool that produces positive results.

In order to use the approach successfully, you, the trainer, must answer a couple of questions about your participants.

1. What experience/knowledge do they bring to the class? If they have none, you'll need some background information before you can expect much participation.

    I once got a call from an instructor who said, "My class is bombing! I tried involvement, but it isn't working." I asked for details. He had carefully structured an opening discussion for his class of new salespeople. He distributed the discussion questions and chose a member from each small group to read the questions and lead the discussion. Unfortunately, very little discussion followed. The problem lay in his first question: How do you find prospective customers? The reason there was so little discussion was that the class consisted of new salespeople with no experience. If they had known how to find prospects, they probably wouldn't have been in the class.

    The solution was equally clear: The participants needed some information before they could have a meaningful discussion. The instructor then prepared a reference card describing seven different prospecting methods and gave an example of how each could be used. Participants then could consider each method in terms of its applicability to their product, territory, etc.

2. What do the participants need to know when the class is over, and what will they need to be able to find?

    For example, in a class on conflict management, we cover five ways to deal with an angry person. It's important that participants know those five steps. If someone walks into your office, slams a fist on the table, and yells, "I'm fed up, and I'm not going to take it anymore!" you won't help the situation by flipping through the conflict manual to "Step one—acknowledge the anger" and then saying, "You seem upset." You need to know that information—and know it cold.

Group Involvement

Or, to use a more dramatic example, consider cardiopulmonary resuscitation (CPR). When you need to apply it, both hands, your mouth, and absolute concentration are imperative. You can't stop and look in a manual to learn the techniques.

The things people need to know and do almost without thinking are great candidates for participation and involvement. In fact, they almost demand it. These topics probably will take up the bulk of your training time because of their importance. The things your participants need to be able to find, such as material in a reference manual, can also utilize participation; the more familiar they are with the manual, the quicker they'll be able to find things back on the job.

One thing I've learned in training and presenting and almost every trainer or speaker quickly learns as he or she gets involved in a group is that people like to talk to one another. They like to socialize. These basic elements of human behavior can be used to create powerful learning experiences that will get results for our participants.

Insider's Tip

When designing a presentation, remember CPR:

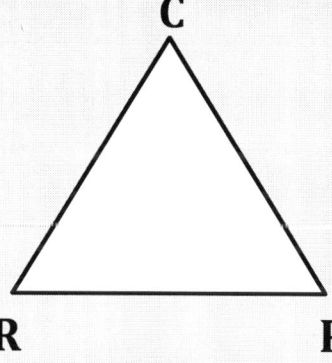

- Make sure the **Content** is relevant.
- Make sure you allow for adequate **Participation**.
- Make sure you find ways to **Revisit** and **Reinforce** the key points.

Research Factoid

"Whenever explanations are given, they should be clear, focused, and in small steps, with student practice after each step (Brophy & Good, 1986; Druian & Butler, 1987; Rosenshine, 1988; Taylor & Valentine, 1985)."

– Reynolds, (1992), p. 19

Research Factoid

> *"Guided practice allows students to transfer new material from their working memory to long-term memory."*
> – Rosenshine (1988); Reynolds, (1992), p. 20

If we are going to use group involvement effectively, we need to consider some simple guidelines.

1. The physical arrangement you use for training can communicate to participants that participation is expected and encouraged.

    Your room arrangement helps determine instructor control, sight lines (how well can participants see each other, the instructor, visuals, etc.), and participation. Here are six common arrangements used in training.

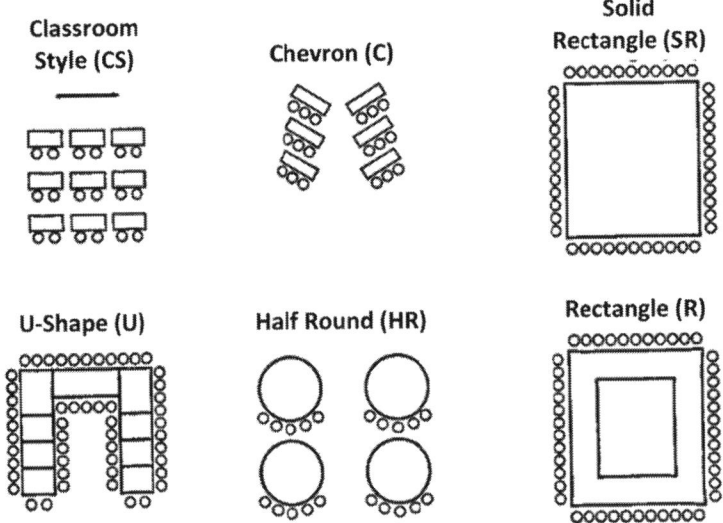

What do you want? High, medium, or low control as an instructor? Understand that often when you have better control of the learning environment, you can give control to small groups and group leaders. You don't have direct control, but you have a more controlled result because the participants themselves have become responsible for the involvement and learning. High, medium, or low eye contact between participants? Remember the greater the eye contact with each other, the greater the responsibility participants feel toward each other. This is another reason for breaking participants into smaller groups and arranging the seating so that they can see you as well as each other. High, medium, or low participation from your attendees? The larger the group, the less participation there will be from individuals. The more difficult you make it for participants to see or hear each other, the lower the participation will be as well. The physical room arrangement can greatly influence these factors.

Control	H	H	M	M	M	M
Sightlines	L	M	H	H	M	M
Participation	L	M	H	H	L	M

2. Numerous techniques can be used to generate group involvement. Some of them involve the entire group—be it 15, 20, 200, or 500 people—as a whole. For example, a lecture is a type of whole-group involvement. Of course, if only some people in the group are asking questions, they're more involved than others.

   Another more effective way to involve an entire group is to break that group down into smaller units. For example, you can get 200 people involved by breaking them up into pairs (dyads) or trios (triads).

   If you're able to, you might seat people in half rounds or herringbone style as described earlier. When this is possible, I recommend seating people in rounds of five to seven each. Leave part of the table open, the part that faces you or is closest to where you'll be speaking and using visuals. That way, people can be involved with one another as you're structuring those opportunities and, at the same time, they can easily see you as you're giving instructions or presenting various parts of the program.

   I recommend small groups of five to seven for good reason. With more than seven people, some will tend to get lost in the group and not participate, particularly if they're shy. If you have fewer than five people, it becomes more possible for one person to dominate the group or the discussion.

3. Group leaders help stimulate group involvement.

   If you break your larger group (for example, 50 participants) into smaller groups (for example, groups of five), group leaders can facilitate group activities in several ways:

   - The group leader leads the group through the activity according to directions given by the instructor. You may give directions verbally, or you may have them printed and handed out. If you hand out project sheets, you have two choices. You can give them only to the group leaders, who then read the assigned project, directions, or discussion questions aloud. Or you can provide each person with a discussion or activity or project sheet so that the whole group can follow along as the project is covered.

   - The group leader reads aloud each project as the other participants at the table follow along. Although some group leaders may want participants to read on their own with a discussion to follow, this is less effective. When the leader reads aloud, participants benefit in four ways.

1) The group as a whole focuses on each individual issue.

2) By seeing and hearing at the same time, participants retain more. This may be very important for participants who are not particularly good readers.

3) The confidence of the group leader increases. The leader reads as the others listen and follow the leader's direction. This can further be reinforced by occasionally giving only the group leader the project.

4) It gives each participant a leadership role. If the activity is read by the group leader, the leader's role is clearly established. The role of group leader is rotated among the participants so that each person in the group has an opportunity.

- The group leader can succinctly summarize the conclusions or discussion of the group. He or she simply stands, facing the other participants, and gives a brief report. Group leaders shouldn't deliver their reports while seated; being a group leader means acquiring basic presentation skills, such as addressing a group, in a variety of settings.

Each group leader's report should be brief. I usually allow only one minute and I stick firmly to that limit for these reasons.

1) Anyone can talk for a minute. Allowing all group leaders the same short time minimizes comparisons in presentation styles—which isn't our primary focus.

2) It helps ensure that each group leader will have something fresh to contribute—even those who report second or third.

3) It keeps the more verbal leaders from rambling. To end a group-leader report, use a simple phrase such as, "Okay, thank you very much." Natural pauses in the normal speaking pattern will allow you to terminate the report. I recommend that you don't comment on group-leader reports but conclude each one in the same congenial, neutral manner.

With groups larger than 25, not every group leader can report on every project. Generally, I will ask for three group-leader reports, and, when those are given, I'll occasionally ask if other leaders have anything else to add.

4) How you distribute materials depends on the size of the group. When 40 or more participants are going through the program simultaneously, you might put all program materials in a single binder, distributed at the beginning. If this is the case, you may not want to sequence all your material in chronological order because some participants tend to look ahead several pages to try to "psych" out the objectives. If you want people to discover and explore their own thoughts, you don't want to tip them off by having them read discussion materials intended for future use. This problem can be solved either by placing some pages further back in the manual, out of

the regular sequence, or by holding some pages out of the manual, to be distributed at the appropriate time.

If you have large groups, you may want to precount your additional materials and have group leaders pick them up at the appropriate times, rather than distributing the materials to each group or to each participant yourself.

Whenever you use the instructor-led and participant-centered approach, you will have to be aware of how much you allow your participants to rely on you. I generally try to clarify instructions if necessary, but I don't let myself be drawn into group discussions or debates—even if the group seems "stuck" or divided about which approach to take. Remember, the emphasis with this approach is on giving our participants experiences that will enable them to apply the content back on the job when their instructors aren't readily available to solve every problem or answer every question. The more we answer their questions and solve their problems in class and the more dependent they become, the less effective they'll be on the job. We want to provide a supportive environment for their exploration, struggle, and discovery so that the insights they gain will truly be theirs—as well as the self-confidence that comes from those discoveries.

The Instructor's Role in an Instructor-Led, Participant-Centered Training Program

If you are going to use the instructor-led and participant-centered approach, which generates maximum group involvement, you must position yourself carefully as the instructor. The more you or I take the role of the expert or the authority, the less likely people are to seek their own answers and to work through their own problems. They become more inclined to regard you as the final authority in terms of whether or not the discoveries reached in their group discussions were "correct." In the belief that the instructor should be more a facilitator or coordinator than an "expert," I offer the following explanation of this challenging role.

The Responsibility

It must be emphasized that the purpose of every training session is to assist the participants in developing their own answers, applying tools and techniques, using reference manuals, and tapping their own resources and those of their colleagues to reach solutions that work, both in class and on the job.

In situations where there are right and wrong answers, participants should be provided with resources and models that allow them to develop their own correct approaches and solutions. They must use what they know and have access to, rather than having the instructor either come to the rescue or play judge by determining right and wrong. Our purpose as trainers is not primarily to counsel, interpret, instruct, or in any other way lead people to believe that we are going to supply the answers to their questions. Instead, we should let the seminar, the instruments, the projects, the case studies, and other materials serve as resources that the participants can draw on to solve their problems and develop appropriate plans of action.

Life is a do-it-yourself project, just as our daily work activities are, for the most part, do-it-yourself projects. This instructor-led and participant-centered instructional approach attempts, as much as possible, to mirror that. It seeks to blend the best from the didactic instructor-led model with the finest from the heuristic participant-centered model while trying to minimize weaknesses of each. It's designed to allow participants to gain insight into how they learn, solve problems, find appropriate resources, etc., so that they can be better equipped to meet their daily challenges. It can also, as a byproduct, help them develop better ways of relating to coworkers in order to be more productive on the job.

For your own benefit, then, and for that of your participants, it is important at the outset that you make it clear that you are there to lead and to guide but not to be the authority (even though your education and profession have made you one). Instructor-led, participant-centered training is designed to be a do-it-yourself project: the participants put the effort in and get a return on that effort for themselves. The insights, discoveries, and decisions they make must be theirs, not yours, for they will be responsible for implementing them after your time together.

This will take greater self-discipline on your part than any other method you might choose to use. But by exercising that discipline, you will help your participants gain self-discovery that cannot be obtained in any other way. Your role may not seem as significant as others you might take in instructing, but it is. Your visibility may not be as great, but your impact is greater.

I once had a participant in a seminar who had moved his family to a farm in order to provide a more wholesome environment for raising children. One day, he and one of his young daughters were watching some ducklings hatch from eggs. As one was struggling to break from its shell, the little girl tried to help by cracking the shell and setting the duckling free. An hour later, the duckling was dead. Said her father, from that experience, "We learned that the struggle to break from the shell was part of the process that equipped the duckling with the survival skills to live life. Without going through that process, it couldn't survive."

The lesson they learned is analogous to what trainers soon learn in the classroom: let participants struggle to attain rewards. Your role may not seem significant, but it is. The approach I recommend limits lecture and maximizes discovery and participation. Sometimes, it may not seem as if you're needed, but you are—often in ways the participants don't perceive. Ideally, you're the best kind of teacher—a facilitator of insight, change, and growth who teaches that answers come from within. Your personal attitudes and your role modeling will set the tone for your participants. And your seriousness of purpose, your personal planning, and your adherence to the guidelines you establish, along with your interest and enthusiasm for both the content and the participants, will facilitate change and learning for each of your participants.

You may face some problems. Some participants may not cooperate. Or they may seem indifferent, be late for sessions, or make critical comments. But that is part of the process. If you are patient, the participants themselves will resolve these problems. It is part of the chemistry of small-group interaction. Small-group members are accountable for one another—sometimes without realizing it—and the behavior of one member reflects on the others. Each person, then, becomes part of the change process for every other person. And you are a part of that process, too. Change can be difficult, but it does happen.

Fortunately, most participants will be supportive and enthusiastic, but some will not. They will complain, criticize, rationalize, joke, or withdraw. Understand this and don't be thrown by it. You would have some participants do this no matter what approach you took. Your patience and understanding in the face of this resistance will eventually produce a breakthrough. By being patient, understanding, and positive, you will empower your participants to achieve the objectives of the course. Your participants will react the way you react. By demonstrating confidence in the ultimate value of this approach and maintaining your subtle leadership role, you will encourage them to react positively.

Don't abandon your role as a leader. Maintain control in a low-key way and stick to your schedule. Respect your participants by starting and ending on time. Show your interest by being available to talk with them for at least 15 minutes before and after each class, and make your planning and preparation evident. These steps will create a strong program. Stick to your outline as closely as possible. Other ideas and enhancements to the program undoubtedly will surface; save them to structure follow-up sessions, either planned or voluntary. If your participants want to continue meeting on some voluntary, self-controlled basis after completing the program, discuss this possibility with them after the program is over.

Group Management

Small-group dynamics begin with participants in a program forming groups of from five to seven people. This helps level the playing field between introverts and extroverts. When I let a small group exist with under five members, an extrovert can dominate the group. When I have a small group with more than seven members, the introvert tends to not participate. Different activities or projects are then given to these groups to be discussed or completed within a specific time.

Adults generally need more physical movement than they are provided in most training programs. If your program consists of day-long blocks, try to rotate the groups twice a day. If, for example, you have five groups, this can be accomplished by having the participants number off one through five and then grouping all the ones together, all the twos together, and so on. This permits all participants to interact with people they may not know. If you have some people who are resistant, it also keeps any one group from having to deal with them for the entire program. In each rotation, you move away from everyone you've been with. If you've been with someone who's resistant and negative, you're now relieved of that challenge.

You can rotate groups about every three hours. The number of ways you can rotate is limited only by your imagination. Assuming you have five groups of five each, here are two of the simplest methods.

1. Number one through five around the room. Rotate so each person sits with the others having the same number. Five completely new groups are formed.

2. Have everyone stand and form groups of three people while standing (there will be one group of four). Each person in the group must be from a different table. Ask each person to share one thing he or she has learned. Next, ask that they form groups of five; again, each person must be someone new to the others. The five now share one idea they've learned from their group of three. After this, they now become a new group and join each other at a table.

Different individuals should serve as group leaders for each project. This can be an opportunity to inject a little fun and humor in the program. Here are some ways I've used to choose group leaders.

- Say, "I'd like one person from each table to volunteer to do something. Once you've volunteered, I'll tell you what you're going to do." Generally, this is greeted by some laughter. After you have one volunteer from each table say, "Great, you've just volunteered to help me find the first group leaders. They're the people seated to the left of every volunteer."

- I ask everyone to point a finger in the air, and then I say, "At the count of three, point to the person at your table who should be the leader." The person with the most fingers pointed at him or her leads.

- The leader could be the person with the largest high school graduating class, or the person with the smallest high school graduating class, or the person with the most letters in his or her first name (or nickname), or with the fewest letters.

- When there are three minutes left in the break, I'll say, "Group leaders, you have three minutes to find the rest of your group and get them back on time. Your new group leader will be the person at your table who sits down last."

At the beginning of the unit, you might want to have each group assign its members a number. Then appoint each "number one" to be his or her group's leader. Generally, after you've been going for a while, the group will simply rotate to be sure that the opportunity is shared. Try to shift the responsibility of group leader around as much as possible.

The Activity/Discussion/Application Approach

The activity/discussion/application formula provides an effective way to structure group-involvement activities. That is, we first do an activity. Then we discuss what went on. How did the participants and observers feel during the activity, and what happened as a result? The final step is to consider application. In other words, how can this activity be applied back on the job? How does it apply to real-life situations?

What I call the "potato activity" makes good use of the activity/discussion/application formula. Early in the seminar, I start giving people potatoes as rewards. If they make an interesting comment, I'll thank them and give them a potato. If they are helpful, I'll thank them and give them a potato. Sometimes, I'll simply give a potato at random. From time to time, I'll ask the "keepers of the potatoes" to pass their potato to someone else at another table. Needless to say, this peculiar potato business piques participant curiosity.

Then, just before a program break, I say, "I'd like those of you who have a potato to take it with you during the break and give it to someone who has not had a potato today. And if you receive a potato, you can give it to someone else who has not received a potato today." During the break, six or eight potatoes are passed around like crazy, as participants discuss with each other the point of this potato caper.

After the break, I generally lecture for a few minutes and then I ask the people who have the potatoes to stand, and I tell them one last time to pass the potatoes to someone at another table. I then ask the people who now have potatoes to come up front, and I give each of them a non-bending drink straw.

I say to the group, "One of the things we've talked about is that the key to motivation is belief. So let me ask how many of you believe I can tell these people how to drive their straws through their potatoes with a single blow. Notice, I said 'Tell." I won't demonstrate this, so they won't actually see it done. I'll simply tell them how to do it, and then they'll do it. How many of you believe that? Could I see a show of hands?" Generally, about a third of the hands will go up. Then I'll reach into my pocket and take out a $20, or a $50, or a $100 bill and say, "How many of you believe so much that you'd be willing to bet $20 or $50 or $100 that I can do it?" Generally, all the hands drop. So I say, "What we're really talking about is that the key to motivation is belief. And if we do believe, are we willing to put our money where our mouths are?"

Now, it's time to explain to the people standing up front how to put the straw through the potato. I begin by stressing that the secret here is following through. First, they must hold the straw in a closed fist with their thumb over the top and say "follow through" out loud together. In their other hand, they cup the potato so their hand forms a "C" around it. No one should hold the potato in the palm of their hand because they could hurt themselves when they drive the straw through. "After all," I say, "we wouldn't want any OSHA (Occupational Safety and Health Act) violations!" If you're working with business-people, trainers, or personnel people, you'll get a laugh at this because they are only too aware of complicated OSHA safety regulations.

I then tell them to practice a couple more times. Then, when they're ready, they can simply drive the straw through the potato. Once again, I remind them that the key is following through, not the amount of power that's used. "Simply draw your straw back when you're ready, and, as you bring it forward, say out loud, 'Follow through.'" Generally, over half the people will do it the first time; with a couple more tries and maybe new straws for those who break them, everybody will get it. I then have everyone give the participants a hand and suggest that they might want to take the potatoes back to their tables as souvenirs.

We're now ready to discuss what just occurred. This discussion can involve the entire group together, or you can break the group into small units for discussions. The purpose of the discussion is to consider the following questions. What was the difference between showing and telling? Did it matter whether or not the participants believed entirely that they could accomplish the activity at the beginning? How did a willingness to try affect their ability to participate and succeed?

Here are three other methods that can be used for making sure that content is well taught.

1. E–T–A—Experience Theory Awareness

We first provide people with an experience; we then give them the theory behind what happened or why the experience worked the way it did, and that leads to awareness.

For example, people come into a training room that has half-round tables rather than a traditional classroom style. They begin interacting with one another and later we start to explore the differences between room arrangements. When you're seated at a half-round with five to seven people, you instantly form a group and that begins to develop a sense of accountability to the group both in terms of involvement and participation and behavior. Our behavior now reflects on our group. Having discussed this theory, people then become aware that half-rounds may be much more useful for teaching than the traditional classroom style.

2. E–A–T—Experience Awareness Theory

Sometimes we'll provide people with an experience and they won't even need the theory until later almost as an after-thought. This approach is the most antithetical to the traditional learning order of Experience Awareness and Theory. Consider how one might teach the subject of customer service in a traditional manner. First, there would be the PowerPoint lecture about the correct way to deliver good customer service. This is putting the theory first. The trainer hopes that by giving them the theory, awareness will be created. Then the trainer might use a role play to have the participants try and use the theory just delivered. Now consider how much more powerful and involving it would be if the trainer came and had everyone involved in the role play first (this would be putting the experience component first). Then they would discuss in small groups what they found difficult in the role-play. Only then would the trainer deliver the theory as an embellishment to what the students were discovering for themselves. Finally, the trainer might have them conduct the role-play again—seeking to improve based on the insights they had gained from their first experience and their exploration of the theory.

In the very process in going through the experience, they get an "A-HA!" The theory merely gives them a reason for why it worked, though intuitively they now know it works because they've experienced it. Later in this chapter, you'll be given a wide variety of methods for delivering your content in an experiential manner without resorting to lecture.

In a seminar, after presenting information in a variety of ways for about an hour and a half, you stop and have participants make an action idea list. They begin to list the ideas that they've picked up that they can use back on the job. Once they've had a couple of minutes to do this, you now have them share with their table their action ideas. As they listen to others at their table, other action ideas they're hearing may appeal to them, and they can add them to their own list.

Then you have each table share an action idea with the other participants in the room, and you go from table to table until a master list of all the action ideas is formed. Again, at this point, if anyone hears an idea that appeals to them, they can add it to their action idea list. As you go through this process, there may be people who say to themselves, "Gee, this is a really good process! It's good to stop and take time to list these action ideas. I'm going to use that in my next class." Later you talk about the importance of reflection time—the importance of taking time occasionally to stop and give people a chance to reflect here and now on what they're learning rather than simply continuing to dump content and never allowing any time to reflect.

You could also emphasize the importance of reviewing without calling it review. In allowing a reflection time, people are basically reviewing their own content. In allowing people to share their action ideas in a small-group setting, there is review and reinforcement going on. Some of it is reinforcement, because people are hearing others talk about the same action ideas they have listed. Review is going on because they may hear ideas that hadn't occurred to them because their focus was someplace else as that particular idea was being demonstrated in the classroom. The theory that you've discussed about the importance of reflection and review simply reinforces the awareness that they gain because they realized that, in the action idea process, they liked the idea and were going to use it. They had an experience that created awareness—this theory simply reinforced it.

3. T–E–A—Theory Experience Awareness

Sometimes participants may have no information or experience on the subject at all, so we need to present some theory first, and then we can give them an experience that then leads to awareness.

If you were teaching a sales training program, it might be important to discuss the theory of closing—what needs to be done before asking for the order and what the basic steps in closing are that might also include handling objections and put-offs. Then you can provide people with the experience of actually using the tested closing pattern or handling the most common objections using answers that have been worked out through experience. That then leads them to an awareness that having a method and a planned way for closing and dealing with objections is much more powerful than "winging it" or simply hoping that people will buy.

Things to Remember about Instructor-Led and Participant-Centered Training

1. Start on time; end on time. If you wait for stragglers before you begin, each session will start a little late; and you will, in effect, be teaching them to be late. If the members know you start precisely on schedule, they will learn to be prompt. I always try to start with some value-added material that is useful but not critical. That way, I can start on time and reward those who are punctual but not have those who are late miss vital information.

2. Not every project has to be completed. If I introduce an activity where sequence is not critical, I can have each group start on different parts of the activity. During the reporting process, all the participants become familiar with all the information. This method keeps everything moving along briskly. If the participants are always wishing they had a little more time, you will retain their appetites for the program.

3. Try to maintain your role as a facilitator. Do not preach, lecture, or inject your own thinking. Do not top off discussions and reports with your own opinions. Obviously, you're familiar with the content of the program and could, therefore, give summaries filled with dazzling insight. But that's not the purpose. People value their own discoveries. If they feel they're competing with you, they'll give up and take an "Okay, wise guy, you tell us" stance that will kill any participation.

4. Avoid the "boss" image. Lead by example. If you criticize, embarrass, or make jokes about participants, you'll lose the respect of the group. If people express differing viewpoints, value them even if you don't agree with them.

5. Learn the names of your participants. Be available to everyone.

6. Encourage the participants to mix. Change the groups frequently to build a cohesive split among your entire class and to discourage the formation of cliques.

7. Make individuals' problems the group's problems. If an individual asks you a question, respond by saying, "That's an interesting question. Do you mind if I ask the other members for their impressions?" You should become an example of correct attitude rather than an authority. By turning individual questions into class projects, you help participants grow.

8. Don't engage in debate with participants about who is right or wrong. Instead, help them use the resources that are available to find the right answers in those cases where there is a right and wrong.

9. Help each participant work with all the other participants. We can't always choose the people we work with or for. Understanding and growth can be fostered by focusing the small groups on common problems and helping them use their combined resources to find solutions.

10. Be the first one there and the last one to leave. Check out the facilities. Arrange your material so you are fully prepared to conduct the session.
11. Personify the spirit of the program—that is, be enthusiastic, cheerful, positive, and considerate.
12. Use a casual leadership style. Avoid abrupt commands such as "Stop!" Comments such as "Let's get started" or "The time is up" indicate a more relaxed approach. Remember, the participants are adults who like to be in control, so try to suggest rather than order.
13. Avoid eavesdropping or sitting in on discussions.
14. Maintain the time limit on group-leader reports. Be gentle but firm on this point. Not maintaining this control is the cause of most participant complaints.

Insider's Tip

Music can be useful as a group involvement aid:

- Bright, uplifting music as people come in can set the tone.
- Reflective music can help as people work on an individual basis.
- Moderately-paced music can help keep small-group discussions moving, and help mask nearby conversation.
- Game show style music can add a new dimension to games and simulations. Either raising or lowering music volume can serve to indicate the wrap-up of any time period.

The Instructional Design Grid is a powerful tool for helping select appropriate methods for a variety of situations. There are three simple keys for understanding the grid, which first appeared in an article I co-authored for the 1987 University Associates Annual for Developing Human Resources.

First, looking at the chart, notice the bar across the top indicating Information Receiving, Discussion, Information Finding, and Dramatization. The 17 instructional methods covered are listed in order of the degree of group involvement with lecture being least involving on the left side of the chart, and games and simulations being the most involving on the far right.

Instructional Design Grid

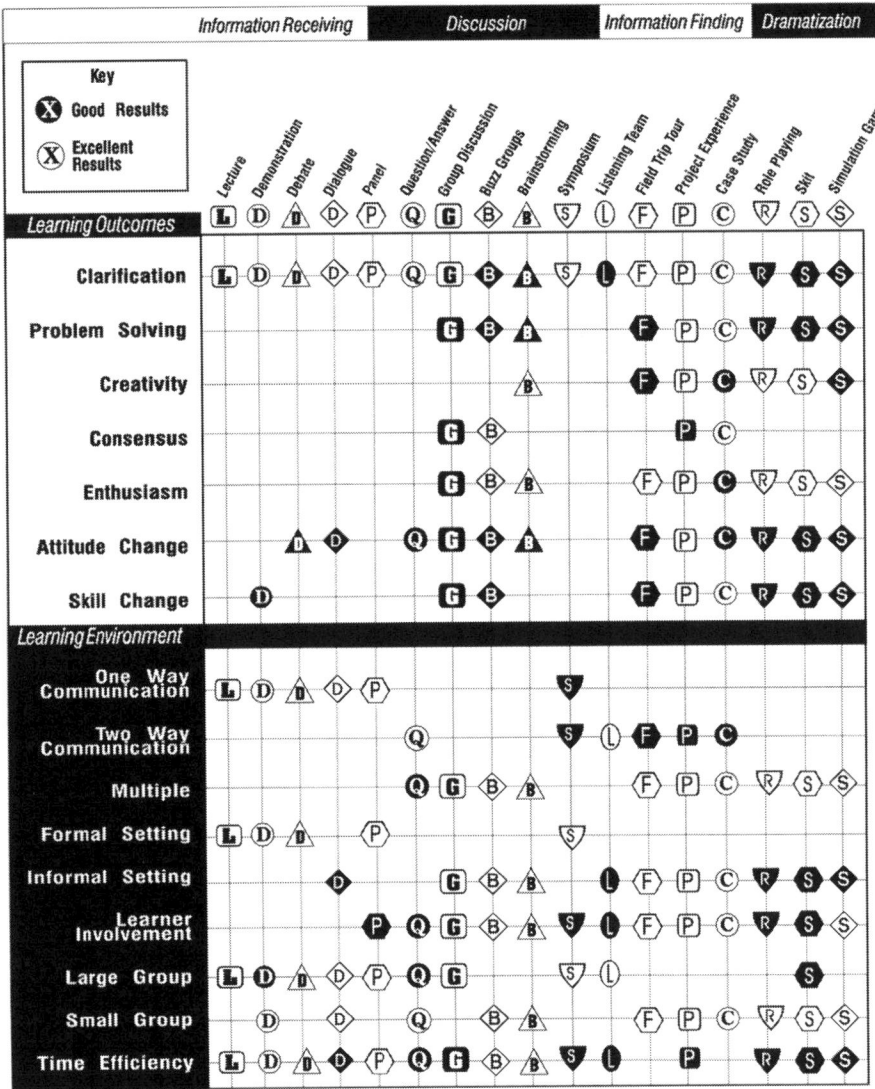

Used with permission "The 1987 Annual: Developing Human Resource," Article by Robert W. Pike, et al.

Second, notice that seven possible Learning Outcomes that you might desire are listed at the top of the left column. As you go across the chart, each method is matched to the outcome so that you can understand that a method is not recommended at all for that outcome (for example, Lecture is not recommended for Problem Solving), or can provide good results (for example, Brainstorming is a good method when Problem Solving is the outcome, but excellent if Creativity is the outcome), or can provide Excellent Results (for example, a Case Study or Project Experience can help provide Excellent Results when the desired outcome is Skill Change).

Third, notice that factors in the Learning Environment available to you have an impact on which instructional methods you can use. Nine common learning environment factors are listed starting with One Way Communication down through Time Efficiency. Here again, each Instructional Method is matched against the factors to show you whether the use of that method when the environmental factor is present is either Not Recommended (for example Buzz Groups when only one-way communication is available), will provide Good Results (for example a Panel when Learner Involvement is an important factor), or will provide Excellent Results (for example Games and Simulations with Small Groups). Using this chart to help you select appropriate methods for your classes will provide you with both variety and better results.

Methods of Instruction

A method of instruction is a system by which information is presented or sought for the purpose of solving problems, gaining new understandings, developing, or experiencing new attitudes.

Research Factoid

> *"Effective teachers provide alternate explanation, demonstrate skills and procedures, and use activities requiring student participation. Effective teachers do not expect students to teach themselves by having students interact independently with the curriculum materials. Effective teachers become actively involved with teaching and require students to become actively involved with learning."*
>
> – Good, T. L., & Brophy, J. E. (1994)

There are numerous ways to present content; here are some of the most common.

Method:	Lecture
Description:	One person systematically presenting information
Advantages:	Presents maximum information in a limited time. Makes it possible to arrange diverse materials and ideas in an orderly system of thought
Limitations:	Uses one person's point of view, one channel of communication, and no group participation; is strongly influenced by the personality of the speaker
Pattern of Interaction:	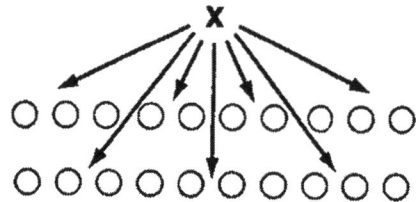

Method:	Question and Answer
Description:	One person provoking response by inquiry, usually from person to person
Advantages:	Provides for clarification of information to answer specific needs of the learner; easily combined with other methods
Limitations:	Tends to become too formal, threatening, and embarrassing; group may become bored and lose interest
Pattern of Interaction:	

Method:	Group Discussion
Description:	Two or more people sharing knowledge, experiences, and opinions, building on ideas, clarifying, evaluating, and coordinating to reach an agreement or gain better understanding
Advantages:	Meets the needs of group members by providing a high degree of interaction, interest, and involvement
Limitations:	Does not provide authoritative information nor is it helpful for large groups; requires time, patience, and capable leadership
Pattern of Interaction:	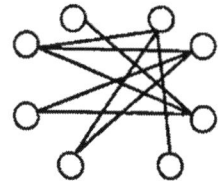

Method:	Lecture Forum
Description:	One person combining the lecture with asking questions for clarification of specific points
Advantages:	Combines with the lecture a two-way communication for clarification of ideas and meeting specific needs
Limitations:	Presents one person's viewpoint in answering questions that will tend to be perfunctory and limited to a few people
Pattern of Interaction:	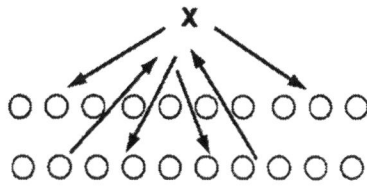

Method:	Symposium
Description:	Three or more people with different points of view presenting short speeches followed by questions and answers under the direction of a moderator
Advantages:	Presents several viewpoints and, through questions, clarifies information to meet specific needs
Limitations:	Requires speakers with equal ability, a skillful chairperson, and freedom of participation
Pattern of Interaction:	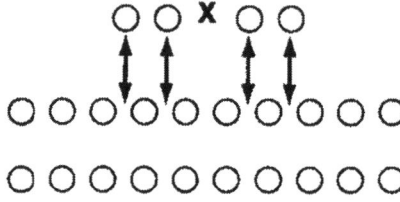

Method:	Panel
Description:	Three or more people discussing an issue before a group under the direction of a moderator, followed by a group discussion
Advantages:	Presents different viewpoints to stimulate thinking
Limitations:	Needs a skillful moderator to keep the panel on subject and to keep a limited number of questioners from monopolizing the discussion; needs a balanced panel to keep personalities from influencing opinions
Pattern of Interaction:	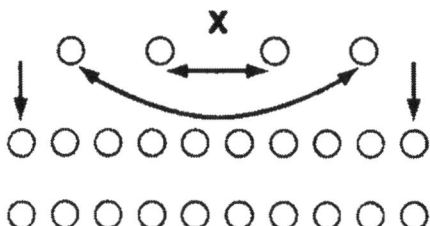

Group Involvement

Method:	Debate
Description:	Two speakers, under the direction of a moderator, presenting two sides of an issue
Advantages:	Sharpens the issue for a group by presenting both sides; holds interest and clarifies questions
Limitations:	Tends to become emotional, requiring a skillful moderator to mediate differences
Pattern of Interaction:	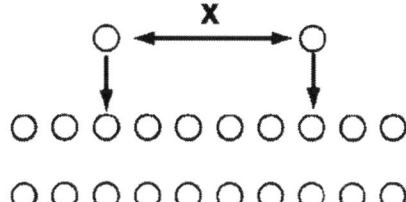

Method:	Conversations
Description:	Two people informally discussing a topic before an audience
Advantages:	Provides information in an informal setting, adding interest and emotional appeal as it encourages discussion
Limitations:	Needs careful planning to keep from becoming disorganized or dominated by personality of participants
Pattern of Interaction:	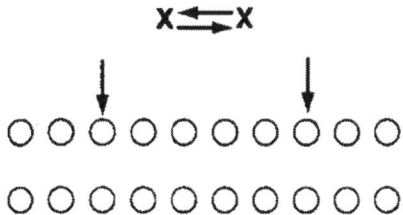

Research Factoid

> *"Students learn more if they are actively involved in discussions than if they set passively without participating... distributing response opportunities [to various students] helps keep [students] attentive and accountable..."*
>
> – Good, T. L., & Brophy, J. E. (1994)

Method:	Buzz Groups
Description:	A large group divided into smaller groups of five to seven discussing a particular topic and then reporting back to the larger group
Advantages:	Promotes enthusiasm and involvement as it provides opportunity for maximum discussion in limited time
Limitations:	Discussion tends to be shallow, disorganized, and easily dominated by one or two in the group; needs a skillful leader to handle the process
Pattern of Interaction:	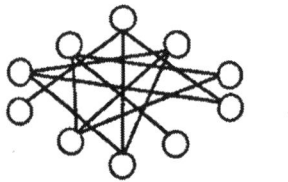 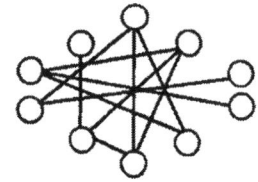

Method:	Role-Playing
Description:	Selected members of a group spontaneously acting out a human relations situation or incident, followed by analysis and evaluation
Advantages:	Provides the opportunity to "feel" human relations situations and experiment with possible solutions
Limitations:	Tends to be artificial and merely entertaining unless carefully handled; may become an end in itself, unrelated to the group problem
Pattern of Interaction:	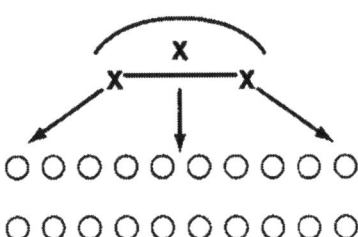

Group Involvement

Method:	Demonstrations
Description:	One person illustrating a process before a group
Advantages:	Illustrates techniques and skills and shows the results of particular procedures
Limitations:	Provides limited participation by group members
Pattern of Interaction:	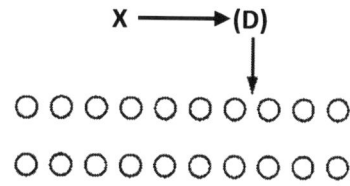

Method:	Laboratory
Description:	One or more people solving problems through testing and experimentation
Advantages:	Translates theory into practice, providing actual experience and first-hand information; appeals to many senses and shows results by doing
Limitations:	Generally requires more time, special skills, and equipment
Pattern of Interaction:	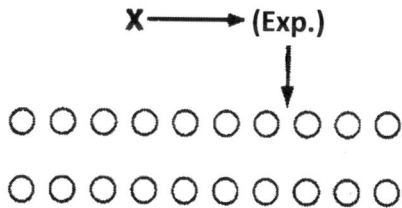

Method:	Exhibits
Description:	Showing an arrangement or collection of materials
Advantages:	Displays needed information in visible form
Limitations:	Uses visual appeal only, lacking communication and discussion; requires time and preparation
Pattern of Interaction:	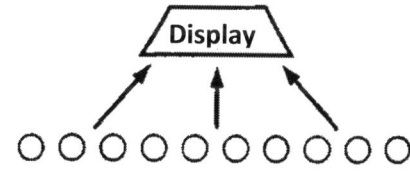

Method:	Projects
Description:	Group members cooperatively investigating a problem
Advantages:	Offers first-hand information, stimulates interests, allows pursuit of personal interest, provides practical experience, and builds group closeness
Limitations:	Requires time for completion; activity tends to become an end in itself
Pattern of Interaction:	○○○○○ ○○○○○ ○○○○○ ○○○○○ → Projects

Ways to Get Participants Back from Breaks

Time

Use odd times, like "We'll break until 11:06."

Music

Play music during breaks and either significantly raise or lower the volume to signify the end of the break.

Rewards

Offer points for activities you want people involved in. For example, one point for each person who is back on time. Double the point value if the whole table is back on time.

Town Crier

Appoint someone whose job it is to ring a school bell and announce the end of break. A participant can do this much more forcefully than an instructor.

Lights

Blink the lights on and off as they do in the theater to signal five minutes until the curtain goes up.

Trivia

Offer a trivia question word puzzle, or some other activity right near the end of the break to get people seated, reconnected, and reinvolved.

Tips

Offer a quick training tip or two just as break ends. If someone chooses to be late, they've missed a great tip or two.

Group Leader

Have each table go on break with a group leader responsible for on-time return. The group leader could be the first person to stand as the group starts the break—or the last person to stand, etc.

Participant Centered = Results

 **Instructor-Led, Participant-Centered**

Ways to Get Participants Back from Breaks

- Time
- Music
- Rewards
- Volunteer Board
- Town Crier
- Lights/Camera
- Tips
-
-
-

Chapter 6:
Creative Materials

Projects, Case Studies, and Role Plays (or Skill Practices)
that Encourage Students to Learn from Each Other
and Their Shared Life Experiences

"Experience keeps a dear school," said Benjamin Franklin. "A fool can learn in no other." Experience requires that we pay the price of learning ourselves. But we have a choice; we can choose to learn from others who already have paid that price. We can learn vicariously from their experiences and thus accelerate our own learning experiences.

Research Factoid

> *"A juggling act occurs in working memory when students try to learn from a lecture or an oral presentation. It takes about 10 seconds to transfer one bit of information from working memory to the more permanent store of long-term memory (Simon, 1974). If we consider that the typical speech rate for lectures is 150 words per minute, and an idea occurs every five words, we have students being bombarded with 30 ideas per minute (E. Gagne, 1985)! For the sake of discussion, let's assume that only half the ideas are new or important. Even then, the students are faced with 15 ideas a minute, but they're only capable of processing six. When this happens, students grasp at what they can get or out of frustration, tune out altogether."*
>
> – Eggan & Kauchak, (1988), p. 313

This chapter is about creating situations where participants can learn from their own experiences, as well as from experiences that you, the trainer, can provide. Sometimes, you'll want to create the situations in advance. Other times, it makes sense to have the participants go through the process of creating their own, using their own experiences and information. Whichever direction you choose (and you may choose both in the same program), you'll follow the same basic model.

Step 1: Select the Issue

What *issue* do you want to focus on? Is it managing conflict, resolving conflict, solving problems, or showing appreciation?

Step 2: Select the Incident/Situation

How are you going to approach the issue you've selected? If, for example, you are dealing with how emotions affect communications, you might choose an incident or a situation involving a boss and a subordinate.

Step 3: Provide Enough Details to Enable Participants to Reach Decisions

For example, the role play described on pages 109–110 takes place between a department head and a supervisor. There is sufficient detail to conduct the role play and set the agenda and objectives.

Step 4: Tell Specifically What Kind of Product You Want

Do you want the group to answer a series of questions and be prepared to deliver a summary? Are participants supposed to devise an action plan that ought to be followed to resolve the situation? Make clear what you expect to get back from your participants when the project is over.

Step 5: Set the Group Size

Are people going to pair off? Are they going to work as a group on a project, case study, or role play? Will they do the task individually? Each of these options affects the dynamics of the activity.

Step 6: Set Your Group Mix

In other words, are you going to have men working together, women working together, managers working together, subordinates working together? Are you going to mix these kinds of groups? Are you going to have outside and inside salespeople separate or together? Take the time to think about the participants in the group. Is there value to rearranging them in specific ways to take advantage of the unique background or experience that certain members may have? Or perhaps random assignments will work just as well? In either case, think it through before you decide.

Step 7: Set Your Time Limits

How much time are you going to allow? In some projects we structure, we develop more material than any group can cover. This keeps everyone fully occupied during the time available. The most important discussion questions are at the beginning and the end. Assuming there are eight questions to discuss and 20 minutes available for discussion, after 15 minutes we'd ask the groups to move to question six, if they're not already there. This way, each group gets to the key material.

The Role Play (or Skill Practice)

Research Factoid

> *"Effective teachers provide opportunities for students to practice and apply the new information."*
>
> — Good, T. L., & Brophy, J. E. (1994)

You can ask people to approach a role-play situation in one of three ways:

1. Approach the role play exactly the way you would a real-life situation. In other words, you are this person, so handle the situation the way you would if you really were confronting it.

2. Approach it exactly as it's written in the project. Forget the fact that you don't agree with certain opinions, biases, etc., in the written project; just "follow the script," as it were.

3. Do it ideally. In other words, seize the opportunity to say and do things in the role play that you would never say or do in a real-life situation.

Even though as trainers we are familiar with and use the term *role play*, I recommend describing it to your participants as a skill practice. Role play gets a bad rap. People often say the situations are not real. But no one argues with the practice a sports team needs. You'd be upset with a team that did not want to practice—only play the real game. Skill practice allows us the opportunity to use skills in an environment where there is no real-world cost (lost sales, upset customers, etc.) if we do not apply the skill perfectly the first time, the second time, or even the third time!

In this skill practice, one participant will play the role of a department head. Tell that person: "Be forceful in presenting your argument; remember, you believe you are right."

> You are the head of a 75-person department in a large organization. You are proud of the fact that you started out as an office clerk 20 years ago and that, by working hard and taking advantage of on-the-job training opportunities and a few night courses, you're the only high-school graduate in your organization to have a similar position.
>
> In spite of your experience and expertise, however, one of your six supervisors is constantly bucking you. This person has been in the organization about a year and has received several promotions, largely on the strength of a recently earned master's degree. Particularly annoying is the way he interrupts department meetings with suggestions that are ill-timed and that throw your schedule out of kilter.
>
> You believe that meetings should start and end on time, so you've called a private conference to discuss the matter. You feel the best solution is to meet privately before department meetings to review suggestions and select those that should be discussed in the general meeting. You know you need to make your points quickly and with no interruptions. You resent being interrupted and sidetracked from the issue at hand, and you expect others will respect your solution.

The other participant in this skill practice will play the supervisor. Tell this person: "Be forceful in presenting your argument; remember, you believe you're right.

> You are a supervisor responsible for 15 people in your organization. You have achieved this position in a little over a year, more because of your master's degree than your work experience. Others in your department look to you as an innovator. Your fellow supervisors seem to think you're headed for bigger and better things.
>
> The one stumbling block seems to be your boss, the head of your department who is responsible for 75 people including yourself and five other supervisors. The boss seems to be irritated with the perfectly valid suggestions you bring up in your department meetings. You get the feeling that the boss is threatened by your master's degree, perhaps because he himself didn't finish college. You also feel there may be some jealousy because you keep coming up with these great suggestions. You're scheduled for a personnel interview. You want to make sure you get full credit for your ideas; that's why you bring them up in front of everyone. Whatever your boss says, you want to be sure to clear the way for a time at each department meeting to suggest new ideas. Scheduling a specific time, say 10 or 15 minutes, would give you a forum for your thoughts and, at the same time, would appease your boss, who constantly harps about the importance of starting and ending on time.

You will notice that a number of factors were considered in this role play between the department head and the supervisor.

Each role is structured so that the players have specific opinions.

- Each person enters the role play with a specific agenda.

- The role play can be used for several purposes:

    1) People tend to get emotional in this role play so that we can observe how they listen (or choose not to listen!) to one another's points of view.

    2) Observers can focus on what happens when people enter a meeting with their minds already made up about the outcome.

    3) We can discuss how to unblock emotions in certain situations.

    4) We can consider alternative approaches to solving this problem. Sometimes, we encounter difficulty solving problems because we approach them with preconceived solutions. We're then blocked by these preconceptions from looking at other possible solutions.

Written Role Plays

Group involvement can also be generated by introducing an individual activity followed by a group activity. The following two projects illustrate this approach. The first, titled "Living Up to Your Potential," was given to participants to do individually in seven or eight minutes. Without sharing what they had written, they were asked to do the second project, "Achieving Your Expectations," as a group with a leader reporting their conclusions afterwards. Approximately 20 minutes were allowed for discussion.

You'll notice that we started with a project that individuals completed on their own. Then, in the group project, individuals worked together—exploring their feelings and expectations and realizing how these related to goal setting and other issues.

At the end of the individual activity—"Living Up to Your Potential"—no report was required to the larger group. But at the end of the "Achieving Your Expectations" activity, three or four group leaders summarized their discussions to all the groups in the seminar.

Ask participants to do one of the following exercises:

Living Up to Your Potential

1. You are given access to your personnel file. In it is a glowing letter of recommendation about you written by your boss. It is the most gratifying letter you can imagine receiving.

   Write what you would want the letter to say:

   _____
   _____
   _____
   _____
   _____
   _____
   _____

2. You are in your hometown. An old friend of yours and your spouse are having lunch with you. The friend asks, "Do you have any idea how much you are loved?" and hands you a letter. Your spouse wrote it, extolling your virtues and gave it to your friend.

   Write what you would like the letter to say:

   _____
   _____
   _____
   _____
   _____
   _____
   _____

After participants have completed writing their letters, ask the following questions to stimulate discussion:

Achieving Your Expectations

1. What are your feelings about the letter you have just written? How would you feel if such a letter were written about you? How would it affect your expectations for yourself? How would it affect your relationship with the person who wrote it?

2. In writing that letter, you were, in a way, writing out your own ideal expectations for your life, painting a picture of the person you would like to be. What could you do to move closer to this ideal?

3. We hear a lot about the expectations of others and their effect on our ability to perform, but how about our own expectations? How do they affect how we perform?

4. Do you have expectations of the kind of person you would like to be and of what you would like to achieve? What are they?

5. What would it take to achieve these expectations?

6. How do experiences relate to goals and goal setting? How could goal setting help you realize your expectations?

7. How do experiences relate to goals and goal setting? How could goal setting help you realize your expectations?

8. How could affirmations help you to realize your expectations? What are some affirmations you could put to use in achieving your expectations?

When Role Reversal Can Make a Point

Role reversal is a concept that applies not only to role plays but also to other kinds of projects. Sometimes it helps us put ourselves in another person's shoes. This can be accomplished very effectively and can best be illustrated by this example of an activity that I use in a seminar about persuasion.

Very simply, what I do is have everyone in the group become either the editor of a union newsletter or the editor of a company newsletter. Then I announce to the group that the president of their company is about to come in and read the following prepared statement. Assuming the role of the president, I deliver this announcement.

"As you all know, the economy has hit our company particularly hard. Taking into consideration the substantial capital equipment purchases we have made in the past 12 months and the fact that we are able to operate at only 60 percent capacity due to significantly decreased sales, I must request that all employees agree to a 10 percent pay decrease and a freeze on raises for the next six months.

"Agreeing to this proposal should help insure that any necessary layoffs will be minimal. I would also hope that we would not have to extend our annual plant closing beyond the usual two weeks. Senior management of your company has already agreed unanimously to accept a 10 percent cut in their salaries.

"I regret having to make this request, but I feel it is in the best interests of the company and—in the long run—in your futures.

"Please sign the attached card stating your agreement and return it to the personnel office immediately."

After I read this statement, I ask the "editors" to write a four- or five-paragraph article from the viewpoint of their newsletter on this announcement. People can work on this individually, or they can work in groups. The union-newsletter groups, maybe at two or three tables, work together, and the company-newsletter group works at a separate table. When they're finished, several of the groups will read aloud their news articles, which obviously express certain biases.

As a final step, I ask the groups to reverse roles: those who were editors of the company newsletter are now editors of the union newsletter and vice versa. This produces a slingshot effect. Sometimes the groups are able to reverse roles very well; at other times, they're not. Either way, the point is made. If role reversal is difficult, the discussion centers on why. Frequently, the groups have become so biased that they can't switch positions. This situation stimulates discussion about the importance of keeping an open mind toward issues in order to solve problems and resolve conflict.

Quick Tips for Role Play (Skill Practice)

- Work in smaller groups of three to six. This minimizes the discomfort of "everyone's watching."
- Add a coach to the role play. The coach stands behind the person and either the coach or the role player can call a "time out" to talk about what to do or say next.
- Make the coach a "tag-team" member. If the role player gets stuck, the coach can be "tagged" to switch places with the role player.
- Position role play as "skill practice." No one would dream of playing a sport by participating in competitions with no prior practice. This is our chance to practice before the real game, the game of life, begins.

Designing Effective Projects and Case Studies

There are a number of strategies that can be used to make projects and case studies more effective. I'll use two projects that I developed for some of my programs to illustrate.

> **Project 1:** Janice Bell is the office manager of a small office with the responsibility of overseeing five clerks and typists. The job started small and has grown to where she is crowded for space. She has been on the job 20 years and this is the only job that she's ever had. Janice was fresh out of business school when she joined the firm. She likes the company and the people she works with. One day her boss asks for a private conference and says, "You and your people have been doing a wonderful job, but the load seems to be getting more than your people can handle. I've been giving it some thought and have checked around pretty carefully. I think the solution would be to get some scanners and begin to use optical character recognition (OCR). There's also a new version of our word processing package that allows file sharing and on-line editing and file mark-up that would save time and effort as well. They have a special two-week school that you and one of your people could go to that would teach you everything you need to know. What do you think?" Janice responds rather touchily, "My people work hard. The workload is growing, but we've solved that problem in the past by adding an extra person." Her boss feels the technology upgrades would be a better idea. Janice finally says that she'll send two people from her department, but she will not go herself.
>
> Why do you think Janice was so touchy? Why would she turn down the opportunity for this training? What could her boss have said to make the situation more acceptable?
>
> **Project 2:** For the past six years, your family has gone to the same lakeside cottage for your two-week vacation. This year, you feel it's time for a change. You have secretly put aside a little money each payday, and a month before the vacation you say at dinner, "Surprise! I've been saving all year and this year our vacation is going to be special. We'll not only have the lakes, but also the mountains and the ocean." You pull out a fabulous full color brochure and describe the fantastic resort spots that your family can choose from this year, rather than the "same old, same old." To your dismay the plan is greeted rather unenthusiastically. No one seems to want to make a decision. Finally someone suggests that you just go back up to the lake and use the money to buy a new flat screen TV. Now it's your turn to feel upset and dismayed. All your sacrifice—and it's not even appreciated.
>
> Why do you think the family is acting this way? Is their resistance to a different vacation spot—or perhaps the fact that you didn't let them in on the planning? What could you have done to smooth the way for a favorable decision and enjoyable vacation?

1. Offer participants a choice. Rather than simply one case study, I offered two. You'll notice the first is business oriented, the second more personal. In some settings, I might want to use one or the other—or both. Designing more than one provides me with flexibility—and my participants with a choice.

2. Be careful of your language. In the case of Janice Bell, if you read the material, you cannot tell whether Janice's boss is male or female. Don't make roles gender specific unless you absolutely have to. In the family vacation incident, I've asked people how many thought the person saving the money was male? Female? Then I point out that the case says *you* have been saving money. Many times people miss that. Men raise their hands saying they saw the person as female and vice versa. You might also consider the use of gender neutral names throughout (i.e., Chris, Pat, Terry, etc.).

Challenge of Change

Group leader: Read aloud and discuss.

1) You have been discussing a difficult subject for people to grasp—change. Do you feel that people are naturally resistant to change—or do they resist the manner in which change is presented? Share any personal experiences where you may have resisted the manner change was presented rather than the change itself.

2) Why do you feel people are resistant to change? Were the "good old days" really that good? Or is it that we realize that time is moving on and if the good old days were back so would be our youth? What are some other things that might cause this resistance?

3) Many people have set habits for literally everything they do—which shoe is put on first in the morning, where their coffee cup is, etc. Change is difficult because it means changing habits. How could changing little habits—like the route you take each morning or getting up 15 minutes earlier or taking a walk around the block before breakfast—make changing other things easier? Discuss some things that you could do to alter your routine and bring a little change into your life.

4) What are some things that you've heard people say that might indicate to you that they are resisting change? (For example, have you heard, "But we've always done it that way"?)

5) Seeing the bigger picture can help you prepare for change. Where do you think the railroad would be today if industry leaders had seen themselves 50 years ago in the transportation industry rather than railroading? How about if leaders in the motion picture industry had seen themselves in the entertainment industry? What other illustrations can you think of where people and industries were bypassed because they refused to change when they had the opportunity?

6) What are some habits that you have that you would not want to change? Why not? What are some habits that you might want to develop? Why?

7) How does your attitude affect the benefits that you get from change? Are there some changes that you have made (or been forced to make) in your life that you could see no benefits in at the time? What possible benefits can you see looking back? Can bigger benefits be derived from change by expecting positive results and benefits beforehand? Why?

3. Develop discussion materials that help debrief the activity. In this example, after people have discussed the mini-cases, they debrief with a series of questions designed to help them look at the issue behind the cases—the challenge of change. Notice the questions begin with general questions (e.g., Why do you feel people are resistant to change?) and end with more specific application questions (e.g., What are some habits that you might want to develop?).

4. Develop value-added questions. In most classes, you'll have two groups of people—the quick and the analytical. Developing value-added questions can help the analytical have the discussion time they need without the quick feeling as if they've wasted their time. Let's say you have seven discussion questions. The important questions are Questions 1, 2, 3, and 7. The value-added questions are 4, 5, and 6. Once you see that an analytical group is on Question 4 you can say, "If you're not already there, please drop down to Question 7 and spend your last two minutes on it." In all likelihood, the quick can't get through all seven before the analyticals get through their four.

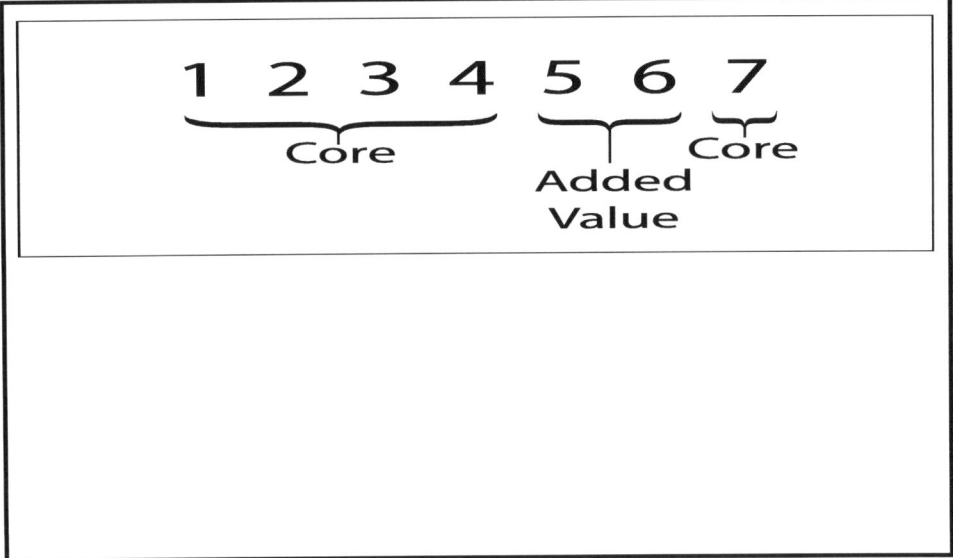

5. Use the power of choice to overcome inertia. For example, let's say there are seven problems to solve. I'll say to people, "You have a choice. Start with 1 and work to 7 or start with 7 and work to 1." People will usually look at both 1 and 7, choose the easiest and start there. The model is this: Questions 1 and 7 are the easiest, 2 and 6 next easiest, 3 and 5 more difficult, and 4 almost impossible. No one gets through all of them. When I debrief, someone gives a solution for 1, then someone 7, and so on. For half the group, they're checking the solution. For the other half, it's new because it's a problem they didn't work. It's another strategy that creates energy and interest.

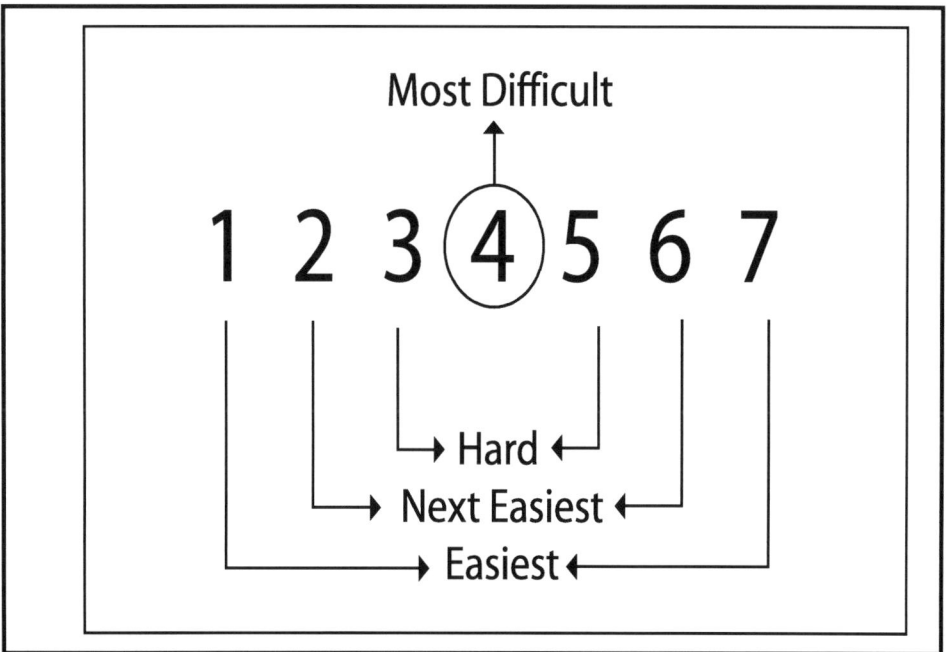

The Grid Concept

This exercise works particularly well with groups of people who have some knowledge about or experience in the area you're exploring. One of the benefits of the grid concept is that it can be customized to the particular group you're working with.

The first example I offer here relates to training. The participants—say, 40 trainers or so in groups of five or six brainstorm at their tables about the qualities and characteristics necessary for a person to be an effective trainer and/or speaker. Then I ask the groups, one at a time, to give me one characteristic from their list. Group 1 gives an item, Group 2 an item, and so on, until every group has named all its items, which I write down. While the participants are involved in the next project, I take the groups' suggestions and make them into an effectiveness grid.

Here are the results of one such effectiveness grid that was developed for the Central Wisconsin Chapter of American Society for Training and Development.

Central Wisconsin ASTD's
Training Effectiveness Grid

	10	20	30	40	50	60	70	80	90	100
Communication Skills (Good)										
Enthusiastic										
Nice (Friendly)										
Tests (Evaluates)										
Ready (Prepared)										
Adaptable (Flexible)										
Listener										
Wisdom										
Innovative										
Sales Ability (Persuasive)										
Conscientious										
Organized										
Neat (Well-dressed)										
Sensitive										
Interest in Others										
Natural Warmth										
Assortment (Variety)										
Sees People (Eye contact)										
Tolerant (Patient)										
Dedicated										

Three Greatest Strengths   Three Greatest Needs

1. _____   1. _____

2. _____   2. _____

3. _____   3. _____

    Each trainer received a copy of this grid and then did a self-rating on how effective he or she was in each of the areas listed. They circled the three they saw as their greatest strengths and the three they saw as their greatest needs on the grid and then, at the bottom of the grid, they could list their three strongest and three weakest areas. They did not necessarily rate their three weakest areas, those that needed improvement, as the lowest because they may not have had to use those skills in their particular function as trainers.

I concluded this exercise by saying, "The qualities and characteristics listed on your grid are those mentioned when people are asked, What do you need to be a successful trainer? Actually, most of these qualities could be applied not just to being successful as a trainer but to being successful in general.

"One of the most important things to notice about the grid is that every one of us can acquire and manage each of the qualities and characteristics listed. Even energy, for example, can be managed. It's been discovered that we burn three times as much energy when we think negatively as when we think positively and are in control of our emotions and actions.

"By way of illustration, imagine for a moment that you're all single. For those of you who are, that's easy. But the rest of you imagine it as well. Now, you're all single, and you've had a lousy day. No one loves you, and the day just seems to drag on and on. Every time you look at your watch, it seems as though it's going backwards.

"Finally, this lousy day ends. You slump into your car, drive home, walk through the door, collapse on the couch. You don't even have enough energy to turn on the television.

"As you're lying there in a stupor, the phone rings. You answer it, and it happens to be someone of the opposite sex whom you've admired—hopelessly, you thought—from afar. 'I know it's really short notice,' says this person, 'but I happen to have a couple of tickets for (an event you've been dying to go to). I wonder if you'd like to go with me tonight?' And you say, 'Well, I really appreciate the offer, but it's been such a lousy day. I think I really just want to take a nice hot bath and go to bed.' Right? Wrong!

"In that situation, each of us would suddenly have all the energy we need to go out and enjoy that evening's activity, because something crucial has just changed. And it's changed pretty dramatically. What is it?"

When people answer "attitude," they're absolutely right. Remember we burn three times as much energy when thinking negatively as when we're thinking positively and are in control of our emotions and actions. All the things we've discussed here can be acquired, developed, and managed by each of us. The area on the left side of the line we made on the Central Wisconsin ASTD grid represents what we are right now. The area on the right side represents our potential, what we can be. The entire focus of our training should be to help those we train acquire, develop, and manage the skills and characteristics needed to be effective.

This concept can be used for other topics as well. It could, for instance, be a problem-solving or decision-making or sales-effectiveness grid. In the example that follows, it happens to deal with customer courtesy.

Caesars Boardwalk Regency's Customer Service/Courtesy Effectiveness Grid

	10	20	30	40	50	60	70	80	90	100
Courteous										
Appearance (Good)										
Eye Contact										
Smiles										
Acts to Solve Problems										
Responsive										
Self-Image (Positive)										
Be-of-Service Attitude										
Organized										
Amiable (Friendly)										
Reliable (Follows through)										
Detail-oriented										
Withholds Judgment										
Attitude (Positive)										
Listens										
Knowledge of Job & Hotel/Casino										
Remembers Names										
Empathy (Understanding)										
Genuinely Helpful										
Energetic (Motivated)										
Needs to be Responsible										
Communicates Clearly										
Yourself										

    This grid was designed for Caesars Boardwalk Regency, a hotel/casino in Atlantic City. It's based on interviews my partner and I conducted; we asked people what they looked for when they went to a hotel or casino or restaurant. What were the hallmarks, from the customer's perspective, of real courtesy? We took the 85 characteristics from the interviews and boiled them down into the qualities represented on the Caesars Boardwalk Regency acrostic. This became the company's customer-courtesy effectiveness grid, and it formed the basis for a training program on customer service and courtesy for all 3,500 employees of Caesars Boardwalk Regency.

    This third example is a computer literacy grid that was designed for our Computer Literacy for Executives and Managers seminar. This grid was based on the actual course content to be covered. We wanted a self-rating at the beginning of the course to find out how much each manager already knew so that their expertise could be incorporated into the course as we proceeded.

Computer Literacy Grid

	10	20	30	40	50	60	70	80	90	100
Computer Software										
Operating Skills										
Memory (Storage)										
Printers										
Utilities										
Terminology										
Electronic Spreadsheet										
Records (Database Management)										
Lease/Purchase Decision										
Information Services										
Tele (Comm.)										
Elements (Concepts)										
Remote (Distributed)										
Application										
Components (Hardware)										
You and Change										
Graphics										
Requirements (Needs)										
Information Processing (Words)										
Documentation										

Developing Your Own Grid

Here are the steps for developing your own grid:

1. Develop the list of concepts, characteristics, etc., that you want participants to be aware of and interact around. As demonstrated from the three examples given here, they may be provided by participants, based on your research, or generated from customers or some other stakeholder group as appropriate for your purposes.

2. Prioritize the concepts in order of importance. This is because you may have more concepts, characteristics, or qualities than you can effectively cover in a single grid. You want participants focusing on those that are going to have the highest value.

3. Choose a word or phrase that will help create a custom grid just as we did with each of the three examples.

4. Match the highest priority words to appropriate letters within your chosen word or phrase.

5. When you need letters that don't exist in the phrase that you've chosen, either change the phrase or look for synonyms that convey the same basic meaning, but start with the letter you need. You'll notice in the Central Wisconsin ASTD'S Training Effectiveness Grid that good communications was one characteristic of good customer service. I needed a "C" though, so I put "Communication Skills (Good)" on the grid.

6. Decide whether you want people to select their three greatest needs and strengths to list at the bottom of the grid.

7. Voila, you've created a powerful customized tool to use in your own training!

Summary

Projects, case studies, and role plays are just three of the methods we can use to create more involvement and learning on the part of our participants. Most of the creativity that we bring into the classroom is because of the preparation that occurred before we ever entered the classroom.

Chapter 7:
Creating Effective Resource Materials

*Materials That Put the Need to Know, Nice to Know,
and How to Find at People's Fingertips*

All things being equal, people like "stuff." When we walk into a seminar or workshop, and we see a lot of neat "stuff," we start the seminar with the feeling that there's going to be something here for us to benefit from. Now, the instructor can quickly demonstrate that that's not true, but the initial impression that we have as participants is that there is something to be gained.

There are at least six benefits of providing resource material to participants:

1. **Enhancing the Educational Offering.** Participants can't possibly take complete and accurate notes of everything that happens in the classroom, so handouts can help participants fill in the gaps. The handout can also go beyond the classroom time by providing additional materials that couldn't be covered in the classroom.

2. **Enhancing Marketing Opportunities.** As instructors, we need to constantly be selling the value of the training that we're delivering. When participants go back to the workplace with well-organized materials that they can show to supervisors and coworkers, those materials are saying, "This seminar is worthwhile."

3. **Ensuring Instructor Preparation.** When instructors have deadlines for preparing course materials that they'll be using, it helps to ensure preparation. Preparation of handouts and resource materials take time, but it also helps to ensure that the instructor spends time in advance of the class thinking about the content, thinking about the sequence, etc., simply because those affect how the materials are put together.

4. **Helping the Instructor Get through the First Critical Moments of the Class.** It is possible to be nervous in starting a new seminar. When resource materials are available, an instructor can take time leading participants through the materials so that they have an awareness of the overall class and of the materials that are available. This helps the participants get comfortable and also helps the instructor develop some momentum and eliminate any nervousness.

5. **Providing a Way of Demonstrating the Instructor's Competency.** When the instructor is the one who has prepared the course materials, participants look at those materials and, without the instructor saying anything verbally, the material shows the participants that the instructor has expertise in this area.

6. **Creating a Job Aid that Will Help the Participant Transfer the Information Back to the Job.** When support materials are used (particularly when the participant personalizes that material through participation in the class), that material becomes a valuable reference/resource for reinforcing the principles taught back on the job.

   Here is a checklist, along with example pages from various seminars I've developed over the years.

Part 1. Table of Contents

On page 1, we have a table of contents so that any participant picking up the workbook can say to him- or herself "This is organized." Analytical participants can relax a little bit knowing that there is a structure to the program.

---

*Developing, Marketing, and
Promoting Successful
Seminars and Workshops*

Table of Contents

Introduction
  Robert W. Pike's Bio 3
  Seminar Flow Chart 5
  Conference Flow Chart 7

Chapter One: Information Services
  Practical Tips to Improve Information Services 11
  Newsletter 13
  Increasing Your Income, Exposure, Credibility, and
     Profits with In-House Programs 15
  Sample Proposal 29
  10 Marketing/Business Development Tips 43
  How to Price Your Programs for Maximum Profits 47
  Basic Program Costs/Pricing Spreadsheet 53
  Advanced Program Costs/Pricing Spreadsheet 1 55
  Advanced Program Costs/Pricing Spreadsheet 2 57
  Creative PR Boosts Program Attendance 59
  Using Advisory Boards 61
  Sample Invitation to Advisory Board 63
  Meeting Promotion—Measuring Direct Mail Effectiveness 65

Chapter Two: Marketing
  Considerations for Workshop Timing 69
  Marketing Plan Form 71
  Cost-Effective Promotion and Advertising and Test Market Considerations 77
  Mailing List Summary Sheet 79
  Public Relations 81
  Publicity Do's and Don'ts 87
  Before You Advertise 93

Part 2. Welcome

On page 2, we have a welcome letter that helps orient participants to the seminar and gives them an idea of what to expect during the seminar.

Introduction

Welcome to Bob Pike's Master Class in Instructor-Led, Participant-Centered Training. I began training full time in 1969. In 1983 I published *Creative Training Techniques* as a spiral bound manual. After selling 30,000 copies, it was published as *The Creative Training Techniques Handbook* in 1987.

Since then it has sold over 330,000 copies, making it the best-selling train-the-trainer book ever published. More than 125,000 trainers on five continents have been through programs I designed around the CTT Handbook. (The Fourth Edition has been retitled as *Master Trainer Handbook*.) This 2015 edition represents the latest iteration. You will focus not only on the delivery of training, but on the entire training process—including transfer strategies.

The format is that of a workshop. I like this metaphor because both my father and grandfather were carpenters, as was I in my early years. It was one of the ways I paid my way through college. When I went to either my father's or grandfather's workshops, I knew that I was there to work hard—but I also knew that it would be fun. And I knew that I would be helping to create something that would add value and be useful. Years later, I would use that knowledge, skill, and experience to build a grandfather clock for my grandmother.

You will be doing the same thing. Get ready to roll up your sleeves, gain new skills and knowledge, and apply them in real time during the workshop so that you leave with not only an action plan to implement, but with things that you have already created that will immediately start to transform your training.

My goal is to add value and make a difference for you and your organizations with this experience. Working together, I know we can do that. Welcome.

God bless,

Bob Pike

Bob Pike, CPLP Fellow, CPLP Fellow CSP, CPAE Speaker Hall of Fame
Founder/Past Chairman—The Bob Pike Group
Founder/Editor—CTT Press, Inc.
Past Chairman—Lead Like Jesus

Part 3. Credibility

Next, we have my biosketch. No one is ever as famous or as credible as they'd like to be. Oftentimes in seminars, it's not appropriate because of the size of the group to provide introductions. For example, you wouldn't have a colleague give an introduction of you to a seminar group that consisted of four people. But a written biosketch can help the participants be aware of what gives this instructor the right to be teaching this seminar. People may not be aware of the years of experience or the specialized training that you may have gone through in order to get ready to do this seminar. A biosketch can help develop your credibility.

Bob Pike, CPLP Fellow, CSP, CPAE

Developing, Marketing, and Promoting Successful Seminars and Workshops

Bob has developed and implemented training programs for business, industry, government, and the professions since 1969. Beginning as a representative for Master Education Industries, he received nine promotions in three and one-half years, to Senior Vice President. His responsibilities included developing an intensive three-week Master Training Academy covering all phases of sales training, management development, communications, motivation/platform skills, and business operations. During his five years as Vice President of Personal Dynamics, Inc., that company grew from less than 4,000 enrollments per years to more than 80,000. He pioneered undergraduate and graduate credit on a national basis.

As founder and past Chairman Emeritus of The Bob Pike Group and Chairman of CTT Newsletters, LLC, Bob leads sessions over 100 days per year covering topics like training the trainer, instructional design, business planning, marketing seminars and workshops, leadership, attitudes, motivation, decision-making, problem-solving, personal and organizational effectiveness. More than 125,000 trainers on five continents have attended versions of Bob Pike's Master Class for Instructor-Led, Participant-Centered Training Workshop. As a consultant, Bob has worked with such organizations as Pfizer, Upjohn, Caesars Boardwalk Regency, Exhibitor Magazine, Hallmark Cards, Inc., and IBM. A member of the American Society for Training and Development (ASTD) since 1972, Bob has been active in many capacities including three National Conference Design Committees, Director of Special Interest Groups, and member of the National Board of Directors. He also served on the Board of Directors for the National Speaker's Association (NSA) and the International Alliance of Learning.

An outstanding speaker, Bob has presented at regional and national ASTD and TRAINING Conferences as well as global training and performance conferences around the world. In 1991, Bob was granted the professional designation of Certified Speaking Professional (CSP) by the National Speaker's Association. This designation has been earned by less than 9% of the more than 3,800 members of the NSA. In 1999, he was granted the professional designation of CPAE (Council of Peers Award of Excellence) Speaker Hall of Fame. In 2013 he became the second person to be named a CPLP Fellow by ASTD.

Bob has a regular column, "Trainer Talk", in TRAINING Magazine. He is editor of Bob Pike's Master Trainer newsletter (formerly the Creative Training Techniques Newsletter). He is author of *Master Trainer Handbook* (formerly the *Creative Training Techniques Handbook*) and co-author of *One-on-One Training, Dealing with Difficult Participants, 50 Creative Training Openers, 50 Creative Training Closers,* along with more than 25 other books and a dozen videos.

Part 4. Workbook Orientation

Part four is a workbook orientation. In our workbook, we include a page entitled, "How to Use this Workbook" that lets users know that there are three parts to the workbook. The first section, "Need to Know," is on the white pages and those pages are going to be covered very thoroughly during the seminar. The second section, "Nice to Know," is on the purple pages. They're supplemental and depending on the needs of the group, some of those pages will be in the seminar. It's important to note that any partial pages are in the "Need to Know" pages, whereas the "Nice to Know" pages can stand alone. People are not going to be frustrated by finding blanks and wondering what those blanks represent. The third section, "Where to Go," is located in the yellow pages. In other words, these are resources that are going to be useful to them later and are easily accessible.

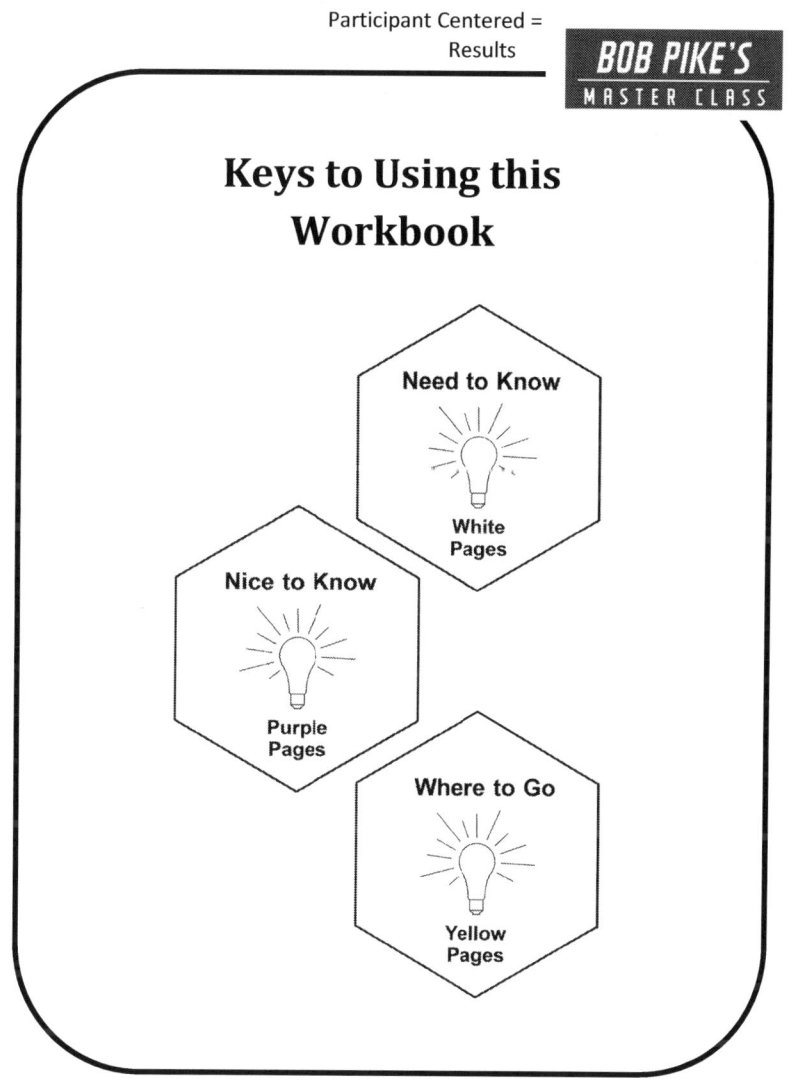

Research Factoid

> *"Students are more successful when lessons are structured."*
> – Brophy, J., & Good, T. L. (1986)

Part 5. Partial Handouts

Here is the handout we use for openings. It includes key blanks that need to be filled in. The instructor uses PowerPoint or flip charts to provide the participants with the key words. This way the participants can focus on what's happening in the class, have a track to run on with the partial handout, and, if the participants choose, need only to write in the key word to have the handout be complete, yet will frequently take many more notes.

Participant Centered = Results

BOB PIKE'S MASTER CLASS

Purpose of Training = Deliver _____.
Training = Do It To _____ Project.

E ____	E ____	T ____
A ____	T ____	E ____
T ____	A ____	A ____

Pike's Five Laws

1. Adults are _____ with big bodies.
2. People don't _____ with their own data.
3. Learning is directly _____ to the amount of fun you have.
4. Learning hasn't taken _____ until behavior has changed.
5. _____.

Part 6. Note Pages

In the "Need to Know" section of the resource material, every left page is a note page so that if participants need more space than the actual handout they're writing on, they can take additional notes right next to the handout that they're working on.

Part 7. Activity Guide Sheets

Some people can hear verbal instructions and completely understand what needs to be done. Others find it much more comfortable to hear the instructions, but then have the instructions in front of them.

Openings

Four Facts

Part I. On this sheet, please list four facts about yourself. Three of them should be true. One of them should be false.

1. _____   2. _____
3. _____   4. _____

Part II. Now, as a group, do the following steps, in order, one at a time.

1. List below the name of each person in your group (other than yourself).
2. Each person reads their four statements aloud.
3. As each person reads the four statements, list next to his or her name the number of the statement you think is false about them and why.
4. Once each person has completed sharing the statements, take one person at a time and have each of the remaining people tell which statement is false and why. Then the person who shared the four statements originally can reveal which one was really false.
5. Do this for each of the people in your group.

   1) Name_____ Statement number_____ is false because
   _____.

   2) Name_____ Statement number_____ is false because
   _____.

   3) Name_____ Statement number_____ is false because
   _____.

   4) Name_____ Statement number_____ is false because
   _____.

   5) Name_____ Statement number_____ is false because
   _____.

   6) Name_____ Statement number_____ is false because
   _____.

There is an activity that we do in many of my train-the-trainer programs called Four Facts. The first part of the activity is completed individually. The instructor reads the instructions out loud and then models the instructions by providing four facts about him- or herself. Participants then list their own facts on the page. A group leader is then chosen and leads the group through the activity based on the instructions given. Once again, the instructor has given these instructions verbally, perhaps picked out one group and walked the entire room through how the activity would work with this one group, and then has each of the groups in the seminar do the activity based on the steps that are listed.

Part 8. Follow-up Discussion Sheets

Almost every activity that is done in a seminar needs to be processed in some way. Sometimes that processing can simply be done verbally through a discussion. At other times, it is more helpful to let smaller groups within the seminar discuss what happened and why, and discussion sheets can really help make that much easier. Once the Four Facts activity is over, participants are then given the Four Facts discussion sheet, which is then used in small groups.

Openers

Four Facts
Sample Discussion

Group Leader Read:

1. Were you surprised at some of the "facts" that people shared? Which? Why?

2. How good were you as a group and individually at picking the false statement? What does this tell you about making assumptions and judgments about people?

3. Were some of the statements made by different people similar? What reasons could you give for this?

4. Were some of the "facts" quite different? What reasons could you give for this?

Part 9. Reference Lists

Reference lists can be given complete or they can be developed by participants themselves. We give people a training tools sheet so that as they go through the seminar and notice a training tool that they like, they can create their own reference list in the workbook. Examples of tools that might appear on this list are Mr. Sketch® markers, special water-based markers that don't bleed through on the flip charts, 3M® tape flags that can be used to create reference points that are easy to get back to in the manual, and perhaps checklists in the seminar.

Props/Tools

Training Tools

-
-
-
-
-
-
-
-
-
-
-
-
-
-

-
-
-
-
-
-
-
-
-
-
-
-
-
-

We have seven different methods that we can use to get participants back from breaks on time, so we give them to participants in the form of a checklist and ask them to discuss when, where, and how these were used to get them back from break on time. Sometimes participants will come up with additional ways that the instructor didn't even realize were being used and for that reason there are some blanks on the bottom of the page.

Part 10. Charts

In the seminar, we spend time looking at an instructional design grid that was part of an article that several of us contributed to in the 1987 *University Associates Annual for Developing Human Resources*. The diagram or grid can help to convey a lot of information in a very condensed space. When talking about room setups, diagrams are much more helpful to give participants than simply giving them a verbal explanation.

Instructional Design Grid

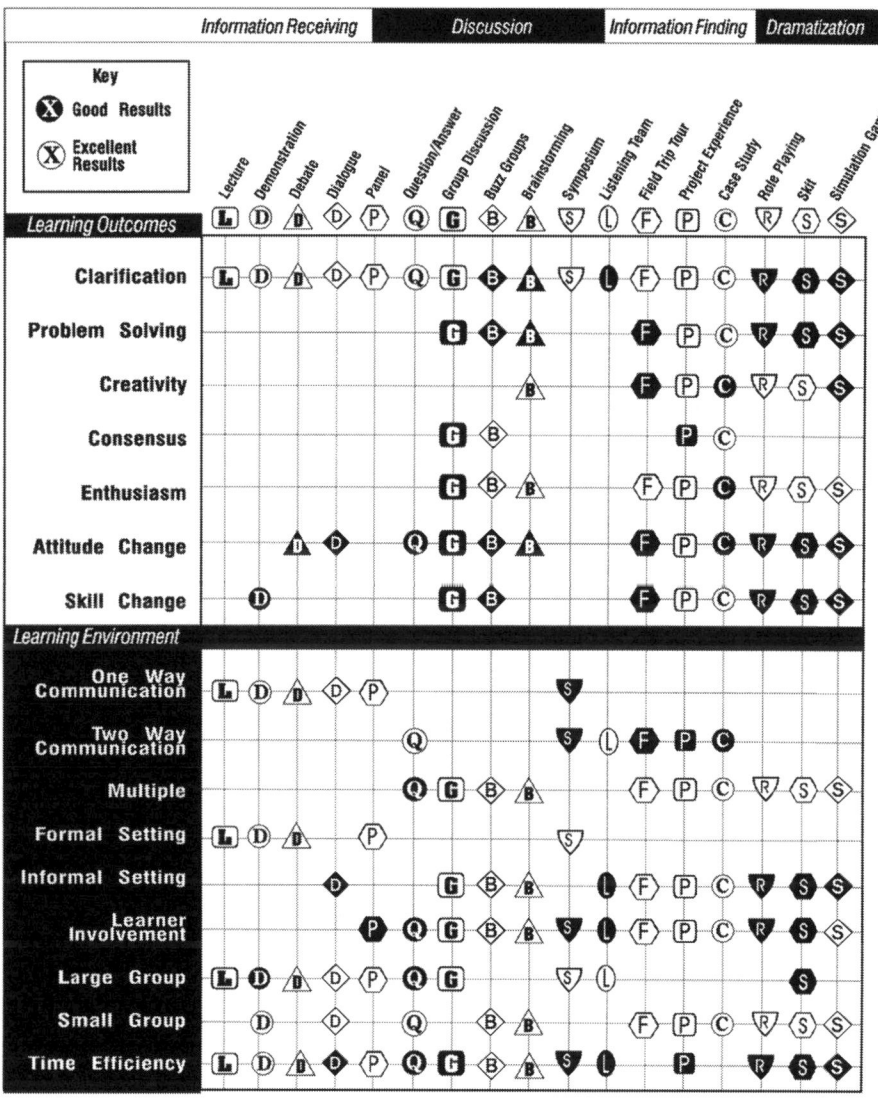

Used with permission "The 1987 Annual: Developing Human Resource," Article by Robert W. Pike, et al.

Part 11. Reference Sheets

Once information is covered in the seminar, it may be helpful to provide a summary of the things that have been covered, or a bonus sheet that covers that information plus additional information such as the list of "Difficult Participant Strategies" below that we include in the workbook.

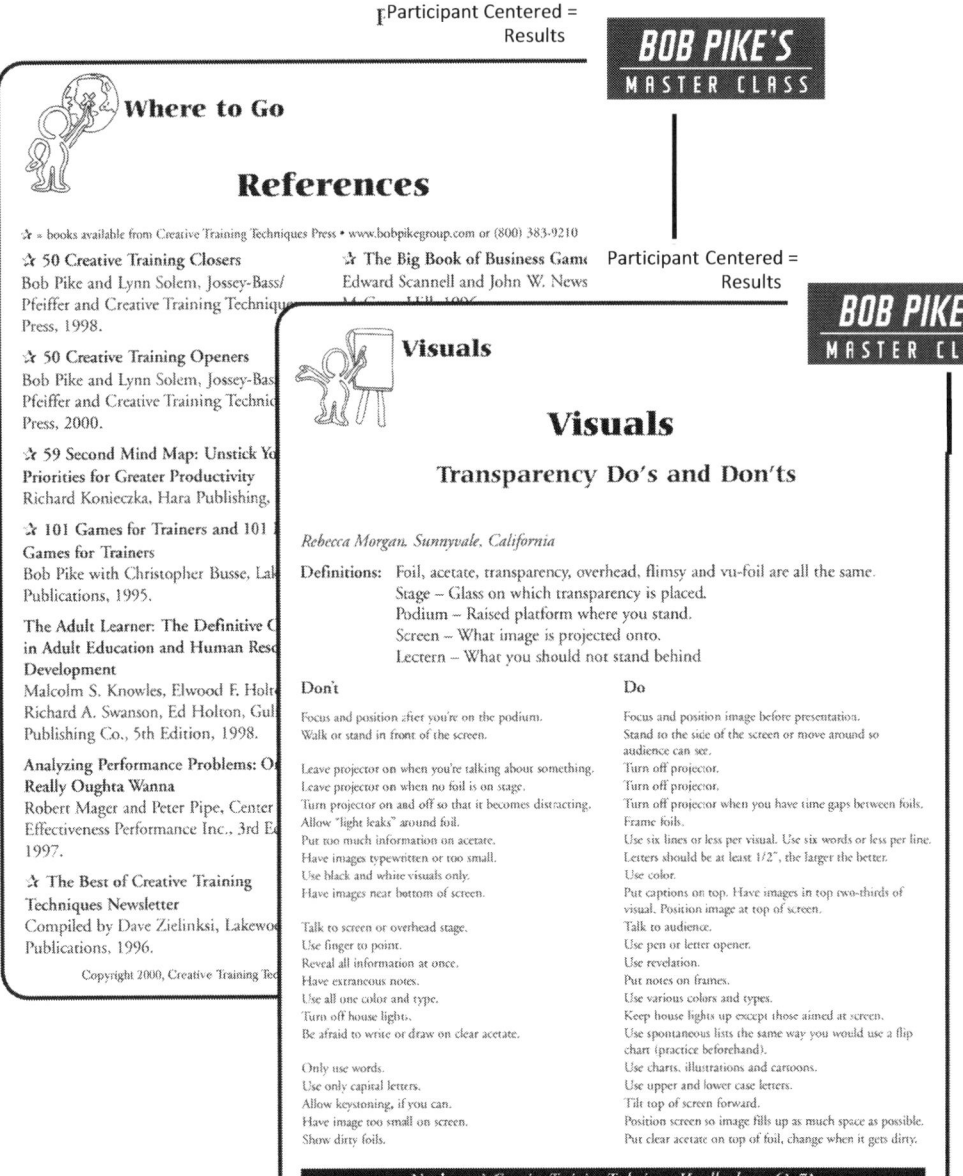

Part 12. Diagrams

We've heard the saying, "A picture is worth a thousand words." Diagrams can help convey that meaning. Here's the room layout that we use for a typical instructor-led and participant-centered seminar. As part of the workbook it helps participants be able to recall later many of the small details that made the room setup work in their seminar so that they can recreate it in their own classroom environment.

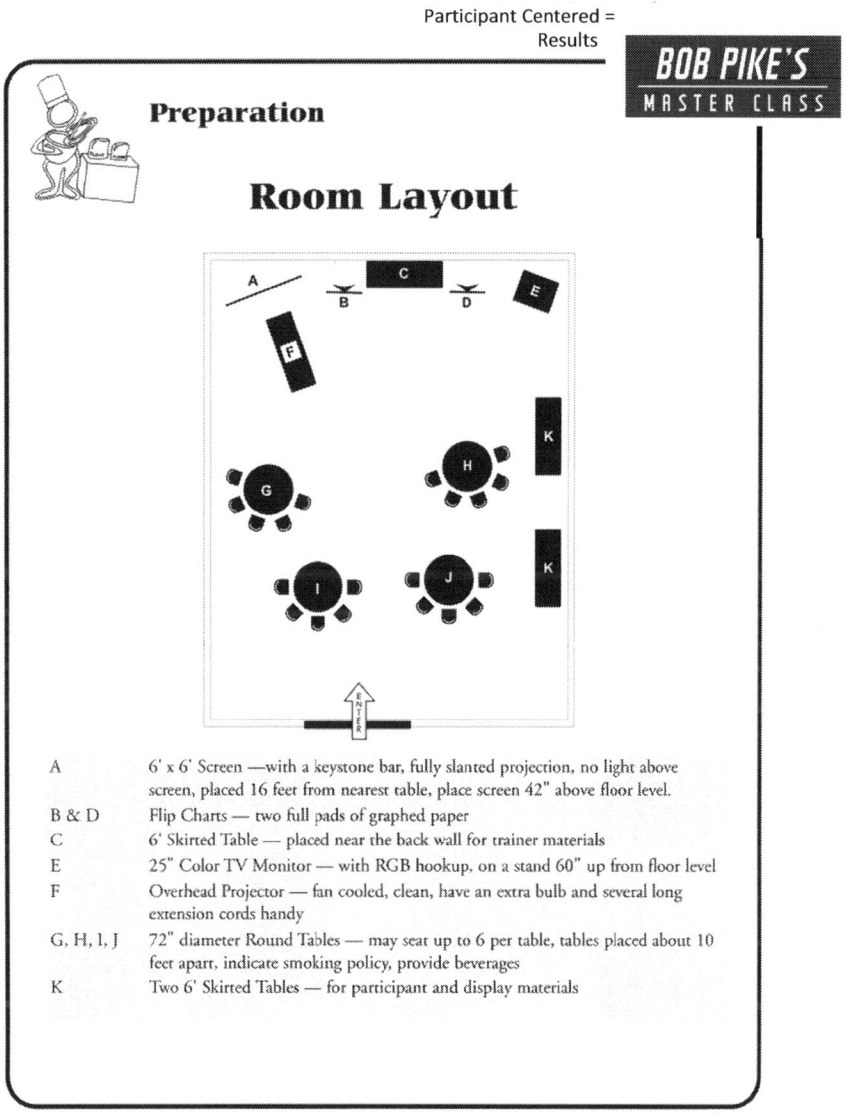

Part 13. Flow Charts

Participants can more readily visualize a process that has steps when it's presented as a flow chart. Here is the flow chart that we use in many of our proposals to help clients realize that developing powerful training programs is in many ways like manufacturing a new product. There are many steps, some of which can occur simultaneously. Good design and implementation doesn't happen by accident.

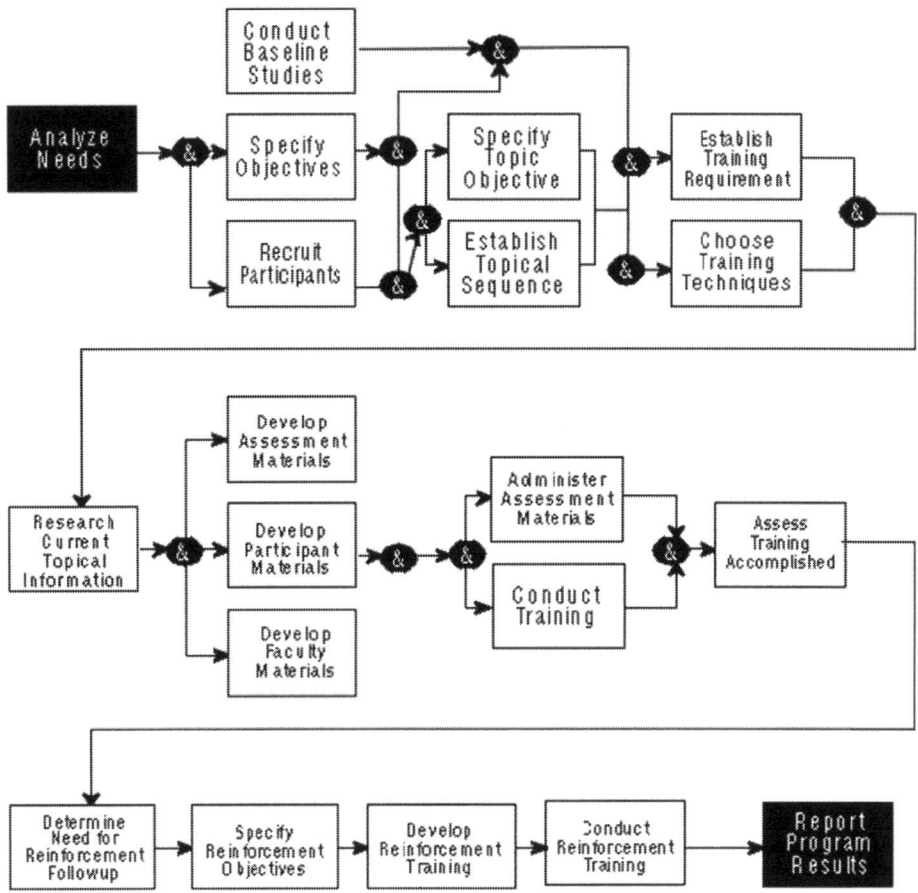

Why Handouts Can Be Almost as Important as the Presentation Itself

Throughout this book, I've emphasized the need for application. One involvement technique that I've mentioned several times is that of giving people handouts for them to complete. Two examples are partial PowerPoints on which they fill in key words and partial outlines that they complete as the session proceeds. This activity keeps participants involved in the learning process and gives them something of value that they can refer to in the future.

This simple involvement technique also allows you to cover more material in less time. A well-prepared handout indicates in a nonverbal way that you're thoroughly and thoughtfully prepared for the presentation. It tells your participants that you cared enough about this presentation to prepare superior supplemental materials.

The Seminar Workbook:
A Checklist of Additional Ideas

The seminar workbook usually is not designed to stand alone; it is a support to the seminar—a supplement. It may contain materials to be used in the seminar, as well as resources to be consulted after the program is over. If you do include material for use both during and after the seminar, consider printing the materials on two or three different colored papers. Title the sections as we do in our Workbook "Need to Know" (white), "Nice to Know" (purple), and "Where to Go" (yellow). This keeps participants from being overwhelmed by the amount of material they may be receiving, and it keeps them from thinking you are behind in the program because you haven't covered all of the material in the manual.

In addition to the examples we have already given in this chapter, here is a checklist of 14 more types of handouts to consider to create a workbook that is practical during class—and a fantastic resource after the class is over.

1. A checklist that attendees can actually use on their jobs. (This can be a sequence of steps to take in a process, items needed to perform a task, elements to include in a project.)

2. A list of points that will be fully or partially covered, but that would require extensive note keeping to record in full.

3. Schematics of a technical process.

4. Reprints of articles (including those by the seminar leader).

5. A summary of key points. (This material would typically be projected on an overhead as well.)

6. A humorous perspective on the topic.

7. A bibliography.

8. Formulas. (This material should be projected.)

9. Graphs (projected).

10. Photographs (projected).

11. Definitions that the seminar leader will discuss but that are time-consuming to write down.

12. Section dividers. (Divide your workbook into modular sections.)

13. Sample correspondence.

14. Case studies.

All of these types of handouts will enable you to create a workbook that automatically involves your participants in the learning process. By requiring that the participants be involved in a variety of ways to make the handouts within the workbook complete, it also ensures that participants understand that the real value of the workbook is in the interaction that they have with it as a part of the seminar, not the workbook by itself.

Chapter 8:
Presentation Techniques

How to Build and Deliver Powerful Presentations

What makes a powerful presentation? Just what can we do to get people to listen and respond in a positive manner to what we have to say? Each of us has had the experience of being captivated by a presentation, one that would have held our attention indefinitely. We've also probably shared the experience of being "trapped" in a presentation that felt as though it lasted 10 times longer than necessary. So how do we design presentations and training programs that fit into the first category and avoid the pitfalls that put us in the second category?

My operational definition of a presentation is the systematic discussion, explanation, or demonstration of skills, knowledge, or attitudes. A presentation is not necessarily a lecture, though lecture may be part of it. A powerful presentation enables participants to expand skills, reinforce or change attitudes, and gain new knowledge. For the trainer, presentations are not limited to training programs. There are executive briefings and overviews, problem-solving meetings, budget meetings, meetings to consider proposals for new programs, reports, etc. Presentation is a part of all of these. Some presentations are delivered on short notice, but a knowledge of presentation formats can help the presenter use even a short amount of preparation time effectively. Now, what are the keys to building powerful presentations?

Next, let's remember that every person in our program is going to be tuned to two radio stations—WII-FM: What's In It For Me? and MMFI-AM: Make Me Feel Important About Myself. Whatever we design and deliver must be based on those two points. Since all the participants will be asking, "What's in it for me?" we must, in preparing our presentation, continually reinforce the payoff for those participants if we're going to achieve the impact we want. Furthermore, we want to build the confidence of our participants so that we can ensure the transfer, back on the job, of the skills they've learned and the knowledge they've developed. That means keeping the focus and spotlight on the participants as much as possible. The greater their sense of accomplishment in the class, the greater the transfer back on the job.

Research Factoid

"Effective teachers expect students to successfully reach the instructional goals."

– Rosenthal, R., & Jacobsen, L. (1968). Pygmalion *in the Classroom: Teacher Expectation and Pupils' Intellectual Development.* NY: Holt, Rinehart & Winston

Where, we must ask ourselves, do we want to be at the end of the presentation?

Interestingly enough and a little counter-intuitive, this is actually the first question to ask in preparing a presentation. As has oftentimes been said, you can't hit the bull's-eye of a target if you don't know where it is. Too many presentations just sort of dribble off inconclusively; in others, the instructor races through the latter part of the content because time is running out. A strong conclusion is a must for any training program and, as a matter of fact, for every segment of a training program. It is not enough to capture the attention of participants at the beginning and/or to deliver strong content in the middle; it is also imperative to have a strong wrap-up that drives home the point(s) you've made.

Research Factoid

"Effective teachers achieve closure to their lessons. Effective teachers plan how to bring a lesson to a close and how to make the transition into the adjoining lesson."

– Gage, N. L., & Berliner, D. C. (1984). Educational Psychology. Boston, MA: Houghton Mifflin

Training programs can last for days, weeks, or even months, but the length of each presentation must be in tune with the attention span of the participants. If the focus of our training is results (and those results being significant behavioral change back on the job), as it should be, then we must work within limits appropriate to what participants can absorb.

Try this little test on yourself, carefully following the instructions in order to derive maximum benefit from this illustration. Clearly read aloud the following series of numbers:

6, 9, 12, 4, 14, 7, 5, 8, 11

Now jot down your answers to these three questions without looking back at the series of numbers.

1. What was the first number in the sequence?
2. What was the last number in the sequence?
3. What was the middle number in the sequence?

In my seminars, 95 percent of the participants usually recall the first number correctly, 65 to 90 percent correctly recall the last number, but 20 percent or less correctly recall the middle number. This would indicate that people remember beginnings and endings rather than what comes in the middle. One conclusion for presenters is to design programs that have more compelling beginnings and endings—and to find ways to reinforce the middle.

People have limited short-term memories. Remember in chapter four our voicemail example of hearing a ten-digit number and not being able to recall all of it when dialing because it was too long? For most of us, it's a common experience; once we get beyond seven "bits" of information, we start to lose that information. Perhaps that's why there's so much emphasis on the "30-second sound bite" in political advertising and why most commercials last 30 seconds or less.

To accommodate participants' limited short-term memories, we should present a limited amount of new information that can be absorbed before adding more information (see the Insider's Tip on page 83 regarding the concept of CPR for more insight into this area). Imagine pouring liquid through a funnel. If we pour too fast, the liquid spills over and is lost. But if we pour either at a rate less than or equal to the maximum we'll prevent spillage. Or we can stop periodically to allow the liquid to drain before we continue. Here—and in the presentations we deliver—the delivery rate and the amount delivered are key.

There are seven keys to memory that can help us build more powerful presentation— and help our participants to remember the key content as well. They are illustrated in the windowpane you see on the following page.

Master Trainer Handbook

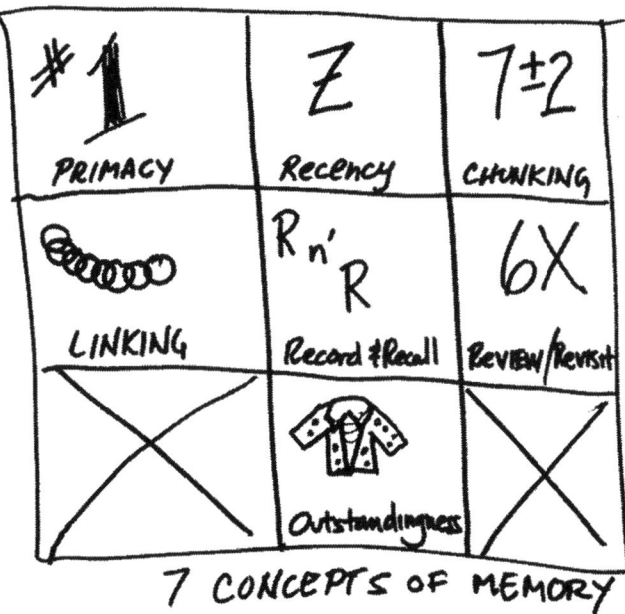

7 CONCEPTS OF MEMORY

1. Primacy says that we remember first things best—the beginning of a list, etc. For those of us who train, this reinforces the fact that the opening is one of the most impactful times of trainings, yet often it gets squandered with housekeeping or lengthy personal introductions. We must reconsider how we want to invest this memorable moment.

2. Recency says that we remember last things next best—the last thing that was heard, presented, etc. Remember the numbers you looked at a few minutes ago? In classes I've taught, 95 percent remember the first number, 65–90 percent the last number, but less than 20 percent the middle number. Therefore, let's have more beginnings and more endings and reinforce the middle! If we follow the principle of chunking, we will have more openings and closings!

3. Chunking says that we remember best when presented with bite-sized or small chunks of information. AT&T did research in the 1950s regarding phone numbers. They discovered that the average person could remember seven bits of information, plus or minus two. So local telephone numbers had seven digits that were further chunked into three digits followed by a hyphen and four digits (for example, 829-1954).

4. Linking says that we remember best when we can connect new information to information we have already learned. For example look at the letters in the box below:

IUZEILT

5. After looking at these letters for five seconds turn the page. Without going back to the previous page can you recall the first letter? Can you recall the last letter? Can you remember *for sure* the middle letter? Would you be willing to bet a substantial sum of money that without turning back you could remember the *exact* position of each letter? Most people in seminars can't remember much more than the first and last letters for sure. Go to the end of the chapter and look at the letters in the box on page 162.

6. What if I asked you the same questions about the positions of these letters in the box on page 162? Would you have the same challenge? Probably not. Why? Because you recognize these letters as forming a word you know. One glance and you knew the position of all seven letters (the same seven letters as in the previous "example"). (I also cheated a bit and put the first letters in all uppercase. You'll remember from the chapter on visual aids that this makes reading the letters much more difficult than simply upper- and lowercase!) This is the concept of linking. Seven bits of information are now recognized as one. We must work hard as trainers to always find something that is already in our participants' long-term memories to which we can link the new information. When teaching a new software, is there a current software that is similar to the one being taught to which the new information can be linked? When we step into a class and say in word or attitude "What I'm about to teach you is unlike anything you've ever seen before," we make learning very difficult.

7. Record and recall. People remember better when they write things down themselves. This phenomenon is increased when they draw the icons that are used in the windowpane as well.

8. Revisit not review. Review is when the trainer says it again. Revisit is when participants engage in some way with the content again. We need to revisit content six times with interval reinforcement to move information from short-term memory to long-term memory.

9. Be outstanding. We remember the silly, the ridiculous, the unusual, and the out of the ordinary. The sketch here represents a Hawaiian shirt. I point out to audiences that when I present in a business suit, there is really nothing memorable—it's expected. However, what if I showed up wearing a yellow and green Hawaiian shirt open to the navel with a dozen gold chains? You'd probably remember. Why? Because it was out of the ordinary (and you might think even inappropriate). However, it does make it memorable—and that's the point here.

As you think back to your education, you can probably remember an instructor who had the courage to be different (and hence memorable). Possibly it was that history teacher who came to class dressed as King George or a math teacher who had you figure the weight of a car based on the pressure in its tires. They had the courage to stand out in their teaching practices for the sake of making their content more memorable to their students. I wish that for us all.

As mentioned in Chapter 2, in his book *Use Both Sides of Your Brain,* Tony Buzan estimates that the average adult can listen with *understanding* for 90 minutes but with *retention* for only 20 minutes. To me, that means that I need a distinct change-up, or change of pace, at least every 20 minutes in order to create a new learning cycle. Another illustration: Imagine pouring liquid from a container holding nine quarts into one that holds two quarts. After you pour out two quarts, you must empty your smaller container and begin the process again. As trainers, we often reach the "two-quart" limit with our participants but keep on "pouring" because there's so much to cover. Just because they're listening, nodding, and smiling doesn't mean we have achieved our goals of retention and application.

Also in Chapter 2, I mentioned Albert Mehrabian's research on retention: When people are exposed to an idea one time, they retain 10 percent or less of it after 30 days. Yet when they are exposed to the same idea six times, with interval reinforcement, their retention is 90 percent at the end of 30 days. The implication for trainers is that we need to build opportunities for review and reinforcement into our presentations.

Presentation Design Methods

Several models can be used for designing presentations. Which method you choose will depend on the type of information you cover, the amount of time you have, the experience level of your participants, and whether you want your participants to attain familiarity, mastery, or something in between.

Since 1969, I've used all of the following outlines to build and deliver powerful presentations: problem-solving approach; past, present, future approach; and new-twist approach.

Problem-Solving Approach

A full outline for the problem-solving approach includes the following:

A. **History of the problem**—Why is there a problem? Where did it come from? What makes it a problem? Who does it affect?

B. **Current condition of the problem**—What is the status of the problem now? How widespread is it? How likely is it to continue? What are the consequences if we don't act?

C. **Possible solutions**—What are the alternatives? What are the advantages and disadvantages of each? How quickly can each be implemented? What is the likelihood of success?

D. **Analysis of solutions**—What do these solutions mean to your listeners? How does each affect them? (Remember, they are tuned to WII-FM!) How does it affect others, especially those who are important to them?

E. **The best solution and why**—Given all the available information, what's the best course of action to take?

F. **Call to action**.

If your time is short, present most of the information in the preceding approach in hand-out form and follow this abbreviated outline:

    A. **Problem:** I found myself using the same opening for every training program I delivered. It seemed to be worn out—for both my participants and me.

    B. **Solution:** Then I asked myself, "What makes an opening effective?" and I came up with three things:

- It breaks preoccupation.
- It facilitates networking—and generally, anything involving a small-group approach does that.
- It makes a point about the training. If the opening I use helps people discover a deficiency of knowledge or execution, helps them recognize the existence of a problem, or helps them open their minds and be less judgmental and/or hasty, then I've succeeded.

    C. **Call to Action:** By asking—and answering—that question about openings, I could begin to deliver more powerful, meaningful openings to my training programs and presentations.

Past, Present, Future Approach

This approach is especially appropriate for extemporaneous presentations, especially those that chronicle personal experience or knowledge:

- **Past**—What was it, or what were you, like in the past in terms of the topic at hand? For example: In the past, I had difficulty knowing where to start when developing a presentation. My brain seemed to freeze, and I couldn't get my pencil to move. Everything was bottled up inside, out of reach.

- **Present**—What is it, or what are you, like now? For example: Now things flow more smoothly when I develop a presentation. By applying brainstorming techniques and reviewing different outline formats, ideas start to come, and I can begin to fill in the blanks.

- **Future**—What will happen in the future? For example: In the future, I plan to add new outlines to increase my options. I also plan to look for stories, illustrations, and poems that can spice up my presentations so I can continue to increase my effectiveness.

New-Twist Approach

The components of the new-twist approach are:

    A. An old idea
    B. A new twist on an old idea
    C. How the idea was discovered
    D. How it worked for participants
    E. How your participants or listeners can use the idea
    F. Call to action

Here is an example of how I used the new-twist approach myself:

A. **An old idea**—For as long as I can remember, I've used flip charts, especially in brainstorming sessions I facilitated. However, the sessions seemed to bog down when the ideas started to come fast and furiously.

B. **A new twist on an old idea**—Then I started asking two or more participants to volunteer as recorders. They would do the writing, leaving me free to facilitate the discussion.

C. **How the idea was discovered**—When I was a participant myself in a brainstorming session, I observed a facilitator who used a volunteer to record ideas. The technique kept things moving briskly, but I thought, "If one works reasonably well, why not use two volunteers to really speed things along?"

D. **How it worked for participants**—My brainstorming sessions haven't been the same since. They move as quickly as the ideas surface.

E. **How your participants or listeners can use the idea**—When asking for volunteers, clarify what you're asking them to do. I try to make it less intimidating to volunteer by joking, "If you can't spell a word at least two ways, you're not being creative." Also, give each volunteer recorder two markers of different colors; printing alternating ideas in different colors helps people see each one separately.

F. **Call to action**—Just stock up on markers, and the next time you are tempted to pick them up, ask for not one volunteer but two.

Theory and Skill Sessions

In the mid-1980s, I worked with Mike Berger, who was then director of the Corporate Learning Institute at Vanderbilt University, in developing a Technical Education Forum for IBM. Mike said that every theory or skill session should MOVE participants in the opening and RECAP for participants at the close. I think it's great advice.

Motivate	**R**eview
Orient and preview	**E**licit
in**V**estigate	**C**onnect
Explain objectives	**A**nswer
	Punctuate

Eight Dynamite Motivators and Energizers

1. **Describe an incident.** I want you to imagine that it is a warm August evening, the night of your organization's annual awards banquet. For four years, you've worked hard, been loyal to your company, and, over time, made an increasingly greater contribution at work. You're excited because you are certain (or almost certain) that tonight your efforts will be recognized.

You've flown to Denver, picked up a luxury rental car, and enjoyed a leisurely drive to Colorado Springs, 90 miles to the south. The majestic scenery of the Colorado Rockies unfolds on your right as you drive. At the off-ramp into Colorado Springs, you exit and proceed up a wide, tree-lined boulevard. Ahead of you looms the fabulous Broadmoor Hotel, one of America's few five-star, five-diamond, five-everything hotels.

The doorman opens your car door promptly, and you're ushered up the marble steps. At the top, you begin a long walk down the marble-floored, wood-paneled corridor leading to the ballroom. Fifteen-foot-high mirrors reflect your progress. Gold and crystal chandeliers light the way.

You enter the ballroom and join 400 of your coworkers. Every moment of the evening is fantastic. The dinner is superb, the service exquisite. You almost want to pinch yourself. It's too good to be true.

Finally, the awards begin. As the presentations continue, you realize that either you are going to be recognized as your company's outstanding contributor—or you're going home empty handed.

The company president steps to the podium to present the final award. When he glances your way, you realize instantly that tonight's your night. The award is yours.

The president begins. "Our recipient doesn't know this, but four years ago, every manager he'd had recommended his termination. The feeling was, this person could never live up to the high standards I have personally set in our organization. Only I was able to see his potential. So I began to act as mentor to him, carefully laying out a step-by-step development plan. I spent hours of one-on-one time, sharing my wisdom and insights and explaining to him the ideas, concepts, and techniques that have made me the leader I am in our industry. As our recipient began to implement my development plan—never wavering, never deviating, never questioning the course I'd set—the results became obvious. This past year especially, my plan has paid dividends as this person outperformed all others in our organization. It's my privilege to recognize our company's outstanding contributor.

As you hear your name called, how do you feel?

When I've described this scenario and asked this question, I've heard such answers as: "Cheated," "Angry," "I'd feel like crawling under a rock," and "I'd feel like giving the award back to the president—he obviously thinks it's his." Almost everyone who is asked to comment on this incident feels motivated to offer his or her reaction. And that's the whole point; you want to motivate participants to become involved in your presentation.

2. **Ask for a show of hands.** However, the show of hands must be meaningful. If people want to look around to see who else has a hand up, then you've probably asked a good question. Here are two I've used.

1) How many of you have ever observed a "dynamic duo" in your class? You know, two people who walk in together, sit down together, fold their arms together, and both give you body language that says, "I don't want to be here, so this better be good." Can I see a show of hands? (Wait for a response.) Good, that means you've been in training longer than a week. (This usually gets a laugh.)

2) In one opening activity, I ask participants to interview other participants in a scavenger-hunt type of activity. The objective is to find people for whom various statements are true. For example, find someone in this room who

- was an only child
- is a downhill skier
- reads *Popular Mechanics*
- drives a pick-up truck
- has been a trainer for five or more years
- has worked for three or more companies in his or her career

I ask participants to check the two or three items they think will be hardest to find among the group. When the activity is over, I ask people to volunteer which items they checked, and then I ask people to raise their hands if the item was true for them. For example: "How many of you are downhill skiers? Let's have a show of hands." People are often quite surprised by the number of hands that go up in response.

3. **Ask a question.** We are so conditioned to answer questions that we often answer even those we may not want to answer. The only thing we're more conditioned to answer than a question is the telephone. (Try not answering yours the next time it rings!) Try this. Don't think of the answer to this question: What is 4 + 4? Try another: What is 5 + 5? Again, don't think of the answer. We can't do it. The mind's need for closure is so great that when a question opens it, we have to answer it in order to achieve closure. You can direct the question to an individual, leave it to an individual to volunteer, or elicit a group response by a show of hands. To maximize involvement, however, I'll place people in groups of five to seven. Then I'll ask a question such as, "What are the two most important ideas you've picked up so far?" or "What are the two biggest complaints customers have about (fill in the type of product or service)?" "Take two minutes to come up with answers in your group." Now I've got the entire group involved rather than several of the most verbal.

4. **Make a promise.** One promise that I made in the Creative Training Techniques workshop is: "By the end of these two days, you'll have at least five ways you can improve your next training program without redesigning one handout or creating one new visual." That promise always gets the participants' attention. I check back with them from time to time to see if they think that I'm fulfilling my promise and to elicit specific techniques that they're

going to use. This serves both to demonstrate my intentions and to encourage periodic review.

5. **Get them laughing.** Notice I didn't say, "Tell a joke." Humor in this context should always make a point. I believe that natural, timely humor is the most effective. When I ask the question about the "dynamic duo" and then say, after the participants respond with a show of hands, "That means you've been in training longer than a week!" they almost always laugh because the humor has a real-life basis.

Effective, natural humor that comes from our own life experience does three things:

1) It makes a point.
2) It shares a story or illustration participants have never heard before because it comes from our personal experience.
3) It draws our audience closer to us because we all can identify with the foibles and triumphs of others.

Humor should fit naturally and logically into a presentation. Don't use an illustration just because it's funny; it must be relevant as well.

You don't *have* to be funny. People aren't expecting Jerry Seinfeld, Chris Rock, or Ellen Degeneres. They expect you and what you have to share on the topic at hand. If you do decide to use stories or jokes outside your experience, make sure they're appropriate for the group. Stories that someone in business would find amusing may not draw a chuckle from a construction worker, and vice versa. If you select humor that's not funny, you may find yourself trying to make it funny with accents and theatrics. Don't. Both you and your audience will regret it.

Every occupation is filled with its own kind of humor. And those who share that occupation can identify with it. Your stories don't have to be embellished, embroidered, or delivered with an accent. By simply sharing an amusing story, you'll have the audience laughing with you—and getting the point.

Over time, you may have repeat participants from previous programs who may not find your stories funny the second time around. So keep looking for fresh stories and experiences to share, and avoid those that have become time-worn. People who hear you repeat an illustration they've already heard umpteen times may decide that you're lazy and don't care.

Finally, consider these rules of thumb about humor:

- It's wonderful when you know how and when to use it, disastrous when you don't.
- It's a tool to drive home ideas, not a substitute for them.
- Use humor based on caring, never on contempt.
- If the story is going to be "on" someone, it should be "on" you.

- Forget off-color humor or humor that uses offensive language.
- Be careful about any story involving race, religion, sex, and politics. When in doubt, don't use it.

Here are two other ways that I've gotten my groups laughing—and neither is a joke:

1) When I have a group activity I want carried out I'll say, "You're going to need a group leader for this so I'd like everyone to point a finger in the air." I wait a second and in case not everyone has understood, I'll point my own finger in the air and look around as I say, "Everybody is pointing a finger in the air." This usually draws a small laugh. Then I say, "When I count to three I want you to point to the person you want to be group leader. The person with the most fingers pointed at them is the group leader. 1, 2, 3!" As I reach the number three with my finger still pointed in the air I make a quick pointing motion over the heads of the audience. Everyone else does the same thing. As people realize who they have selected in each group, laughter usually follows. If it doesn't (and sometimes with a very analytical group it might not!), that's okay. The purpose was to get a leader, not a laugh. The laughter was a bonus!

2) When it's time to go on a break I'll say, "Everyone likes to be liked—and I like to be liked. So rather than me trying to get everyone back from break, it will be the responsibility of the new group leader. When there is three minutes left in the break, I'll say 'Group leaders you have three minutes.' When you hear that those of you who are the new group leaders will have three minutes to find your other group members and get them back on time. If you're wondering who the new group leader is, it's the person in your group who stands up (and here I pause) LAST." Some people jump up right away. As what I've said sinks in others jump up. There's usually a lot of laughter as each group recognizes who their new group leader is! I can then vary this (and usually do!). On lunch break, I may say that the new group leader is the person who stands... first! Again, there is laughter. If not, fine. I still have a leader, which was the point.

6. **Make a provocative statement**. I've said things like: "There are four reasons a trainer ought to be shot on the spot." That usually gets people's attention. They didn't think there was one reason for shooting a trainer. (And there probably isn't, but the statement sure commands attention!) In Chapter 16, you'll be reading about the 22 deadly sins of training. Now I could have merely said "22 Things You Ought to Try Not to Do." However, it would not have commanded the same attention. Don't be afraid to take some dramatic license. I'm guessing your industry has at least 22 deadly sins too.

7. **Cite an unusual statistic.** I recently used some facts that I'd come across in a study. They showed that a person starting work at age 25 and working full-time until age 65 spends an average of 16.8 percent of his or her time on the job. I wanted to show the advantage to an organization of helping employees

develop skills that can be used both on and off the job. If people spend 82.8 percent of their time off the job and if they have problems, it certainly affects performance— negatively. And if things are going smoothly, it also affects performance—positively. However, when I used the statistics, they were challenged by my audiences. What were the demographics? What companies? Where? How was the sampling done?

So now I use another approach when citing those unusual statistics. I involve the participants by saying, "An average person starts work full-time at age 25 and works full-time through age 65. Write down what percent of that person's time you would guess is spent on the job. We're not talking about how productive the person is, just whether or not he or she is physically present."

After a moment, I ask for a show of hands. "How many of you think a person spends 90 percent-plus of his or her time on the job?" I work down to 10 percent by 10 percent increments. The average of this tally usually is roughly 40 percent. I draw a circle on the board and split it into a 60 percent piece and a 40 percent piece.

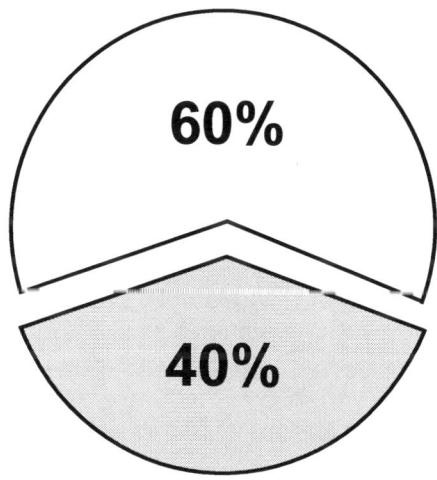

I then ask, "If a person has problems in 60 percent of his or her life, how likely is that to affect the other 40 percent?" The answer usually is "a lot." Then I write 365 (the number of days in a year) on the board. But the average person doesn't work weekends, so we subtract 102 days. Then we subtract the average number of paid holidays—8. Next, the number of vacation days in an average year—about 15. The number of sick or personal leave days? Generally 6. Subtracting all these from 365 gives us 232 days. The average person works 8 hours a day, so we divide by 3 to get 77, which is approximately 21 percent of 365.

Remember, the perception was 40 percent, but the statistic is 16.8 percent. Using their own data, the participants got close to the provocative statistic. Now, the final question: "If the average person spends 80 percent of his or her time off the job and if he or she has a problem, how likely is that to affect performance on the job?" If the answer is "a lot" at 60 percent (and it always seems to be), how much greater the impact when their data show 80 percent!

My guess is that your industry has many unusual statistics embedded in its history and processes. Here is a fun way for getting some information into the minds of your participants.

8. **Use a visual aid or prop.** I've used all kinds of them—cookies, potatoes, pointers for overhead transparencies that looked like small human hands. All of these grab attention and gain interest. And they motivate, too, because they create curiosity, and because people want one—of whatever it is. They may not know what the objects are, but they'll start thinking of ways to contribute to get one.

I remember carrying a pair of baby shoes into a presentation once. I didn't have to wonder if people were watching me as I carried those shoes to the front and hung them over a corner of an easel. I ignored them at first. However, I noticed that participants were understandably preoccupied with them. So I explained that they would be hanging there throughout the training to remind all of us that the training we were about to embark on was a little like learning to walk. We'd fall down from time to time in learning the process. However, if we kept trying and took only little steps, we would all be successful. Now I could have just said all of that. However, the metaphor of the baby shoes made it that much more powerful. Think about metaphorical objects that might help your participants better grasp your content.

Orient and Preview

Having participants answer and discuss the following questions will help reinforce the importance of what you're about to cover. Why is this material important? Why have you been chosen to be here? Why was this material chosen? How will you be able to use this material? What's the road map for the time we're together? Where are we going to start? Where will we end?

Investigate

What level of knowledge do participants already have about the subject? What is the extent of their experience? How soon will they be using what they're about to learn?

Explain the Objectives

It's important that participants enter a theory or a skill session knowing what's expected of them. What will they know when the session is over? How will their feelings or attitudes change? What will they be able to do?

Revisit

We want to review without necessarily calling it review. I've used a variety of techniques to do this. Sometimes I have participants keep track of "action ideas" for use back on the job. They start by sharing them in small groups, which then feed back to the entire group. This process covers most of the content. I then hit any additional points I want to reinforce.

I've also had participants make up test questions they think people ought to be able to answer after the presentation. I split the group into at least three subgroups, each of which develops a test. The tests are then rotated to a second group, which reviews the test for completeness, clarity, and fairness, and then to a third group, which takes the test.

Elicit New Ideas

What new applications do people see for the content? What problems does it solve? Perhaps someone will offer a better way of doing what has been done or, at least, a creative alternative.

Connect to the Future

What's the on-the-job application? What are the possible barriers to application? What strategies can be used to overcome the barriers? How could the participants support one another in the application of the new skills and knowledge?

Answer Questions

But I never ask, "Are there any questions?" I usually break the group into subgroups and give them two to three minutes to go over the content and develop two or three questions they would like to ask. This allows for another review or revisit of the content. Many of the questions will be answered within the group itself. The questions that eventually are asked are of general interest to the entire group.

Punctuate Finish

We don't want the conclusion just to trail off, nor do we want it rushed—by throwing out lots of content in the closing minutes just so we can say it was covered. We want to end with punch, with impact. Here are seven ways to do just that:

1. Summarize the total program in a few well-chosen words.

2. Restate the main points.

3. Present a call to action. For example, you might say, "Involvement is important to building retention and ensuring on-the-job application. You've experienced it here. You've actively participated in discovering ways to involve your own participants. You can generate the same energy in your own classes if you'll keep applying the techniques you've been using."

4. Use humor. David Peoples, who was one of IBM's three consulting instructors, frequently closed his presentations in this good-humor note:

   I fully realize that I have not succeeded in answering all your questions. Indeed, I feel I have not answered any of them completely. The answers I have found only serve to raise a whole new set of questions, which only lead to more problems, some of which we weren't even aware were problems. To sum it all up, I feel we are just as confused as ever in some ways, but I believe we are confused at a higher level and about more important things.

If the presentation has been heavy with content, this serves to lighten the mood. Wrap things up on a high note.

5. Close with a quote. For example: "Remember the Chinese Proverb from 451 B.C., 'What I hear, I forget; what I see, I may remember, but what I do, I understand.' It applies today. Involvement is the key to realizing results."

   Another example. "Remember what you've experienced in this time we've had together. As C. S. Lewis, the English philosopher, said, 'A man with an experience is never at the mercy of a man with an argument.' You know that the techniques you've been using do work. We haven't just talked about things; we've done them. Keep on broadening your experience."

6. Recite a poem. An example. "We've been talking about giving recognition, encouragement, and approval, about letting people know they count. With that in mind, I'd like to close with a poem by Charles Jarvis:

   > *Life's a bother, Life's a worry,*
   > *Life's a busy, crowded way,*
   > *Good intentions go astray.*
   > *I had a friend the other day.*
   > *I haven't any more. He passed away.*
   > *I meant to write, to phone, to call*
   > *I didn't do any of those at all.*
   > *I only hope that he can now see*
   > *How much his friendship meant to me.*
   > *Life's a busy crowded way,*
   > *Good intentions go astray.*

   Let's not let our good intentions go astray. Let's show appreciation now to the people who count—on the job, at home, in the community."

7. Offer an anecdote. For example, "We've been talking about managing and coaching people. I believe that it's important to support people, but we can't do their jobs for them. If you and I will support our people by using the skills we've been developing here, then we'd have fulfilled our responsibilities.

   "I'll never forget my first management position. I had responsibility for a field sales force, and I was determined that none of my people would fail. After all, I had personally experienced every failure behavior, so I could help them avoid all the traps I had fallen into.

   "One day, one of the first people I had recruited called me and said, 'I quit. I can't do this.' I was in shock for two days. Where had I gone wrong? What didn't I do? After a lot of soul searching, I realized I had done everything I could. This fellow had received three weeks of intensive training at the beginning. He had come into the home office for an additional two days of training after 60 days in the field and after 120 days in the field. We had done field selling together. He had received bi-weekly mailings of additional support material. He had audiotapes to reinforce all the training he had received. He had audiovisual aids to help him make his presentations. I had, to the best of my ability, done everything I could but do his job for him.

"If we'll take that approach in coaching, guiding, and counseling our people, we'll be effective managers. But we have to balance our responsibility with the fact that the people we manage must respond to their own opportunities as well. We'll never be able to do that for them."

The Body of Theory and Skill Sessions

While the openings and closings of theory and skill sessions can follow the same pattern, there are differences in the body of the session.

For a theory session, we want to

- explain the theory;
- activate the participants, or involve them in an activity so that they can experience the theory in practice;
- summarize the theory; and
- conclude the session.

For a skill session, we want to:

- show the skill—performing it in its entirety without commentary;
- show and tell—performing the skill with a running commentary about each step;
- practice (participants practice the skill on their own); and
- provide feedback so that participants can learn how they've performed the skill.

Effective Openings

An effective opening announces four things to your participants:

1. Your time will be used well here.
2. I understand who you are, including your background and the expertise and experience you bring.
3. Because I respect you, I'm prepared.
4. I know my content by both training and experience.

Ten Tips on Effective Openings

1. *Open with energy, enthusiasm, and animation.* No one is interested in listening to another dull, dry, listless presentation. Project your interest and enthusiasm. Bring vitality and intensity to the presentation. Challenge your participants.

2. *Don't apologize.* Prepare so thoroughly that you don't need to. Remember, if you feel you must apologize, probably 85 percent of your audience won't know what you're apologizing for, unless you point it out, and the other 15 percent won't be affected by it.

3. *Make eye contact.* There is power in eye contact. To build that power, focus on the eyes of one individual. Look at that person eyeball-to-eyeball, and move about the room establishing the same intense eye contact. Don't stare at the floor, the ceiling, the walls, or the back of the room.

4. *Be "others-oriented."* Instead of being self-conscious, be "others-conscious." If you focus on putting your message across, delivering your content, persuading and influencing your listeners, you won't have to worry about whether or not you're putting on a "good performance." People will appreciate and respect you if you make a sincere, honest effort to benefit them. Thomas Carlyle said over 100 years ago, "Care not for the reward of your speaking, but simply, and with undivided mind, for the truth of your speaking."

5. *Give the audience an overview.* Remember to "tell them what you're going to tell them, and then tell them what you told them." Early on, lay the foundation for the material that you'll cover. Define key terms. Establish a common ground with your audience.

6. *Focus attention.* Ask participants, "What are the key questions that need to be answered? What makes them urgent? What's the first question?"

7. *Be open.* For the most part, the audience should know exactly who you are, what your attitudes are about the subject, and why you feel confident to handle it. They should be able to sense your sincere interest in communicating and sharing your ideas with them.

8. *Be aware of your appearance.* How you look can either encourage people to be receptive to your message or discourage them from heeding it. Appearances do count and so do first impressions.

   - Clothing—Are you dressed professionally? Are you properly groomed? I believe that how we dress shows our respect for the participants. Dress a little more formally than you think you need to. It's a lot easier to dress down if you're slightly overdressed, by removing a jacket, rolling up sleeves, etc., then it is to try to dress up a too-casual outfit. I personally believe that to help maintain their position as the presenter, s/he needs to be dressed one level (only one level and not three or four) better than their best-dressed participant.

   - Gestures—Do you use your hands and your head comfortably? Are your gestures compatible with what you are saying?

   - Facial Expressions—Is your face animated. Does it communicate an interest in your audience and your subject?

   - Posture—Do you stand alert and erect, without being stiff?

- Body Movement—Do your movements and changes in body positions serve a communication purpose? Do they focus attention on the subject at hand?

9. *Be aware of your voice.* Kathleen Hessert, president of Communication Concepts in Charlotte, North Carolina, is a specialist in executive communications. After years as a journalist, newscaster, and anchorperson, she has developed a presentation titled "How You Sound Is So Awful I Can't Hear What You Say." Her point is that a presenter's voice can significantly affect an audience's receptivity.

    - Tone—Do you communicate enthusiasm, seriousness, interest, excitement in your tone of voice?

    - Enunciation—Do you clearly pronounce, or enunciate, each word, or do you slur or slice certain sounds?

    - Pace, Speed—Do you time pauses? Do you fill those vocal pauses with er's and uh's? Do you speak fluently or haltingly? Are you too fast or too slow?

    - Word Choice—Do you use the appropriate words to convey your thoughts? Will your audience be lost because you use words with which they're unfamiliar? Will they be insulted because you define words they already know? Remember "Goldilocks and the Three Bears": Not too hot, not too cold, just right. Your word choice should be the same—not too difficult, not too easy, but just right.

10. *Establish and maintain audience contact.* Do you reach out and figuratively touch the audience? Do you establish rapport that will help them identify with your thoughts and ideas?

An excellent resource exploring the above presentational subtleties is a book by my friend, Dave Arch, entitled *Showmanship for Presenters.*

Building the Middle of a Presentation

Support

Build support for points that the audience may not fully understand or fully agree with. It's important to support your ideas, first, when the audience is skeptical of the truth or value of an idea and, second, when you're presenting a concept that is difficult to understand.

You might consider using some of the following means of support:

1. *Figures*—numerical representations of facts

2. *Statistics*—express factual relationships based on numbers

3. *Facts*—statements about present or past realities that are verifiable, either by third-party support or by direct observation

4. *Definitions*—inquiries into understanding the nature of something, usually by going from general to specific—e.g., "A ranch-style house [term] is a type of building [general class] that consists of only one level [particular qualities]."

5. *Anecdotes*—stories or experiences that are used to illustrate a point, but not necessarily prove it

6. *Examples*—representative instances that prove or clarify a general statement

7. *Illustrations*—more detailed examples that generally offer more specific clarification, point by point

8. *Authorities*—reliable, recognized sources other than yourself who support your point

9. *Analogies*—descriptions of a set of similar conditions that shed additional light on the subject being discussed.

People often remember vivid illustrations, examples, anecdotes, etc., longer than even the key points they are intended to illustrate. If you speak only in broad, general terms, you may be indicating to your audience that you're not sure of your facts, that your research was superficial, and that you really didn't prepare your presentation thoroughly. If we don't support what we say with evidence, we may fail to persuade or influence the audience completely.

Unfortunately, it's easy to use slipshod support, to say "Research shows..." "They say..." or "Everyone knows...." But, what "research" and who are "they" and "everyone"? Invariably, at least one or more listeners will ask those questions and reduce the credibility of your presentation. Be accurate; avoid vague generalities. Train yourself to speak and think clearly. When citing examples, use specific names of people, places, and things, when possible and permissible.

Support is effective only when it is relevant, clear, accurate, strong enough to withstand counterarguments, and easy to explain.

Transitions

There are at least seven transitions we can use to connect the various parts of our presentations:

1. *Questions and answers*—Allowing participants a minute or two to collect their thoughts and generate questions, whether alone, in pairs, or in small groups, can serve as an effective review, as well as a transition. Place a time limit on this type of Q & A, however. And, make the time limit known before the Q & A period begins.

2. *Physical movement*—Moving from one side of the room to another can indicate a transition. The physical movement of participants themselves can be used as a transition. For example, I often ask participants to stand up after they have jotted down their responses to a question. When everyone is standing, I ask for several to volunteer their responses. Then everyone is seated. This process not only uses physical movement as a transition, but it gives participants a controlled stretch break.

3. *Use of media*—For example, you haven't used any media, but now you turn to the flip chart. By introducing a new tool, you signal a transition.

4. *Change media*—You move from the flip chart, for example, to the overhead projector to indicate a transition.

5. *Mini-summary*—From time to time, I may stop and ask participants to share, either by volunteering individually or in small-group discussions, the action ideas they've picked up so far. If I use small groups, I then ask a leader from each to share one or two of the ideas generated. This mini-summary serves as review, gives me feedback about whether I've driven my key points home, and acts as a transition to the next segment of the program.

6. *Refocus*—At times, a participant may sidetrack discussion. I then make a comment such as, "Just before Frank made that comment, what were we talking about?" Someone will name our previous topic. That puts us right back on track without wasting any more time—and without embarrassing the participant.

7. *Pause*—Silence can indicate that we've completed one part of our presentation and are about to move on to another.

Questions

The first transition technique is questions and answers. Let's consider that in a bit more detail.

Asking Them

Questions are great tools for stimulating conversation and guiding communication. Here are some key points to remember in using them in your presentations.

1. Plan your questions. Know, in a general way, what you are going to ask and where in your presentation.

2. Know the purpose of each question. In general, questions either elicit information, e.g., "Where do you live?" or "How many employees are there?"—or opinions, e.g., "How do you like this idea" or "Do you think this plan will work?"

3. When you ask a question, relate it to your audience's or the individual listener's point of reference and background.

4. Go from general questions to more specific ones.

5. Confine your questions to one topic area at a time.

6. Ask questions that are short, clear, and easy to understand. Don't, for example, ask a question like this: "Which of the five steps in the selling cycle—prospecting, appointments, presentations, enrollments, and referrals—do you feel is most important?" On paper, this may seem like a simple question, but, asked orally of an individual or an audience, it becomes confusing. If you are going to ask a lengthier question, then illustrate, by use of an overhead or

flip chart, the key points. For example, you might use an overhead transparency that would show the key parts of the selling cycle and then ask which is the most important. That way, your audience isn't trying so hard to remember the parts of the cycle that they don't even hear your question.

7. Make logical transitions between your questions.

8. When you're leading a discussion, ask questions of the group first and follow with questions to individuals. The purpose of a question asked in a learning situation is for learning to take place, not testing to take place. Asking the question and letting small groups discuss the answer allows more people to be involved and allows everyone to revisit and better anchor the content in the minds. Questions are not appropriate vehicles for waking people up or shutting people down by making them feel stupid.

9. Avoid questions that can be answered by a yes or no and questions where the answer is implied. Avoid answering questions before your audience has a chance to. Avoid cross-examining.

10. Once you've asked a question, don't interrupt the person who's responding.

Answering Them

Be sure to listen for both intent (what's meant) as well as content (what's being asked). In other words, listen for the feelings, the emotions behind the question.

Acknowledge each question, and show that you understand by paraphrasing it. If necessary, get clarification. "If I understand what you're asking, it's this…."

Try to answer the question completely and accurately. Verify the questioner's satisfaction. "Did I say enough about that?" "Did I really tell you everything you wanted me to?" Be ready to give additional proof, support, or clarification of your response.

Avoid these five behaviors when answering questions:

1. Being unresponsive—Even if someone is asking too many questions, don't ignore him or her.

2. Showing that you feel the question is inappropriate, stupid, or ill-timed.

3. Diverting the question—If possible, answer questions as they come up.

4. Going off on a tangent—When somebody asks a question, don't say, "This reminds me of a time when…" and tell a 10-minute war story. By the time you finish, nobody will remember what the question was.

5. Treating two questions as one—Even if two people ask very similar questions, answer them separately.

Tips for Communicating Ideas Effectively

1. *Present single ideas.* Don't throw too many ideas at your audience at one time. If you do, most of them will get lost. Encourage participants to react to an idea once you've presented it. You might say, for example, "Can you think of a use for this idea?"

2. *Get people to "buy off" on one idea before presenting another.* Ask them to respond or react to your ideas so that you're sure they understand and accept the material before you go on to another point.

3. *Be specific.* Communicate as accurately as possible. Use examples, analogies, and illustrations to clarify your key points. Avoid generalizations.

4. *Respond to emotions.* Encourage people to share not only their thoughts but also their feelings. When a person expresses emotion, try to draw that feeling out by providing praise and empathy. Accept the negative emotions people may have. Look for signs of irritation, confusion, or frustration that may indicate that your participants are not listening, understanding, or accepting the content the way they could be.

5. *Share yourself.* Be open to giving all you have and all you know. When you are open to your attendees, they will be open to you. You'll have better, deeper, richer communication from other people when you open yourself to them.

6. *Know what you want to say.* Make sure your thoughts and ideas, the points you want to cover, are clear in your mind and that you have a total grasp of the content you want to communicate. If something isn't clear to you, it almost certainly won't be clear to somebody else.

7. *Use a logical sequence.* Organize your thoughts and ideas in a sequence—chronological, topical, or from more important to less important—that makes sense to your listeners and enables them to apply what you have to offer.

8. *Communicate when people are in the mood to listen.* If people are worried, frustrated, angry, upset, or irritated, don't even try to communicate with them. First, deal with those feelings in an effort to eliminate them.

9. *Use a language common to your listeners.* Avoid jargon, unfamiliar terms, and difficult words. These may prove to your audience that you're with it and/or smart, but they often hinder effective communication and application.

10. *Involve your audience.* Draw your audience out by asking for their reactions. Listen attentively when they speak.

11. *Give feedback.* When someone says something that can be interpreted several ways, give your interpretation to make sure it matches the speaker's. Don't merely parrot back the remark; paraphrase it, and see if the speaker agrees.

12. *Create interest.* Demonstrate the importance of the topic to the attendees. Answer their question "What's in it for me?" Be brief, be specific, and make sure you find common ground by considering the feelings, opinions, and attitudes of your attendees regarding the subject under discussion.

13. *Think first, talk second.* A car won't run if there's no gas in the tank, and a speaker can't communicate effectively if there aren't clear thoughts in the brain.

14. *Know your aim.* Ask yourself, "What is my purpose in communicating this information?" Be specific. Determine exactly what you want attendees to know or feel or do when you finish.

15. *Take into account the total environment whenever you communicate.* Be aware of lighting, the room arrangement, the time of day, and the circumstances under which people are coming to the presentation. That is, are they here voluntarily, or were they ordered to participate?

16. *Get the opinions of others.* Ask other people for their feedback and their interpretation of your ideas. Get a clear perspective of how other people actually see the ideas you're trying to communicate. Don't assume you're being clear; get feedback that tells you you're clear.

17. *Be aware of intent as well as content.* Your tone of voice, posture, facial expressions, dress, receptivity to the input of others—these all communicate your attitude toward your content and your audience.

18. *Follow up.* Feedback tells you that your message has been received. Check to make sure you're actually conveying your content. Encourage feedback and input during the presentation, and then follow up afterward to make sure you did a satisfactory job.

19. *Communicate for long-term, as well as short-term, change.* People often resist change. To ensure that they see not only short-term effects but also long-range benefits of new ideas, actions, and directions, provide information in a way that instills confidence, not fear.

20. *Make sure actions and attitudes support your presentation.* Heed these words: "What you are speaks so loudly I can't hear what you say." Be sure that your actions and attitudes support your words.

21. *Be a good listener.* Very few people are looking for a good talker, but they are looking for someone who will listen. And they will give a lot of power to that rare individual.

Group presentations give you a tremendous opportunity for personal public relations—to make yourself known as a polished professional. You can wait to be called on, or you can volunteer to participate in seminars, panels, conventions, conferences, and sales presentations.

Using the strategies in this chapter can help you "go for it" now with confidence. Just remember that Proper Preparation and Practice Prevent Poor Performance.

$$\boxed{\text{Utilize}}$$

Chapter 9:
Customizing Training

Getting Your Needs Met Outside and Inside Your Organization

It is important to make the best use of your resources. When you don't have all the necessary resources available within your own organization, you have to look elsewhere—outside your organization. Fortunately, there are lots of resources out there: Consultants who can work with you to create what you need, college professors who are experts in specific subjects, larger consulting companies that have experienced staffs, and training companies that have off-the-shelf programs suitable for your needs.

Exploring Outside Options

Here are some key questions you should ask before you decide to select and work with an outside resource.

1. **How are the training objectives generated?** Do the objectives come from you? Are they generated by a needs assessment done by you or by the outside resource you're considering working with on this project? Or—watch out here—are they generated from the prepackaged training program "that will surely meet all your needs"?

   Training must be designed to get results and solve problems. One test you can use with consultants from the outside is to ask what objectives they would have for the program you have in mind. Ideally, their response should indicate a willingness and an ability to focus on what you need, not on what they have available.

2. **For whom have they worked?** Anyone you use should be able to provide references. I once did a consulting project for a large casino/hotel in Atlantic City, New Jersey. During my initial phone discussion with the client's training director, she asked for the names of three other clients of mine whom she could contact. About an hour after our conversation, I called each of those clients as a courtesy, simply to let them know that they might be contacted. Each had already talked with the training director and answered the following questions:

   - What's the largest group Bob Pike has worked with for you?
   - What's the smallest group?
   - What's the biggest problem you've seen him handle with a group?
   - When are you planning to use him next?

   Good questions, aren't they? Notice that the questions do not give any clue as to the assignment the training director might have in mind. You might take a tip from this training director: Get the references when you're in a position to contact them immediately, before the consultant under consideration can. Also, once you've asked for three references, ask for three more. Then contact the second three. Almost anyone who's been around for a while can give you three strong references. But you may learn more that will be useful to you from the second three.

3. **Why should I hire you?** A very direct question and one that should provide you with some interesting answers that can help you compare your options.

4. **Will there be pilot programs?** Generally, I believe the answer to this question should be "YES." Even a program that's been used off-the-shelf with large numbers of people probably should be considered a pilot program the first time it's offered to your group.

5. **How will the pilot program be structured?** A good pilot program will consist of a cross-section of the target audience to be trained. In other words, there should be some marginal performers, some who fall in the middle, and some who are outstanding. The idea is to see how the program will work for your organization. The pilot should reflect, as much as possible, the makeup of a typical class. One modification you might want to make is to have some "senders" in attendance. Who will support and reinforce the training once it has been delivered? You may get better support if those individuals understand what kind of training their people will receive, and this understanding will be enhanced if they are present. If this isn't appropriate, consider scheduling an "executive briefing." This can be anything from a one-hour meeting at which the proposed course is described to an actual presentation of a mini-version of the course. The purpose is the same: to inform and gain the support of those whose subordinates will participate.

6. **Who will do the work?** Sometimes, larger organizations will have a lead consultant, whose name and credentials impress you, but the actual work may be done by others not as qualified. You have a right to know exactly who is going to perform the work. Who will be involved in the presentation? What is their track record? What are their credentials? Check this information carefully. Know what you're paying for.

    The same is true of the contract you execute. Does it specify the people involved as well as the work to be performed? Make sure it does. You are, after all, buying people's time and expertise, so be an informed consumer.

7. **Is this a "turnkey" program?** In other words, when the work is done, will you have everything you need to keep the program in-house, if that's what you need or want? Are you buying the rights to use the materials—necessary instructor guides, visual aids, participant handouts—that are an integral part of the program? Or do you own the materials? Is the program designed in such a way that you, or others in your organization, can run it? Or will you always have to rely on someone from the outside? There's no right answer to any of these questions, but you should know what those answers are. It may cost more if you want to own the materials than simply use them, but that

might be your choice. You might want a higher level of delivery than you can provide from within your organization; again that's OK, as long as it's your choice.

8. **Who else can use the material?** Is it important to restrict access of what's been developed? Would it hurt you if your competition had access to the same training materials? Is anything that's been used in the program proprietary? If so, have you protected yourself against unwanted disclosure?

9. **Are you listening or talking?** Again, I don't think there's a right or wrong answer to this question, but do consider it. Do you want someone who's asking you the right questions? Or someone who's spending time sharing credentials, past accomplishments, etc.? Is the person willing or, better yet, eager to listen to your needs, your problems, the approaches you think might work? Or does the consultant have the solution before you've laid out the problem?

10. **How quickly can the consultant provide an answer?** Nobody knows everything. Beware the person who has an instant answer for every question. The best and brightest consultant ought to be stumped occasionally and have to dig a little before giving a response.

11. **Does the consultant offer to do a needs analysis?** Or does he or she at least want to know about what other approaches you've taken and when? Things change over time. You want to be sure that you're solving the right problem with the right methods. Only a complete and thorough needs analysis can help ensure that you're on track. You may not be in a position to do an extensive analysis, but the consultant should at least offer to assess your needs.

    As discussed in the first chapter, hopefully this needs assessment will go beyond that of merely a survey of management for what they think they need in training programs.

    Here is an example: I was asked to design a curriculum for a department of a large utility. The process would be used at the same time to train the trainers within the department to continue to use the steps to develop future courses as the need arose. I asked about a needs assessment and was told that a very complete one had been done 18 months earlier. I suggested that we schedule a few focus groups to validate the data from the earlier assessment, as well as to increase buy-in for the new training as it was brought online. The focus groups revealed entirely different needs that were, in management's opinion, far more pressing. Therefore, the focus of the project changed, and the organization derived greater benefit. Never underestimate the power of a good front-end analysis.

12. **How complete is the proposal?** A good proposal should do more than just describe the end product and the cost. Does it show the development steps? Does it include time lines? Are there benchmarks or milestones that you'll be able to use along the way to measure progress and ensure that you're on track? A complete and thorough proposal allows you to assess the kind of end

product you're going to get by working with the person or firm you select. Be wary of the one-to-two-page proposal that hits the highlights but offers no substance.

13. **Do they offer a reinforcement component?** We know that true behavioral changes do not occur through an event. There must be an ongoing reinforcement system in order for those newly acquired skills to take hold. Ask the vendor to explain to you the nature of their own reinforcement process following the training.

Selecting/Modifying/Customizing Off-the-Shelf Programs

Before you select a prepackaged program, consider evaluating all program options by asking the following questions:

1. **What are the program's stated goals?** Are they consistent with the needs you've identified? Does the program do more than you need? Does it do less and, therefore, require supplementation? Is the program a good "fit," or will it require so much alteration that you'd be better off building from scratch?

2. **What about program design?** Is the design of the program suitable for your organization? Your culture? Your bias as a trainer? Is it instructor led but participant centered? Does it allow for participation? Is there plenty of real-world application built into the design? Does it take into account the experiences that your participants will bring to the program? Does it overlap with other programs you may already have in place? Will that overlap, if it exists, be viewed critically by others? Can the program be delivered in a variety of formats (e.g., multiple days, daily sessions, weekly sessions), or are you limited to one format? How many participants can the format accommodate? Can it be effective with more? With less? How much expertise is required by the presenter?

3. **What about program pacing?** Does the program offer a variety of activities? Or are the same few repeated over and over again? Does it allow for more involvement and participation later in the day to increase the energy level of the participants? Is the pacing flexible? Can you slow down if the group is stuck on something? Can you speed up if everyone has grasped a concept? Are there alternative activities in case something that's been planned doesn't work and another approach is required to help drive home the point?

4. **Is the time available used effectively?** Is there an appropriate blend of theory and application? Is there a balance between presentation and application? Is the time spent on each topic area too long, too short, or just about right? Are the topics introduced in the proper sequence? Is class time used for things that could be referenced? Does the bulk of in-class time focus on what participants need to know and be able to do rather than on things they can do or find on their own? Do participants become sufficiently familiar with other resources

(such as subject-matter experts, manuals, software, videos, audios, etc.) available to them after the course is over? Can they access these resources and are they comfortable in accessing them?

5. **What is the back up plan?** Assuming the first course is a pilot program, what's the back-up plan? If the scheduled instructor isn't available for some reason, who's the alternate? (Don't assume that an alternate isn't needed. Remember Murphy's Law—"whatever can go wrong will." If the instructor hasn't missed an assignment in 20 years, perhaps he or she is about due to miss one.) Are materials to be shipped in advance? Make sure there's a cushion in the delivery date. Are you being given masters to reproduce? Put a cushion in the date when you're to receive them to ensure proper reproduction. Ordering binders or other materials? Be sure to add a time cushion. Make sure there's a back-up plan for every key element.

6. **Will the program be viewed as relevant by the participants? By the senders? By the payers?** Can each of these three groups see the value of the content from their unique perspectives? Is the content relevant? Do the illustrations fit? Can participants readily make the transfer from the classroom to their work situations? Does the content address the most pressing business needs of the target audience from the perspective of each of these groups?

7. **Does the program use familiar technology?** For example, if you're considering using an off-the-shelf management training program, is the terminology used consistent with the terminology the participants already know? If your organization refers to personal styles as dominant, influencing, supportive, and competent, is it worth it to introduce new terms that may describe the same things, such as driver, expressive, amiable, and analytical? Does the program use terms consistent with your industry?

Do the examples fit? In a selling course, are the examples all big-ticket, long-term sales even though your salespeople sell items that are short-term, one-call close? Are the examples consumer-oriented when your people are manufacturing oriented? These differences can dilute the effectiveness of an otherwise good program.

8. **What logistics are required?** You may have selected a bargain program only to find that it requires small-group breakouts that necessitate expensive off-site arrangements. Overall, you no longer have a bargain. Or perhaps the design requires at least two instructors but you can't spare two for a single course. Or the design depends on small-group video feedback that requires three cameras, three video cassette recorders, three monitors, etc., and you own only one of each. Renting or purchasing the additional units may be possible, but it's an additional cost to consider. Make sure you check all the requirements and the costs for all the requirements before you make a decision.

Eleven Steps to a Program that Meets Your Needs

Whether you're working with an outside consultant to modify or build a training program or working with inside subject-matter experts (SMEs) to meet needs, here's a process that can help ensure that your program is effective.

Step 1. Mind Mapping

One of the most effective program development tools I have ever acquired is the mind map. I was first introduced to the concept when I took a speed-reading course in the late 1960s. In the course, we called it structured recall, and I've heard it referred to by other names, such as branching and spidergrams, but the concept is essentially the same. It worked so well that I continued to use it for several years to structure letters, memos, and papers and to facilitate note taking during presentations I attended and as I read professional materials.

A tremendous amount has been written about the mind and how it works—right brain versus left-brain, linear versus spatial, ad infinitum. My own theory is that most of us have minds like pinball machines: they don't generate thoughts in a linear pattern, but each thought generates two or three spin-off thoughts, rather like the steel ball bouncing around in a pinball machine. When we play pinball, we exercise some control, but the arrangement of the inner pattern of the machine significantly affects where the ball goes.

The human brain contains over one trillion brain cells called neurons. Each neuron is capable of interconnecting with the neurons that surround it in hundreds of ways. Every time we have a thought, it fires a synapse (the connector between neurons) and creates a chain reaction. This makes possible new connections and relationships we might never have logically foreseen.

Mind mapping allows us to see spatially how concepts and information might relate in ways that standard note taking or outlining don't allow.

Research Factoid*

> "...Several research studies have demonstrated the efficacy of graphic organizers in promoting students' learning (Bergerud, Lovvitt, & Horton, 1987; Koran & Koran, 1980; Moyer, Sowder, Threadgill-Sowder, & Moyer, 1984) (Willis and Worthington, p. 55)."
>
> – Ellis, E. S., & Worthington, L. A. (1994)

*Research synthesis on effective teaching principles and the design of quality tools for educators (Technical Report No. 5). Eugene, OR: University of Oregon, Eugene, National Center to Improve the Tools of Educators, College of Education, (ERIC Document Reproduction Service No. ED 386 853)

Here's one mind map (recreated using a Macintosh and MacDraw and Macpaint® software) I created in 10 minutes for a workshop:

Customizing Training

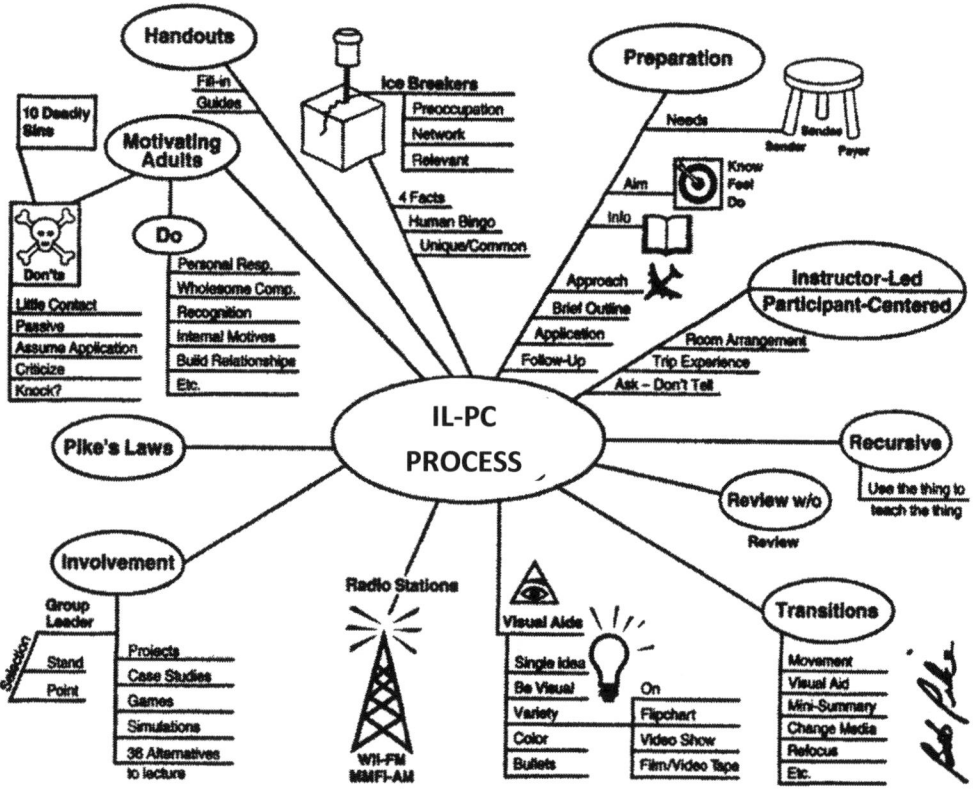

Here are some fundamentals of mind mapping:

- It's free flowing.
- Don't worry about where anything goes for now.
- Use only key words.
- It's your tool; let it work for you.
- Feel free to connect things that relate.
- Feel free to go back and add.
- Try short bursts. Time yourself for five minutes, take a two-minute break, then spend five minutes adding, adjusting, etc.

Mind mapping can be done alone or with groups. Here's a mind map of a Creative Training Techniques workshop that a group produced in 20 minutes to summarize the seminar.

Master Trainer Handbook

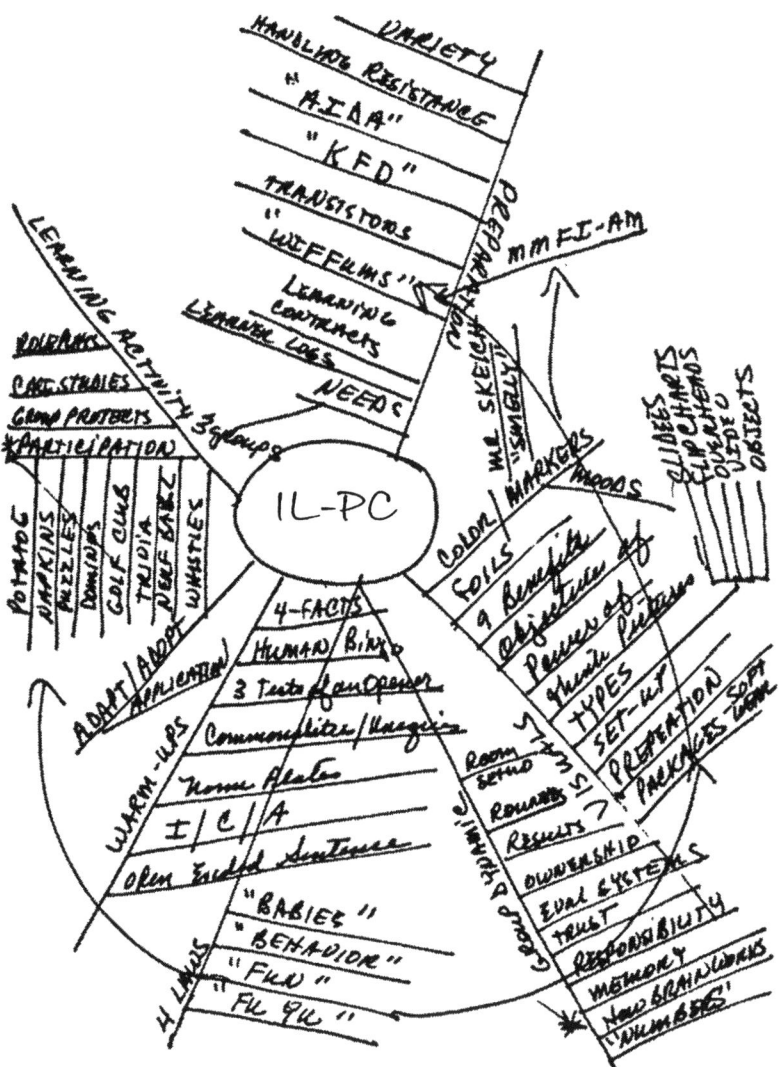

In 1985, I was working with a large computer company to modify some of its technical courses. The model I provided the trainers with whom I was working is the one we're using in this chapter. We started by taping together several large sheets of flip-chart paper and mounting them on the wall where everyone could see what was happening. We determined the core concepts of the course and placed them on the mind map. Then we took the input of the subject-matter experts (SMEs) and added it to the mind map. We continued until we had a thorough picture of the course content.

As you may know, SMEs tend to give you all the information that anyone in the world could ever want about their subject. But the participants of your training program may not need that amount of information or level of expertise. This dilemma leads to Step Two.

Step 2. Minimalist Sets

In any training program, you're likely to have the "Need to Know" and the "Nice to Know," "Where to Go" and the "Never Need to Know."

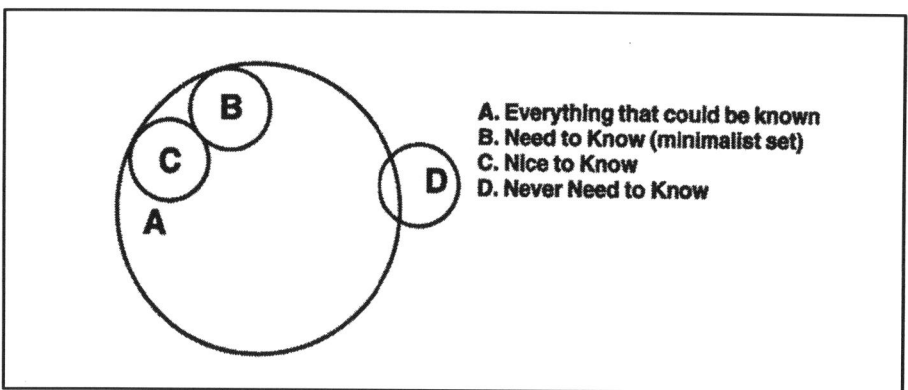

A subject-matter expert or a group of SMEs may generate a content list or competency list so long that the SMEs themselves would be challenged to accomplish it. The question we're asking here is: What's the least somebody in the course would need to know or be able to do in order for the course to be considered successful for that person? This step may involve several things, such as asking those for whom a training program is being designed what's needed in the program. It may involve asking the supervisors of those individuals. It may involve asking the people one level below them. For the program to have the necessary level of support, we need the input of the senders, those sent, and the payers. We want agreement up front of what success will look like. This enables us to pare down the content that we had on our mind map. It also enables us to proceed to Step Three.

Step 3. Choose Order/Methods

What sequence are we going to use in covering the course content? Our choices include these:

- General to specific
- Simple to complex
- Most important to least important
- Primary to secondary
- Whole to parts

These different sequence patterns may all be effective in various parts of the same course.

Step 4. Chunk the Content

Based on what we know about content retention, we would then break the ordering of the content into 20-minute chunks. What will we do the first 20 minutes, the second 20 minutes, etc.

Step 5. Brainstorm Approaches

What are all the possible approaches to delivering the course? What approach/activity am I going to use to communicate the *content* in the first 20-minute chunk? What will I do to have them *process* in that chunk? What will I do when I wish to *revisit*? If participants have information or experience relevant to the content, then discovery methods such as group discussion, brainstorming, games, or simulations can be used. But if participants lack knowledge or experience, then methods such as lecture, symposium, or panel discussions may be more suitable.

Another consideration concerns the time of day each segment will be presented. This is the nitty-gritty. If the course lasts for a day, what do we do to energize people in the afternoon? What parts of our content do people need to master? What should they need to be able to find when they need it? For each part of the program, what are two or three alternative delivery methods? How do we maintain variety, not using any method too frequently or for too long at any one time?

Step 6. Rehearse Individual Modules

Each part is practiced by itself. Does each component have a strong opening and close? Is the middle supported and reinforced? Components that are introduced just before or after program breaks should be especially strong and engaging.

Step 7. Test New Material

Whenever you include totally new material in a program, be sure to test it. If you have new printed instructions, give them to several people beforehand to be sure they can follow the instructions. If you have new visual aids, be sure they communicate clearly the concepts you intend. If you're adding material, ask what, if anything, you should delete to make room for these additions.

Step 8. Dry Run of Program

This dry run will vary, based on the time and money available and the significance of the program. I've had dry runs of a three-day program that were as short as half a day; I simply "walked through" the components because I was familiar with them, but perhaps the sequence was new, or I had made slight alterations I wanted to check. For one major program I helped develop, we had a one-week dry run of a two-week program. The five faculty members were on-site, along with the 10 members of the company's advisory committee for the program. We presented to the advisory committee exactly what we planned to do each minute of each day.

Some parts we talked through, and some parts we walked through, and some parts we ran through. We described how all the assignments would be made, how groups would be formed, etc. The advisory group thoroughly evaluated each part of the program from the organization's perspective. Three weeks later, after lots of revisions, we did the pilot program, which lasted the full two weeks.

Step 9. Pilot Program

This is the real thing. It's a full program just like every other program you'll run; but since it's the first, you won't be able to make all the adjustments that are needed for the program to work as well as possible. Make sure the participants evaluate the program *after it's over,* not at each step along the way. If you're continually stopping to discuss each component, neither you nor they will ever get a feel for the program flow.

Step 10. Evaluate Program

Get all the feedback you can from all the interested parties you can. This may include the senders, those sent, and the payers. You want your program to be as good as you can make it.

There are a number of things you might want people to evaluate:

1. The facilities
2. The level at which the content was developed
3. The instructor's knowledge of the subject
4. The instructor's interest in the participants
5. The usefulness of the content
6. The usefulness of the handouts
7. The effectiveness of the visual aids
8. The applicability of the content back on the job
9. The length of time spent on each topic (too long, too short, just about right)
10. What helped the course be effective?
11. What hindered the course's effectiveness?
12. What would you want to change?
13. The pace (too fast, too slow, just about right)?
14. The content (too advanced, too basic, just about right)?

APPLICATIONS FOR CREATIVE TRAINERS
FEEDBACK/EVALUATION – MINNEAPOLIS 12/6–7/93

We want to make our future sessions and communications as meaningful as possible and we would appreciate your candid evaluation of this program in response to the questions below. Please leave this form with the seminar leader before you depart.

Please PRINT your name and address below for mailing.

Name _____ Title _____

Organization _____

Business Address _____

City _____ State _____ Zip _____

Telephone (___) _____

SECTION EVALUATION:

	Very Useful		Somewhat Useful		Not Useful		Amount of Time Spent: • Too Long (TL) • Too Short (TS) • Just About Right (JAR)		
I. General Concepts of Human Behavior	7	6	5	4	3	2	1	TL	TS	JAR
II. Visuals in Training	7	6	5	4	3	2	1	TL	TS	JAR
III. Interactive Learning Activities	7	6	5	4	3	2	1	TL	TS	JAR
IV. Assessment Instruments	7	6	5	4	3	2	1	TL	TS	JAR
V. Skill Surveys	7	6	5	4	3	2	1	TL	TS	JAR
VI. Skill Practice/Role Plays	7	6	5	4	3	2	1	TL	TS	JAR
VII. Make or Buy Decision	7	6	5	4	3	2	1	TL	TS	JAR

On a scale of 1 to 7, with 7 being the highest, how would you rate the following:

	HIGH						LOW
Overall Course	7	6	5	4	3	2	1
Instructor's Knowledge of Content	7	6	5	4	3	2	1
Instructor's Interest in Audience	7	6	5	4	3	2	1
Instructor's Style of Training	7	6	5	4	3	2	1
Usefulness of Program Materials	7	6	5	4	3	2	1
Effectiveness of Visual Aids	7	6	5	4	3	2	1

What did you like most about the Program?

_____

_____

What would you like to see changes for future programs?

_____

_____

When you develop an evaluation form, be sure that you consider three different types of feedback items on the form. Number one is to use a numerical rating or Likert scale. For example you could use a seven-point scale with seven being the highest. But secondly, also allow open-ended questions. Allow people to describe for you why they gave the various ratings that they did. And thirdly, consider multiple-choice ratings.

Here's an example from one of our seminars. The content area is preparation, and we allow people to indicate on a scale from 1 to 7 how valuable that information was, from 7 being "Very Useful" to 1 being "Not Useful." But notice that there are only three options that we can use:

Was the amount of material covered

a) too long?
b) too short?
c) just about right?

Was the pace of the material

a) too long?
b) too short?
c) just about right?

Was the level that the material was presented at

a) too low?
b) too high?
c) just about right?

This feedback can be useful in improving future offerings of the course.

Step 11. Adjust Program

Based on the feedback you get, recycle all the steps we've just been through to modify, adjust, and adapt to fit the needs of your group.

Chapter 10:
Instrumented Learning

Tapping the Power of Curiosity

Learning instruments (sometimes called assessments) are one of the fastest growing segments of training and human resource development tools today. They tap the power of curiosity because almost all of them tell participants something about themselves. Who wouldn't want to know more about me and how I use time, how I listen, how I learn, how I lead, how I interact with others, etc.?

Name a topic and you can probably find an instrument to go along with it. Stress management, conflict resolution, creativity, problem solving, innovation, personality patterns, leadership styles, time management, and customer service are only a few of them.

For years, I've used an instrument called the Personal Learning Insights Profile to help people understand how they learn best.

However, it is not data generated by the instrument that is important. It is how we use that information to be more effective.

Anyone can create an instrument. It's a simple matter of creating some questions and then having participants respond to the questions. For example, years ago I created an assessment that I called the HOBS Analysis. You'll find it on the next page.

Very simple, ten questions, people took it themselves, scored it themselves—and it was used to help people become more aware of what it takes to **Help Others Become Successful**, hence the name **HOBS** Analysis. I had participants discuss the question below once they had taken and scored the HOBS Analysis:

- Which of your personal values and your organization's values are supported by helping others become successful?

HOBS Analysis Questionnaire

Underline the answer that best reflects your **feeling**.

1. When working on a project, would you rather:
    a. work by yourself
    b. do some by yourself and some with others
    c. help someone else do the project

2. When a project is successfully completed, you care if you get the credit:
    a. seldom
    b. part of the time
    c. most of the time

3. It's okay to help people just so that you get something out of it:
    a. most of the time
    b. part of the time
    c. seldom

4. Believing that people will perform well will help their performance:
    a. seldom
    b. part of the time
    c. most of the time

5. One good reason for helping people is simply to win their favor:
    a. most of the time
    b. part of the time
    c. seldom

6. It would be okay to help another person even if it meant that person would get the approval you wanted:
    a. most of the time
    b. part of the time
    c. seldom

7. The effect of a leader's expectations on the performance of those under his/her direction:
    a. has a great deal of effect
    b. has some effect
    c. has very little effect

8. Feelings of self-pity, jealousy, or envy:
    a. keep you from helping others
    b. are normal and nothing to be concerned about
    c. should be expressed when you feel them

9. Believing in people:
    a. strengthens their self-confidence
    b. requires that you put your own desires aside
    c. should be guarded against or else

10. How important is it for you to be the leader in a task?
    a. relatively unimportant
    b. somewhat important
    c. very important

One of the things I would stress is that in using this, my goal was to create awareness and to foster discussion around helping others become more successful, whether we managed them or not.

HOBS Analysis—Part 2

Score questions 1, 2, 3, 4, 5: 10 points for C, 5 for B, 0 for A
Score questions 6, 7, 8, 8, 10: 10 points for A, 5 for B, 0 for C
Total: _____

Group Leader: Read aloud and discuss.

1. The analysis you have just completed reflects your thoughts and feelings about Helping Others Become Successful (HOBS). How do these thoughts and feelings affect your actions? Did you think there was a right or wrong way to answer the questions? Why? How did this affect the way you answered?

2. The highest possible score is 100 points. The higher your score, the more likely you are to help others become successful. If you were not particularly pleased with your score, what could you do about it?

3. In every adverse situation, we have a choice to let it affect us negatively or positively. Discuss possible reactions to the following:

   Chris helps a new employee learn the ropes. The new employee gets a promotion Chris was expecting. Describe possible negative ways Chris could react? Likely results? Describe possible positive reactions? Likely results?

4. There are three ways to get things done:
   a) Do it yourself.
   b) Get help.
   c) Give help.

5. Individually list two or three ways you can help others become more successful
   a) at work
   b) in your family or social set

There are many commercial learning instruments available today that are much more rigorously developed and much more sophisticated. For example, HRD Press has a Coaching Effectiveness Assessment. It provides respondents with a snapshot of their skills and abilities as a coach. Upon completion of the assessment each person gets a profile of their effectiveness in seven competencies of a coach:

1. Empathizing ability
2. Listening skills
3. Capacity to confront and challenge
4. Problem-solving ability
5. Feedback skills
6. Capacity to empower
7. Mentoring skills

Not only is the assessment available, but a facilitator's guide with suggested activities to process and apply the data to become a more effective coach is also included. Here's an important point to emphasize with any learning instrument—now that you know this about yourself—so what? Unless we can use the data to improve, it simply becomes that—data.

One flaw that I've seen in using learning instruments in training is that participants use the data as an excuse for behavior, not as a tool to manage their behavior. For example, somebody takes a behavioral profile and discovers that they have a personality pattern that includes being blunt. So the next time they're too blunt and direct they say, "I'm sorry, but that's just part of my pattern." Wrong! Part of the value of any learning instrument is to use the data to modify our behavior or learn new skills in order to become more effective. In other words, because a person has now learned that they can be too blunt and direct, they can be aware of that in the interactions and moderate that behavior to interact more effectively.

Inscape Publishing (A John Wiley imprint) has a learning instrument called Innovate with C.A.R.E. The theory behind this instrument is that there are four basic roles needed to take any idea from initiation to completion: Creator, Advancer, Refiner, and Executor. A fifth role makes the others work more smoothly, that of Facilitator. Not everyone is comfortable in all these roles. Sometimes a team can innovate—that is take an idea from initiation to completion far more effectively if each part of the team can play their natural role, and each can recognize the importance of the other roles in the innovation process.

Once again, however, what's important is what you do with the information once you have it. So research and facilitator's kits are available to help participants drill deeper and apply the information to their own situations.

To me, the information has no value unless there's application and we see positive change as a result of people becoming more aware. Getting feedback is important, but more often the instrument should be built into a larger program that allows for action planning as well as skills building so that people gain practical on-the-job value and measurable results as a result of the instrument and the related training. There is an appendix in this book that identifies some of the instruments we use with our clients and lets you know how to get further information.

Here are some things that are important to understand before you choose (or develop) and use any learning instrument. Many of these are questions you should ask a vendor if you're considering a commercially available instrument.

Question 1: What is the difference between a test, a questionnaire, and an assessment?

Answer: A **test** has answers that are right or wrong. It generally measures knowledge, abilities, or attitudes. Tests are objective rather than subjective. A **questionnaire,** on the other hand, is a subjective assessment. It is based on the individual's perception of self with regard to the questions asked. No judgments about the personal traits are made. Finally, an **assessment** invites responses that are used to obtain scores that can be compared to a norm. The scores are based on theory and accrued data. The validity of the inferences must be established.

Question 2: How can I know whether or not an instrument or assessment really measures what it says it measures?

Answer: When an instrument measures what it says it measures it is said to be valid. There are three types of validity that you should be familiar with: content, criterion, and face.

- Content validity is based on expert judgment such as an experienced author, or research, or a review of published literature.
- Criterion validity means that the instrument you are considering correlates well with another proven measure of the same content.
- Face validity says that people responding to the instrument accept the results of the instrument and believe they are accurate.

Question 3: What is reliability?

Answer: Reliability says that an instrument will provide the same measures consistently. In other words, given the same conditions, you will get the same results.

Question 4: Why should I use a learning instrument?

Answer: There are at least five reasons for using a learning instrument as part of a training, team building, or coaching effort:

1. It satisfies participants' curiosity about themselves.
2. Because it is about them, it captures and holds their interest.
3. It makes the subject personal by linking the content to them personally.
4. It enables the instructor to take a step-by-step approach to what can be complex material.
5. It enables the instructor to create interest, increase involvement and participations, and create changes of pace to keep the participants focused on the content.

Question 5: What are some of the benefits of learning instruments?

Answer: There are five key benefits of learning instruments:

1. Because it personalizes complex concepts, it accelerates the learning process for participants.
2. Because participants are involved in a variety of ways, it lengthens retention of the content
3. Because it is personalized, it increases the personal motivation to put the learning to use.
4. It can provide organizations with measurable learning outcomes.
5. It is a well-accepted instructional method.

Question 6: How can learning instruments be misused?

Answer: There are three basic ways people misuse learning instruments:

1. They treat it as a test, which means there is a right or wrong answer.
2. When an individual respondent's scores are shared with others without their knowledge or permission, it may be viewed as an invasion of privacy.
3. In the case of personality instruments, they may be used as predictors of success on the job. Very few instruments have predictive validity.

In addition to the way that we've already discussed, there may be other opportunities for you to use learning instruments. Among them are:

1. As part of a career development, goal setting, or self-development process.
2. To help people with interpersonal problem solving.
3. To help people improve their understanding of their jobs.
4. To help with team building and conflict management.
5. To help people uncover their talents and abilities and better use them.

Ten Questions to Ask in Evaluating Any Learning Instrument

1. What claims are made for the instrument?
2. What research is offered to support those claims?
3. How current is the research data?
4. How easy is the instrument to use—both with individuals and groups?
5. In what ways does use of the instrument engage the learner?
6. How easy is it to interpret the results?
7. Is it low-risk, non-threatening, and confidential?
8. Is it valid and reliable?
9. How much control does it provide the respondent?
10. Can it be self-paced, self-scored, and self-interpreted?

The wise use of instruments can add significantly to the take-away value of your classes. Applying the information in this chapter can help you make a big step in that direction.

Chapter 11:
Transforming Existing Training Programs

How to Transform Lecture-Based Training to Instructor-Led, Participant-Centered Training

Do you have existing training that is labeled as dry, dull, or boring? Or have you gotten this far in the book and said to yourself, "All of this is good, but we've got a lot of existing content we just can't get rid of. What do we do with what we already have?" I cannot begin to count the number of people who have come to our ILPC seminars with exactly the same questions. For some, the instructional content was designed in-house. For others, it is made up of off-the-shelf solutions they have purchased from various vendors. Usually the problem is the same: the content is sound, the delivery is not. The question is: What can I do about it? I can't go back and say that we have to throw everything out and start all over. They probably can't, but they can do many things to existing content without rewriting material.

In this chapter, I'll share with you the five steps we use with our clients to, as they put it, "ILPCize" or "Pikeize" their content. Some of the steps I'll only touch on since we cover them in other parts of this book. Those that are new I'll treat in more depth.

What does it mean to "ILPCize" a program? Essentially, it means that we reconstruct content so that the design of the program does the following:

- Utilizes the CPR concept.
- Follows the 90/20/8 rule.
- Builds in the C.O.R.E concept.
- Includes transfer strategies.
- Includes an elevation plan.

At the end of this chapter, you will find the checklist that we use as we walk through a program with clients to create programs that deliver results. For now, let's go step-by-step through what we look at any time we revise a program:

1. The first step is to utilize the CPR concept. We know that each teachable concept must include the right Content, the right Participation, and the right Revisiting. The first thing that we do is review all of the content. Often we will involve subject matter experts (SMEs) in this. Some new content may be added to ensure that the program is current. We then divide all the content into one of three categories:

    - "Need to Know"
    - "Nice to Know"
    - "Where to Go"

The "Need to Know" will form the core of the program. The "Nice to Know" will be included as an appendix and available for the instructor to draw on as time permits and as class needs demand. Finally, the "Where to Go" will form a reference section for those who need more information than time allows within the class.

As we look at both the "Need to Know" and "Nice to Know" content, we also ask our SMEs what level of mastery participants need with each content piece. We examined the four levels of mastery earlier so that we are asking for each content piece: Do participants need awareness, familiarity, competence, or mastery? For most courses, awareness and familiarity are about 70 percent of the content and competence and mastery the other 30 percent.

Both the "Nice to Know" and "Where to Go" sections will have the ability to stand alone. In other words, if they are not touched on in class, they still add value since the participants can understand them without any explanation on the instructor's part. This means that we do not have fill-in-the-blank materials in these sections. Before we deal with the Participation and Revisit parts of this formula, we need to address the 90/20/8 rule.

2. The second step is to follow the 90/20/8 rule. We know that participants can listen with understanding for 90 minutes and listen with retention for 20 minutes, and that we need to involve them every 8 minutes. Now that we have our "Need to Know" and "Nice to Know" content, we start breaking the content into 20-minute chunks. We look for ways to involve them every 8 minutes within the 20-minute chunk. The involvement can take many forms such as asking a question that participants discuss briefly in small groups, creating a windowpane that they sketch along with the instructor, allowing participants two minutes to generate two questions they have or two most valuable things they've learned so far, etc.

Now we can go back to the Participation part of the equation. For each chunk, we examine how we can involve participants in the content. Here we look at the target audience and ask ourselves questions about the knowledge and experience that some or all of them might bring that can be tapped as a part of the instructional process. What methods can we use to help them discover or uncover what they need to know so that they own the content?

Here is where we use both our Instructional Systems Design Grid and our checklist of "37 Ways to Put Variety in Training" to ensure that we are using the best methods to get the results that we are looking for in each content piece.

Transforming Existing Training Programs

Instructional Design Grid

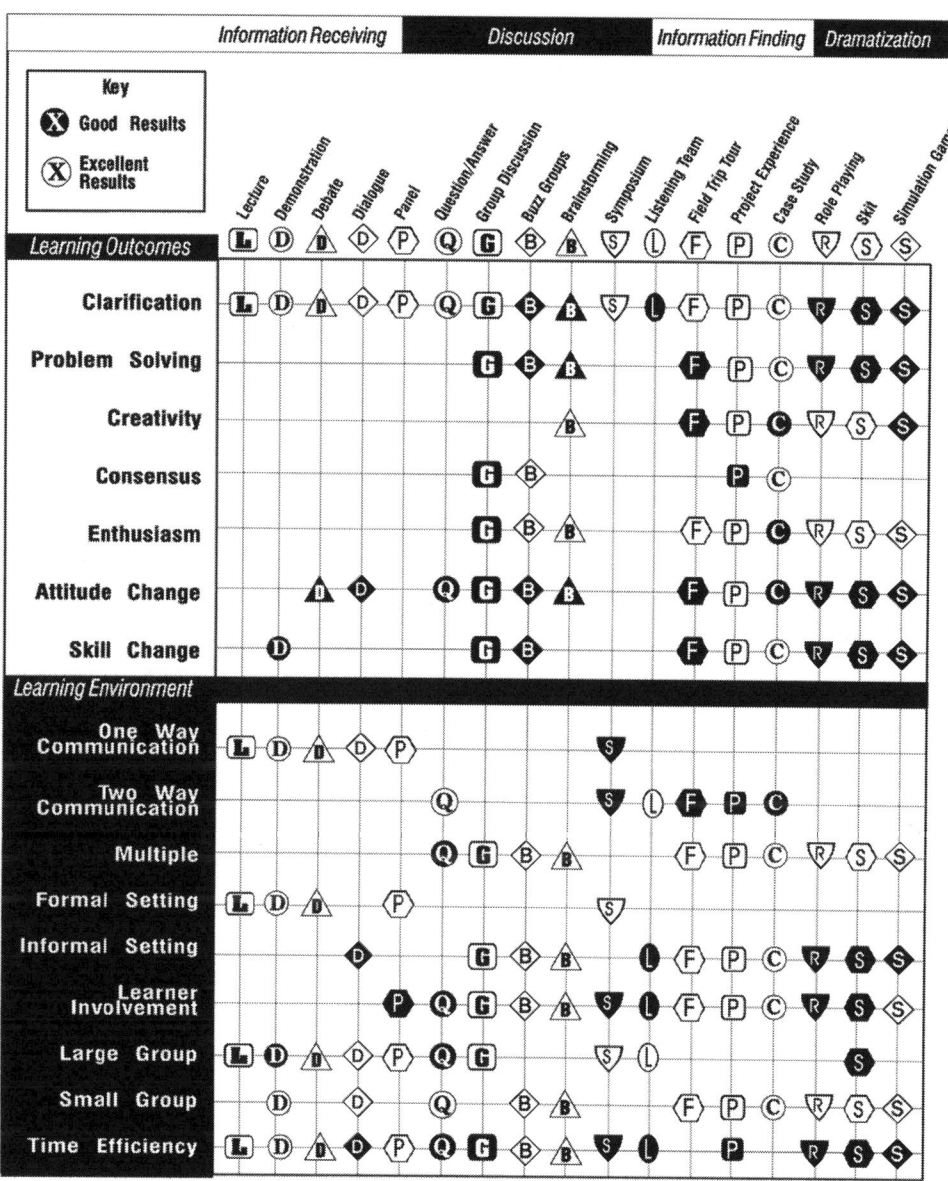

Used with permission "The 1987 Annual: Developing Human Resource," Article by Robert W. Pike, et al.

Bob Pike's
Master Trainer Handbook

Nice to Know

60 Dynamite Ways to Put Variety in Training

1. Action Idea List
2. Brainstorming
3. Brain Teasers
4. Buzz Groups
5. Card Sort
6. Case
7. Charts
8. Coaching
9. Crossword Puzzles
10. Debate
11. Demonstration
12. Field Trips
13. Fill-in-the-Blank
14. Find and Fix
15. Films/Video
16. Gallery Walk
17. Games High
18. Graphic Organizers
19. Group Leader
20. Human Lineup
21. Interactive Learning Activities
22. Infographics
23. Interview
24. Job Aids
25. Learning Partner
26. Lecturette
27. Listening
28. Maps
29. Matching
30. Memorization
31. Mind Maps
32. Mnemonics
33. Models
34. Movie Clips
35. Name Tags (other uses)
36. Object Lessons
37. Paired Shares
38. PowerPoint™
39. Problem Solving
40. Projects
41. Props
42. Questions
43. Quiz
44. Questions and Answers
45. Reading
46. Reflection
47. Report
48. Research
49. Revisit
50. Role Play
51. Simulation
52. Skits
53. Skill Practice
54. Songs
55. Storytelling
56. Teach Backs
57. Testimonies
58. Why Cards
59. Whiteboards
60. Windowpane

3. Next, we look at how we are going to Revisit each content piece. Obviously, for those chunks that fall into the Awareness and Familiarity levels, we will not revisit the content as thoroughly as the Competence and Mastery chunks. For Competence and Mastery, we apply what we know from Mehrabian and we seek ways to revisit content six times so we move the information from short-term memory to long-term memory. We also want the participants themselves to do most of the revisiting of content, rather than the instructor. The more involved they are in this process, the more ways they anchor the information in long-term memory.

   There are dozens of ways to revisit content. Some of the techniques that we use most frequently include the following:

   - Windowpaning, especially when the participants place the key phrase and draw the icons in each of the "panes."

   - Mind mapping, where participants create their own mind maps of content or processes or they fill in a partially completed mind map.

   - Top 10 List, where participants in small groups create a list of the Top 10 best ideas so far, questions to be asked, questions to be answered, most common problems faced, most frequently asked questions, etc. The subgroups then share these with the larger group and a master Top 10 is then developed. Sometimes groups can get very creative! Here's a Top 10 summary—and more, that the trainers at Disney Institute created as a close to one of the programs that I did with them. All of the ideas—and more—are covered in this book. The black and white nature of this book doesn't do it justice.

- Action idea list, where participants periodically go to an action idea page that they've created and add to the list the most important things they've learned that they will use on the job. Perhaps every three to six hours the small group of five to seven that they are part of shares the latest action ideas so that each person can add to their own list of things they hear from other members. This is because we can only focus our attention in one direction at a time. By periodically listening to others, we see viewpoints and ideas we could not consider because their focus was different from ours. Through this process, we benefit from their thinking as well as find our own reinforced. Finally, once a day a master list is created from the entire group. This is posted on chart paper and placed on the wall so that people can continue to revisit the list.

- Triad question form in which we allow participants to create their own list of questions that people should be able to answer if they grasp the content. Each group develops 20 questions based on the content covered. The questions rotate to a second group that reviews the questions for clarity and completeness (one group member goes with the questions so that the review group has someone to provide feedback to). The review group then selects the top 15 of the 20 questions. In the third round, the group of 15 questions is given to a new group to answer using whatever resources they have available. In a very short period of time, the class has revisited in a variety of ways a large amount of content.

Here is what the process looks like in diagram form:

Triad Review

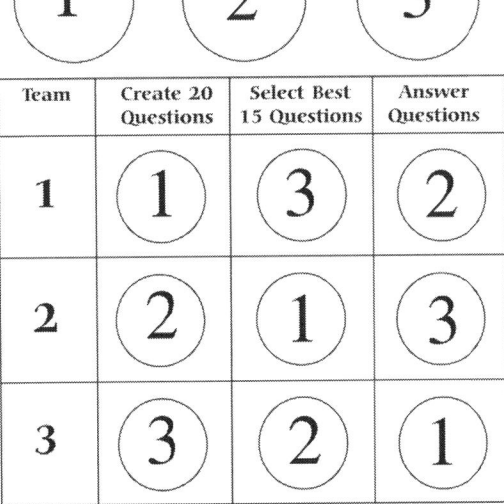

- Gallery walk of various charts that were created during class and are posted on the walls of the room. Participants are divided into groups of three (each person coming from a different subgroup) and invited to rotate through the "gallery" as they might an art gallery. They discuss among themselves what each chart means, what the content was that goes with the chart, any insights they gained in that part of the program, problems that were solved as a result, etc. After this 10- to 15-minute walk through the gallery, the trio breaks up, rejoins their regular subgroups, and the subgroups spend a few minutes sharing with one another the most important insights gained from the experience.

- Graphic organizers to summarize the class. Here is one page of an eight-page graphic organizer that one of my participants in Taiwan put together to summarize an entire two-day program. It is impressive, and all the other participants begged for copies:

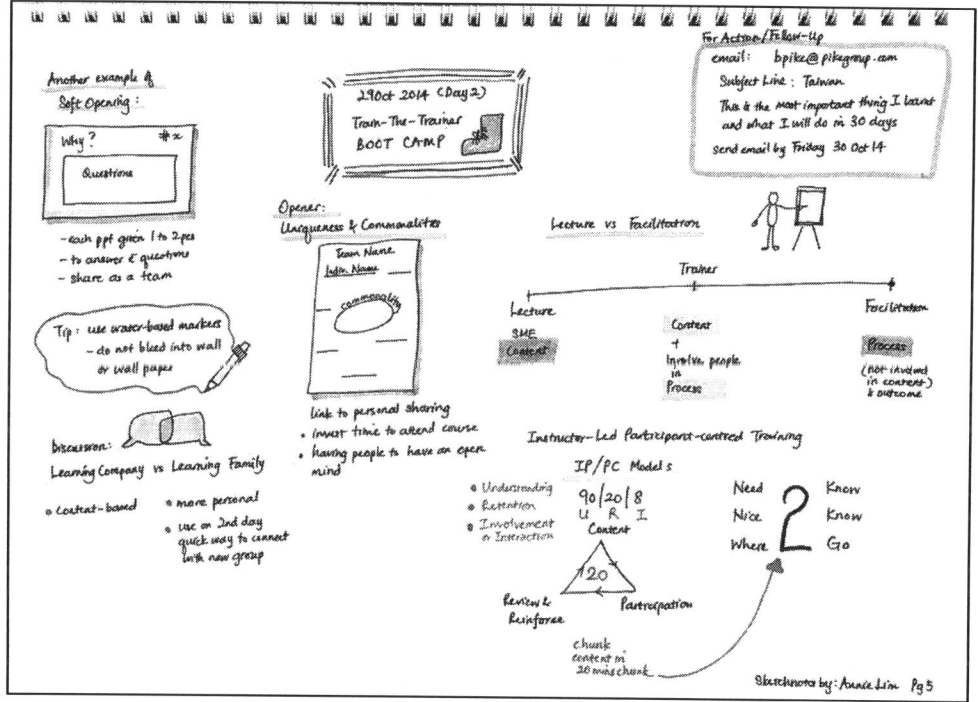

Now we turn our attention to the other three parts of C.O.R.E., which are Closers, Openers, and Energizers, since we've just covered Review and Revisiting.

Closers

How will you close the program—and major segments of the program? In multiple-day programs, you might plan for a close at the end of each day. A closer needs to meet the following three tests that form the acronym ACT:

- **A**ction planning
- **C**elebration
- **T**ie things together

Recently I developed a custom program for a division of Pfizer that we have had as a client for over 25 years. At the end of the day, each person in the small groups of five to seven that we set up gets a certificate, but it's not theirs. It belongs to someone else in the group. Each person shares the most valuable idea they learned that day and how they plan to use that idea. Then the group leader says, I have Juan's certificate, and one contribution I've seen you make to the group today is…." All Juan is allowed to say is, "Thank you." Then Juan says, "I have Chris's certificate, and one contribution I've seen you make to the group today is…." Once again, all Chris is allowed to say is, "Thank you." This continues until each person has their own certificate. The entire close takes less than 15 minutes and creates a powerful way to bring the day full circle.

Openers

Most trainers don't open, they just start. This is a big mistake. Just because people are physically present, it does not mean that they are mentally present. Creative trainers recognize that they need to do at least three things with an opening if they're going to raise the BAR in their training:

- **B**reak preoccupation through involvement.
- **A**llow networking to reduce tension and increase retention.
- **R**elate the opening to the content so that participants see the relevance of the opening. It makes a point. It is not a waste of time.

One powerful opening that we customize for many of our clients is the "Create a Company" opening. For example, if the topic is leadership, then each group of five to seven people is a leadership company. As a group, they come up with a name for their leadership company, a motto for their company, a logo for their company, and then they add the first names of the company members to a chart that is posted on the wall. Throughout the program the company members keep coming back to this chart, adding Post-it notes to the chart with leadership principles that their company uses to create a great work environment, motivated employees, and profitable results.

Because the topic is leadership, participants see the relevance of the activity. Because the entire group participates, networking takes place and tension is reduced. Finally, because there is involvement, preoccupation is broken, brains are stimulated (and in some cases awakened!), and participants are focused on the program.

We've already touched Revisiting techniques, so let's move on to...

Energizers

Almost all participants go through high and low energy periods. For many it happens between 2:00 and 3:00 p.m. in an all-day program. You can't give people breaks all the time, but you can do quick, focused energizers that stimulate people so that you can move on with content. Among the simple, yet powerful ones that we build in to almost every program we co-create with our clients is:

- The controlled stretch break. Participants are given a short individual activity to do. As soon as they complete it, they stand up. As soon as everyone is standing, we have them be seated and move to debriefing the activity.

- Visit the wall. We usually have each table create some kind of chart. Periodically throughout the day they "go to the wall" to add information to their charts. This short move away from their table and back helps to keep people stimulated and energized.

- Teach and Learn. We often place blank charts in the programs we develop. At a given time, we divide groups up and have each group work on a different chart, completing the information that is needed. When the charts are completed, we form new groups so that each chart is represented in the group. Each person debriefs the chart their group had so the others can complete the information.

In my Train-the-Trainer workshop, for example, we have three charts: Training Tools, Ways to Increase Participant Responsibility for Learning, and Ways to Get Participants Back from Break. Imagine we have nine groups of five in the seminar. We post nine letters on a chart—three Ts (for Tools), three Rs (for Responsibility), and three Ps (for Participants). We ask each group to choose a letter from the chart by bringing a marker up and circling their choice—once a choice is circled, it's gone. Participants race up to circle their choices and energy is created—even when people don't know what the choice represents yet! We give each group three minutes, working together to list as many tools as they can that have been modeled in the seminar, to list as many methods we've used for getting people back from break on time, and for increasing the participant's responsibility for their own learning.

At the end of three minutes, we have all the Ts take their workbooks and line up against one wall by group. The same thing happens for the Ps and Rs. We have them number off one through five and form five triads among the Ts, five among the Ps, and five among the Rs. They then have two minutes to compare the charts they've completed, discussing answers and adding responses their group may have missed.

Finally, we have the Ts, Ps, and Rs number of 1 through 15 and form 15 triads so that each of the three charts is represented in the triad. These groups now have nine minutes to debrief their charts so that the others can complete their charts.

Using this activity gets people physically moving around the room every 3 to 5 minutes for about 25 to 30 minutes. It also causes them to review and revisit key content at least three times at the same time. Finally, it maintains and builds self-esteem because each person is constantly sharing ideas learned as well as gaining new ideas.

4. Now we turn our attention to transfer strategies. The entire reason we've used the Instructor-Led, Participant-Centered Process for over 40 years is because our focus is on results. If you've read this book carefully up to now, you'll realize that our system includes not simply techniques to use in design and delivery, but also strategies to ensure that what's taught gets used both on the job and in people's personal lives. We recognize that not everyone attending a training program has full control over their environment. There may be barriers to applying what they learned. Thinking through transfer strategies can help eliminate those barriers.

John Newstrom and Mary Broade developed a transfer matrix, which appeared in their book, *Transfer of Training*. It is based on the idea that three people have the most impact on whether training transfers to the job—the manager sending someone to training, the participant attending the training, and the trainer who does the training. In addition, there are three distinct points in time where these three can influence whether training gets used—before, during, or after the training. Their research with 85 Fortune 500 companies showed that the transfer impact of these three people could be placed in a matrix and a value assigned from greatest impact to least impact. The matrix looks like this:

	Before	During	After
Manager	1	8	3
Participant	7	5	6
Trainer	2	4	9

Transfer of Training
In rank order listing who is in a position to most impact the transfer of knowledge and skills back on the job.

Notice that numbers one, two, and three are the manager before, the trainer before, and the manager after. If you begin to apply everything you're learning in this book to your training, you'll be taking care of most of numbers two, four, five, six, and seven at the same time.

What is important is to ask yourself "What could this person be doing at this point in time that will support the transfer of training afterward?"

Manager Before

For example, the manager before (the number one influencer) could

- be on a manager advisory to provide input on the needs of the target audience;
- hold a briefing with his or her participants so that they understood why they were going and what was expected when they returned;
- ensure that policies, systems, recruitment, or placement were not causing the performance problems;
- gain skill as a coach so that small knowledge and skill deficiencies could be handled on the job;
- schedule a post-course debriefing so that participants understood that they were to come back with an action plan.

Trainer Before

The trainer before (the number two influencer) could

- ensure that managers are a part of the needs assessment process to build ownership of the training program;
- form an advisory board that includes respected managers to gain credibility for the course;
- thoroughly brief managers so that they understand the objectives and they in turn can brief each participant;
- provide training and or coaching to managers on coaching since many may not have seen that skill modeled by their own managers.

Manager After

The manager after (the number three influencer) could

- hold a post-session debrief with each participant as soon as possible to go over each action plan;
- ensure that each participant has time over the 30 days following the training to apply the skills and knowledge gained;
- present a certificate to the participant at a staff meeting and allow the participant to share what they learned and how they see using it.

These suggestions are intended to get you thinking. As a part of our consulting, we've probably used eight or nine strategies for each of the nine areas to maximize transfer and results. If you will visit our website at www.creativetrainingtech.com and become part of our learning community, you'll get an opportunity to share the strategies that you're using and we'll give you access to a private part of the site that includes more transfer strategies as well.

5. The last step is to look at evaluation strategies. As I've adapted Don Kirkpatrick's four levels model, the levels of evaluation are:

   - Did they like it? This is where we develop an evaluation form. We always evaluate at least four things: the content, the presenter, the environment, and the participant.

   - Did they learn it? If the learning is cognitive, you can test it. You can develop a pre-post test that utilizes a blend of multiple choice, matching, true false, fill-in-the-blank, short answer, or essay. It is important that the pre-post test be developed at the same time and that the tests not be the same. Some tests that are computer generated even rotate the correct answer each time the test is given. For example, in a multiple choice the correct answer to the question:

     A single question that is given to you with several possible answers to choose from is called:

     a) multiple choice
     b) fill-in-the-blank
     c) true–false
     d) short answer

     The answer this time is A, multiple choice. The next time the test is accessed, the program rotates the position of the correct answer so that it might be B, C, or D.

     — Did they use it on the job? Here is where we do post-session interviews with supervisors to get feedback on the transfer. If we're going to use this, however, we want to be sure that the participant and supervisor debrief after the program over the participant's action plan. Another method we've used with some clients is to hold a fish bowl session 60 days after the program. The participants return and sit in an inner circle with their managers seated behind them. A panel of senior managers is present. One at a time the participants share their results in implementing their action plans. Knowing after the training is over that this will happen in 60 days provides many managers with extra incentive to see to it that participants have the time to implement their action plans.

     — Did it make a difference? I agree with Don Kirkpatrick here. There are so many variables influencing an organization at any given time that it is both difficult and costly to try to prove that the training program is the one that really made the difference. So, we look for evidence, not proof. For example, if customer satisfaction scores go up in the 60 days following customer service training for those who took the training compared to those who did not, that is evidence that the training had a positive result for the organization.

Transforming Existing Training Programs

We use the data from these evaluations not only to report to the organization on the results, but also to improve the courses the next time they are delivered.

Here is a checklist of nine questions to ask yourself the next time you want to "ILPCize" a program:

1. How can you chunk the content into 20-minute segments?
2. Divide the current content into "Need to Know"/"Nice to Know"/"Where to Go"—will you need subject matter experts (SMEs) for either this question or number 3?
3. At what level of mastery does each chunk need to be?
4. What kinds of participation do you have now? What can you add from the "37 Ways to Put Variety in Your Training" and the Instructional Design Grid?
5. What kinds of review/revisit do you have? How can you build on those? Key Question: Are the participants doing the review—or the instructor?
6. How will you close? How often?
7. How will you open? How often?
8. What transfer strategies will you put in place?
9. What evaluation strategies will you put in place?

Applying the ILPC Process to existing content can increase learning, reduce training time, and build confidence for on-the-job application. Use this chapter as a guide to other parts of the book and get started today!

Chapter 12:
Participant-Centered Techniques for Technical Training

Moving Technical Training from Dry, Dull, and Boring to Interesting, Exciting, and Alive

Almost any time I conduct a train-the-trainer workshop, we have trainers who will ask, "How can you make technical training interesting?" When I ask what technical training is like, the answer is almost always, "Dry, dull, and boring." It is my belief that there is no training that is dull, dry, and boring—there are only dull, dry, and boring methods for delivering it! Look at it this way: we conduct training because we believe that the knowledge and skills will accelerate people's ability to perform on the job. In other words, we're training you because we want you to be a winner. Is that a boring motive? Absolutely not! Remember this the next time you lead technical training. And remind yourself of this as well: "I will look for ways things can be done—not reasons they can't!"

It all starts with our attitude. My attitude has always been that if there is a reason for learning something, then the motivation for learning also exists. If, as the trainer, I think the subject is dry and boring, it almost guarantees that the participants will feel the same way.

Remember that every participant is tuned to two radio stations—WII-FM (What's In It For Me?) and MMFI-AM (Make Me Feel Important About Myself). So how will the training you're offering help people do their jobs faster, better, and easier? What are the benefits they'll gain? What are the losses that they will avoid? As we answer these questions, we begin to lay the groundwork for training that really makes a difference—and a training environment that is high energy!

All of the basics that we've covered in this book apply to technical training. But let's look at some of the specifics so that you have actual examples you can modify, adjust, adapt, and then adopt to your own content. By the way, technical training covers a large area of content. It ranges from teaching CPR (cardio pulmonary resuscitation) to how to run a cash register or a lathe or a computer to how to repair a car, put up wallpaper, or create a computer program. That said, here are four ways you can create a positive mindset at the beginning of technical training by the way that you open.

Four Ways to Open Technical Training

A strong opening is important in technical training just as in any other learning environment. It is even more important that the opening meet the test of being relevant to the content.

1. **Brain Teasers.** Brain teasers are always a good way to wake up the brain. They can either be content related or non-content related, though my preference is for content-related brain teasers. For example, if I were teaching a program on inventory and codes, I might have people match products that we carry in inventory with the manufacturer of the product. Remember that for the most part, I always want people to work on these as groups so that networking is going on. Apart from a formal test or quiz, the purpose of a question in training is for learning to take place. When we allow participants to collaborate with each other, they learn from each other. The byproduct of this is that they strengthen relationships that they can call on for support after the program is over.

2. **Pop quizzes.** Pop quizzes are useful if I think that there may be a great deal of expertise in the class. I might also use it if it were a class updating people who had already been trained. These people may come feeling they don't need any training. What they're faced with is, in their minds, a minor update, but the form and function remain much the same. In my experience, the little things can make a big difference. So I might prepare a pop quiz that contains a lot of the little nuances that might seem insignificant, but that, if not mastered, can lead to disastrous results. When people realize that they do not have the answers, they become more teachable because a need has now been established.

   A variation on this would be to allow people to work by themselves for 5 to 10 minutes, but then allow them to combine into teams to get more of the answers. The point is not that you have all these answers at the beginning of the course, but that you will by the end of the course.

3. **Question on name tag.** Questions on name tags can be a variation on the pop quiz. In this version, I write enough questions regarding the course content for everyone to wear one as they arrive. Their goal is to see if they can find someone besides you as the instructor who can answer the question. If you develop the right questions, the chances are that few will find answers. However, as the class starts indicate that as they find answers, they can mount their name tag on the chart you have placed on the wall titled. "Asked—and answered!" They post a second nametag or a sticky note next to it with the answer. By the end of the class, all of the name tags are on the board.

4. **Grid.** We covered the use of effectiveness grids in an earlier part of this handbook on pages 117–122. Let this serve as a reminder than an effectiveness grid based on the technical skills and knowledge that you'll be teaching can be a great way to start a course by helping people establish a personal baseline on what they already know and can do. It can also acknowledge the experience that is available in the group so that people can seek out other participants as well as tap the knowledge of the instructor.

Bonus: Standing on the Line

Have a masking tape line in the front of the room with a masking tape number 1 on one end of the line and a number 10 on the other. Also have some incremental markings on the tape for 2 through 9. Participants will come to the front of the room and stand on the line in keeping with how proficient they feel about the content being discussed. Although this will not tell you what the participants know, it will tell you what the participants think they know. These attitudes (and who have them) will serve you well as the class proceeds.

If space does not permit standing on the line, you can have participants sit so that they can easily stand up. Then announce topics and do a slow count: 1–2, 3–4, 5–6, 7–8, 9–10. If participants feel they are at a basic level or below, they stand on 1–2. When they are fully erect, they sit down. Some familiarity, stand on 3–4; competence, stand on 5–6; mastery, 7–8; and if they should be teaching this topic, stand on 9–10! (This last statement usually brings a laugh!)

Creating and Maintaining Interest in Technical Training

Getting and maintaining interest is as critical in technical training as in other types of training. Here are some specific ideas from Chapter 8 that have now been taken and applied to technical training.

Use Visuals and Color

Since the mind thinks in pictures, consider how you can make your key points visual. For example, in a technical course on blueprint reading, we reproduce the blueprint on a PowerPoint. However, rather than having it too small for participants to see we have the entire blueprint in the background with a box surrounding the area that we're focusing on. Then we enlarge the part in the box to fill two-thirds of the screen. Some presentation software actually allows you to select and zoom parts of a screen, which accomplishes the same thing.

You have to be careful here, however. A diesel repair class had a great model of the engine that people were learning to repair. It stood in the middle of the shop and various parts were color-coded by function. After a week, the participants went into the repair shop to work on actual engines and were confused. Now they were looking at the engine from the bottom—and the parts on the real engines were not color-coded. Here is an example where we realize that color doesn't always help—and if using a model, make sure that it appears to the participants in the classroom the way it will in the field. See Chapter 4 for more information about the use of visuals.

Add Some Humor

I'm not talking about jokes, but almost every technical topic has humor built into it—especially if you consider the jargon associated with the topic. In a computer class, I might talk about what it means to "boot the computer." Then there's what I thought it meant when I first started using a computer—why would I want to kick my computer? Or my first software manual that told me type a certain command and then hit the "enter" key. I carefully looked all over my keyboard and I could not find a key labeled "enter." In those days, there was only a left arrow, which meant to experienced computer users, "enter." Obviously, I was not experienced. Finally, when I was apprenticing as a carpenter, I was told to get a "butt gage." I thought I was being put on, perhaps undergoing a hazing reserved for those new to the trade. Then I learned that a butt gage helps create the proper size and depth of space needed so that door hinges attached to the door are flush (or flat) with the edge of the door. (This also gives you an idea of my age since most doors for the past 35 years have come preframed; so you no longer have to install the hinges—it's already done at the factory!)

Make a Promise

In a course on medical terminology, I might say, "In the first 45 minutes of this class, I promise to teach you five memory techniques that will reduce the time it takes you to learn the medical terms in this course by 50 percent!" Or I might give a class four keys for doing something and then say, "If you'll remember to ask after the break, I'll give you the fifth and most important key, but you must remember to ask!" After the break, when they ask (and they usually do!), I say, "Before I give you the fifth, take 30 seconds in your groups—what were the first four?" After 30 seconds, I'll ask for a group to volunteer one, then a different group a second, and so on. Then I provide the fifth as promised, but in the meantime, they've revisited the content, we've gotten everyone involved, we've used a question for learning to take place, rather than testing, etc. We've accomplished multiple objectives with one simple technique.

Ask a Question

I ask dozens of questions during training. However, I rarely direct the question at an individual. I usually use the technique just described above to get the entire class involved in revisiting content to come up with the answers. This technique works especially well when teaching a class filled with experienced people because it allows you to honor their knowledge and experience. Here are examples of questions I've used in helping clients create great questions:

- What are the three most common mistakes people make in/when/by (fill in the blank)?
- What are the five most common reasons customers/clients/ patients/guests (complain, leave, sue, send letters of complaint, demand their money back, return, buy more, refer others, etc.)?
- What are the first three things you should do when troubleshooting/repairing/building/fill in the blank)?

You might start keeping a list of the questions you're asked in your classes—and that you ask—and see how you can improve them using some of the suggestions and thought starters here.

Share a Story or an Experience

Stories stick in people's minds. Stories create emotional experiences for people to participate in—and those emotions become powerful aids to memory and learning. If I were teaching a course in basic electrical wiring I might use this story:

> When I was about eight years old, my parents went next door to visit our neighbors. I was left to watch my brother and sister. We played hide and seek. I was very good at hiding. I was hiding in the living room behind the sofa and realized the light from the lamp could give me away. Not wanting to leave my hiding place, I reached out, grabbed the lamp cord, and yanked the plug out of the wall. The game was over and I went to plug the lamp in, but the plug had no prongs—they were still in the socket. I panicked. I had to fix this before my parents got back. I reached out and grabbed the two prongs in the wall to remove them—and got an electrical shock. I was just too slow I thought. If I grab really fast the prongs will be out before the electricity gets to me, I thought. So, I tried again. I discovered I was not quicker than electricity! Finally, I carefully placed the plug over the prongs. I wasn't going to try again. Then I say to the class, "There are at least three things to learn from this story. In your small groups, take 60 seconds, what are they?" Another question I use is, "There are at least three things I could have done to remove the prongs had I understood basic electricity better. Take 60 seconds in your groups, what are they?"

Use a Quote or Statistic

Here are three that I use when working with computer training. Who said:

> "Who would ever need more than 64K of RAM?"
>
> "Why would someone want a computer in their home?"
>
> "I believe that there exists a need for perhaps 10 computers worldwide."

Given what we know today, these quotes seem outrageous, but they came from some of the leading lights in the computer industry. Bill Gates, co-founder of Microsoft said the first, the second came from Ken Olsen, founder of Digital Equipment Corp., and the third from Thomas Watson, founder of IBM. What a great springboard into a variety of technical subjects!

Here's a statistic I like: 43 percent of all statistics are made up on the spot.

Another activity that I use when I want to reinforce the need to be precise is to give participants an index card and ask them to complete the following:

> You need to add someone to your project team. You are reviewing personnel files including performance appraisals. Here are some statements you see. What do they mean?
>
> - When someone is frequently late—what percent of the time is that individual late?
>
> - If someone often volunteers to help—what percent of the time does that happen?

- When someone almost never misses a deadline—what percent of the time is a deadline missed?

- When someone is almost always a team player—what percent of the time is that person a team player?

- Someone owes you a report. You call and ask when it will be ready and are told "soon." In your opinion, how long will it be before you receive the report?

- You're holding a party in someone's honor. They are an hour late. The individual calls and says that they will be there "in a little while." How much time do you think will elapse before you see them?

I then have the small groups compare and get the range of answers for each. We post the ranges and this brings a discussion of how precise communications may or may not be. Then I ask each group to develop three learning points from this example that relate to the technical training they are taking.

Add Some Magic, Props, or an Object Lesson

You've seen earlier in the book how we use a potato as an object lesson—not only as a reward, but also to emphasize the importance of following through. Sometimes I'll have a bowl of eggs on a table in front. I'll crack a couple of the eggs into a glass bowl and comment about how fragile the shells are. Later I pick up a number of them and start throwing them at the participants. They all duck—until they realize that these eggs are soft rubber eggs. Then we begin a discussion of how we assume things—and that making assumptions can create problems. This leads to a discussion of assumptions the participants have seen people make that relate to the class topic—and the problems these assumptions caused when they were treated as fact.

Earlier we shared the example of using potatoes as rewards and then teaching participants to drive a straw through the potato with a single blow to emphasize the importance of following through. This serves as a powerful metaphor and makes the point more eloquently than an hour's lecture—all in a matter of minutes.

I recommend Dave Arch's *Tricks for Trainers* series and, of course, my own *101 Games for Trainers* and *101 More Games for Trainers.*

Use a Game

Games can inject some wholesome competition into a class and allow participants to revisit and anchor important content. We used Windowpaning to teach participants the nine basic steps to performing the Heimlich maneuver. In less than five minutes, using the windowpane, participants understood the steps. Then, I asked for a volunteer, and together we walked through the steps with the volunteer as victim, while I was the rescuer. The class called out each of the steps as I modeled them. Next the volunteer and I reversed roles and the volunteer performed the Heimlich on me while the class called out the steps.

After this, participants paired off and practiced on each other. Then it was time to play "Beat the Clock." Each group received an envelope with the nine steps on nine slips of paper. However, the icons used in the windowpane were not there—instead a more complete word description of the step was substituted. We also included two false steps that were, in fact, the two most common mistakes people make in performing the Heimlich.

Each group had one person in the group keep time while the others laid out the strips in windowpane fashion. When they were done, we had them note the time and then check their work. Each group added 30 seconds for a step out of place and one minute for a wrong step.

We then had a brief discussion about the ease or difficulty of the process. Finally, we allowed them to mix up the steps and play the game one more time. The object was to beat their previous, or baseline, time. Usually every group improves significantly. The result is that people feel a boost in confidence, are impressed with their ability to remember, feel good about improving on their previous time, etc. At no time do we ever compare the groups. Using this series of activities, we can teach the Heimlich in about 20 minutes or so. Participants are surprised to find out that they have revisited the content more than 20 times in a variety of ways.

Let People "Break" Things

I worked with a number of Citibank trainers who were responsible for technical training in computer maintenance. The instructors themselves spent a great deal of time prepping for class because circuit boards, for example, had to be disabled so that the participants could apply the troubleshooting and repair techniques to finding and fixing the problems.

Based on our process, they developed a better teaching sequence that also reduced the amount of prep time for the instructors. In the class, troubleshooting and repair techniques were covered and demonstrated. Then participants were divided into pairs and given a circuit board. Their responsibility was to recreate in the circuit board one or two of the most common malfunctions that past troubleshooting had identified on the job.

After the malfunctions were recreated, one participant went to another group. The person who stayed with the circuit board explained the malfunctions that had been created. The observer signed off that these were common malfunctions that the class had covered. Then the original pairs received a different malfunctioning circuit board than they had either created or reviewed and applied the troubleshooting and repair methods to find and fix the malfunctions.

Several interesting results came from using this process:

- The participants created harder problems for themselves than the instructors had in the past.

- The participants viewed the entire process as fun, exciting, and a challenge.

- The participants revisited the key content at least four times in the process.

- Each individual's confidence level increased with this intense hands-on opportunity.

- Instructor's were freed up to observe and coach as needed.

Six Ways to Generate and Answer Questions from a Technical Group

Questions and answers seems to be a common technique in technical training, but an often misused and abused technique. Often the instructor gets no questions at all—or questions from the same people who often simply want to talk and share war stories under the guise of asking a question.

Here are six techniques that can help you tap the powerful benefits of questions and answers. Any of these techniques can and should be modified, adjusted, and adapted before adopting them for your particular application:

1. **"Ask It" Basket.** A basket is placed in the front of the room. Participants are given a supply of 3" x 5" cards. As they develop questions, they write them on the cards and place them in the basket. The instructor reviews the cards and answers them. As an option, if the instructor knows the answer is either in resources, material already covered, or in the experience within the group, the question can be used as a "toss up" question to the groups. Each group is then allowed a short period of time (varying depending on the complexity of the subject) to find or develop their answer to the question.

2. **"Two Cents Worth".** This is a great process for classes that have very vocal participants. Each participant is given two pennies (cents). They can use a penny any time they want to either ask a question or make a comment. When they have used up their two cents worth, they can't ask any more questions or make any more comments until others have had their two cents worth. Additional coins can be given out for being back on time, completing tasks, etc.

3. **"Capture the Question" Board.** Participants sometimes ask great questions, but the timing of the question is a little off. Participants are provided with a supply of Post-it notes. Whenever a question comes up that needs to be deferred (usually because answering the question would cause more participants confusion than clarity), the instructor asks them to write it out and place it on the "Capture the Question" board. The instructor sets a time by which the question will be answered and asks the participant to remind the class when the time has arrived for the question to be answered.

4. **Create for Other Teams.** This technique can be used in two places. The first place is when you have a group with a lot of technical knowledge and experience (for example, a group that is being recertified in safety or CPR). You divide the group into at least three teams and have them generate questions that people who are certified ought to be able to answer. The questions that are developed are then passed to other teams to review and answer. A second place is where technical content has been covered. Once again, divide up the class into subgroups. Ask them to develop 20 questions that people who understand the content presented should be able to answer and that best covers the content delivered. After a period of time, the questions are passed to a second group to review for clarity. This group then selects the best 15. A third group then answers the top 15 questions using whatever resources they

have available. This enables each group to revisit and reinforce the key content three times, generally in less than 20 or 25 minutes!

5. **Green and Red Dots.** Participants are given small red and green dots (we use Avery file folder dots). Each person is asked to place green dots next to 5 to 10 important concepts, techniques, and processes that they understand best and find most useful. At the same time, they place red dots next to the 5 to 10 concepts, techniques, and processes that need the most clarification. In small groups, they share their green dots and their understanding, along with the red dots. A high percentage of the time, someone's red dot can be turned to green by someone in their group. Those that aren't are tossed to the instructor.

6. **Question List.** Participants are given pads of keynote Post-its. As a group, they brainstorm all the questions they cannot answer (or perhaps all the questions that remain unanswered). After two to five minutes, these are posted on individual flip charts taped to the walls at intervals around the room. Groups circulate from chart to chart with a different color keynote pad either writing down questions that appear that they cannot yet answer. (In this case, the subgroup asks the group for the answer.) Or they use the keynote to answer a group's question that they asked, but could not yet answer.

Bonus: Consulting Envelopes. At the beginning of a class, each participant is given three envelopes. (Sometimes you might post three to four envelopes per person around the room and have them work the activity by moving around the room. On the inside flap of the envelope, they write a content-related question they'd like the group, including the instructor, to consult on. These are then taped to the wall by the flap so that the question shows.

Periodically the instructor allows the group to circulate with 3" x 5" cards. If they have some ideas that can help respond to the question, they write them on a 3" x 5" card along with their name and place them in the envelope. After this process is repeated two to three times, participants are allowed to retrieve the envelopes and examine the contents.

Participants can then take turns sharing with the class the most useful responses they received—and who the respondent was that shared the information. Once again, we have a technique that honors the experience that rests within the group and helps people to feel good about themselves. This process can be repeated throughout the program.

Six Ways to Build Excitement into Technical Training

Originally all these tools were used in the ways listed below within the course. Participants listed the various uses for each. Each group was assigned (or chose) a different tool to begin with and then rotated through as many as they had time for. After 5 to 6 minutes, they were asked to join with other groups to add to or complete their lists. What kind of list could you give participants in your courses?

Dots. Participants can use dots in at least four ways: first, they can place a green dot next to concepts they find useful—and share those. Second, they can place red dots next to ideas that need more clarity and share those to get help from one another and the instructor to turn the red dots to green. Third, they can use dots to vote on topics they most want addressed in the class. Typically this is done by allowing them to place a dot next to one-third of the topics, plus one (this is called the one-third–plus–one rule) that are most important to them. This gives the instructor a sense of the importance of the various topics so that they can be expanded or contracted to fit the needs of the class. Fourth, participants can place dots on the name tags or name tents of co-participants that contributed to their learning. As they do this, they give the person specific feedback on what was said or done that the other person found useful. How else could you use dots?

Tape flags. At the beginning of the class, participants are given several different color 3M tape flags. As a group, they decide what each color represents. The tape flags are then placed within their various handouts, workbooks, and resource materials to highlight key ideas, help them locate key charts, checklists, etc., locate glossaries, and more. This helps them to become more aware of the printed resources they're taking with them and makes the resources easier to use after the class is over. How else could you use tape flags?

Highlighters. Participants are given several different color highlighters and decide what concept each color represents: key points, material that I need clarified, ideas I can use, etc. The highlighter is used throughout the course and periodically participants share with one another what they've highlighted so that they can use each other's experience to bring more clarity to the content. How else could you use highlighters?

Post-its. Each participant table had a variety of 3M Post-its called Keynotes. These were used throughout the course to list ideas, list answers to questions, ask questions, etc. Participants also used them to create game pieces, such as a sequencing game. Each group would list the individual steps to doing something taught in the course (whether discrete steps had been given or not). Other groups then had the challenge of putting the Keynotes in the correct order in the shortest possible time.

An almost carnival-like atmosphere is created. The steps are posted in random order on a piece of chart paper attached to the wall. Groups rotate from chart to chart to try their hand at sequencing while one participant stays with the chart. Groups are timed and as they move to another chart, the chart master randomizes the keynotes to prepare for the next group. How else could you use Post-its?

"Match" games. Participants create games that involve pairs from course content. Examples are words and their definitions, parts and their locations, faults and their fixes, items and their uses, etc. These are handed to another table or taped to the wall, and the other groups take turns rotating among the cards and matching the pairs up correctly as quickly as possible. How else could you use 3" x 5" cards?

Crossword puzzles. These can be created and used in at least two ways: as a pre-course test to see how much people know and as a mid- or end-course review to help reinforce the information. In the first, the instructor prepares the crossword puzzle. In the second example, the participants can create their own puzzles if they wish. How else could you use crossword puzzles?

In many ways, technical training is easier to make participant centered than other types of training because it is frequently skill based, and the practice of skills automatically creates involvement. Because participants often have the focus of wanting to do better back on the job, the practical nature of technical training means that many participants are pre-sold on the importance of the course. By modifying, adjusting, adapting, and adopting the things we've discussed in this chapter, you'll be well on the way to increasing the impact—and the fun factor—in your own technical courses.

Three Tools for Making Technical Training More Memorable (and Visual)!

Participants in my train-the-trainer classes are exposed to a variety of methods to improve memory power. They then come to this page to revisit how these methods had been used during the class to help them retain key concepts. The techniques also demonstrated how important visual cues are to memory (at least for 70 percent of all learners!).

Stacking/Linking. One way to use this method is to have participants turn a list of items into a story. In this way, we are stacking the items on top of—or linking them to—one another. For example, look at these 20 seemingly unrelated items:

wallpaper	nurse	plant
mountain	watch	power
skirt	perfume	safe
string	elephant	melon
ice cream cone	jail	dog
scissors	mirror	necklace
nail	suitcase	

As we made up a story using these words, we used gestures and pointed to various parts of the room. See if you can picture this in your mind's eye. We also had people repeat the various parts of the story and make the gestures. This added exercise brought additional memory and learning anchors into play.

The first time, I told the story complete with gestures and movement. The second time, I paused, and the participants filled in the word. The third time, I made the gestures and movements, and the participants rehearsed the story in their own minds silently. The fourth time, a participant came up and told the story, and the rest filled in the pauses. Once again—all of this took less than 15 minutes.

Over here on the wall, we have (wallpaper) [I rub the wall up and down with my hand]. On the wallpaper is a picture of a (mountain) [I make a triangle or mountain-shaped gesture], and the mountain is wearing a (skirt) [I gesture as though I'm wrapping a skirt around myself]. The skirt has a loose (string) that comes out of the skirt and plops down in the middle of the room on top of a six-foot tall (ice cream cone) [I make an ice cream cone shape gesture in the middle of the room six feet high]. We want to cut the cone with (scissors) [I make an x motion with my arms as though each were a scissor blade cutting], but the scissors are broken so we fix it with a (nail). The person fixing the scissors is a (nurse) [I make a gesture as though wearing a nurse's cap] who is wearing a (watch). She is also wearing (perfume) [I make a gesture as though spraying perfume all over myself] that makes her smell like an (elephant) [I extend one arm in front of my nose and make a sweeping movement as though my arm were an elephant's trunk]. The elephant stomps over and rips open the door to a (jail). On the jail wall is a (mirror) [I make a gesture as though I'm combing my hair in the mirror]. Under the mirror is a (suitcase) [I point to the suitcase]. I open the suitcase and out pops a (plant). Now this is an amazing plant. You touch the plant, the lights come on. You touch the plant, the lights go off. This plant has (power) [I flex my arm to show that I have a powerful bicep!]. Over on another wall [I point to a third wall] there is a (safe) [I gesture as though working a combination]. I open the safe and out rolls a (melon). The melon rolls across the room and hits a (dog) that is wearing a very expensive (necklace) [I gesture as though a necklace is around my throat.]

If we take the time to let people look at the list first for a period of time and then try to reconstruct the list from memory, they usually fail miserably. This is especially true if the list has to be in the exact sequence. Let's say we give one point for remembering a word, and two additional points if the word is in the correct place in the sequence. A perfect score would be 60. Most people average 20 or less.

After rehearsing the story the way we did, most score 50 percent higher at a minimum. Over 70 percent will have a score of 90 percent or better! (By the way, the next day they'll still remember the story!)

Mind Mapping/Brainwriting

One of the greatest challenges when making presentations is preparing for them. Many people sit down, they pick up a sheet of paper, and their minds go blank. They don't know where to start. Or they have so many ideas they don't know how to organize them. Or they don't have enough information to choose a format or decide on the points to be covered.

The book *Use Both Sides of Your Brain*, by Tony Buzan, is very helpful in putting presentations on the right track. A significant part of the book outlines a technique that Tony calls mind mapping. When I use mind mapping, it reduces the time it takes me to develop a presentation, a report, an article, or a letter by approximately 50 percent. Mind mapping allows me to use words to visually relate concepts and information in ways that are more enlightening than note taking or outlining.

Mind mapping a presentation helps me to take a look at how I may want to present the information. It enables me to focus not only on the content, but also on the sequence of the content. A mind map helps me to see not only what is there, but also what is missing.

Here are the fundamental aspects of mind mapping:

- Start with your central thought. Write this premise in the middle of a blank sheet of paper. Then, list the first support idea that comes into your mind in the 12:00 position. Next, note any related points. As you exhaust ideas on a topic, move to the 1:00 position and begin again. Continue around the clock.

- Be free-flowing. One of the models that I use for the mind looks like a pinball machine. It can bounce around very quickly to numerous ideas before it comes up with a logical conclusion. We've all had this experience: someone says something to you. You pause for a minute, and then reply. Your listener asks where in the world your response came from. You reply, "You said this, which reminded me of that, and that made me think of that, which reminded me of that, and that's why I said that to you." For you, the thought progression was very logical, but anyone else looking at it can't see how you got from the original statement to your reply. The mind mapping technique accommodates this type of bouncing around better than either note taking or outlining.

- Use only key words. Often when taking notes and creating an outline, we use too many words. Most people think faster than they write. (The human mind can think 1,200 to 1,600 words a minute. On average, most people only write freehand 25 to 35 words a minute, and the best of us can type little more than 100 words a minute.) So the key concept is to think in bullets and jot down one or two words that capture the concept. This way you won't slow down your thinking.

- Allow yourself to bounce around. It may be that you get to the third or fourth key idea and suddenly you think of something that fits back with idea number one. That's OK—stop, bounce back up, add the idea, and continue on.

- Feel free to connect things that relate. When two topics relate to one another, simply draw an arrow to connect them. The arrow may be drawn with the same color as the rest of the mind map or with another color to highlight clearly the intended connection.

- Try short bursts. Time yourself for five minutes. Then, take a break. Sit back. Look at your mind map. Do something else. Then, spend another five minutes adding, modifying, and adjusting.

Remember, mind mapping is your tool. Let it work for you. Many people, when exposed to mind mapping, say "I could never show this to my boss." A mind map is not necessarily for others. Rather, it is primarily for yourself. Don't use a mind map as a report. Instead, use the mind map to dictate or type the report. Use it to make sure that all the elements you want in the report are there before you start.*

Finally, consider adding windowpanes to your repertoire. In Chapter 4 on visuals, we've given you the basics, along with examples. Windowpaning is especially valuable when you are teaching anything that has an exact series of steps that are performed in a specific order.

---

* The content on mind mapping is adapted from my book, *High Impact Presentations,* and is used with permission.

Applying these techniques, and adapting the many others we've supplied in this book, can transform your training—especially your technical training—and increase the impact and application for your participants. In short, it will increase the results you deliver to your internal or external clients.

My only additional thought has to do with sometimes participants referring to training done on computers as "technical training." We maybe could use our list of computer training ideas in this chapter (i.e., room setup, curtains on the computer, pairing by competencies, redlight/greenlight table tents for the top of computers, etc.). I'm not sure if it fits, but I know that some think of this as "technical training." Note: this last paragraph is put here deliberately to see if participants in my seminars actually read the technical training chapter thoroughly.

Chapter 13:
Participant-Centered Techniques for Computer Training

Moving Computer Training from Dry, Dull, and Boring to Interesting, Exciting, and Alive

In some ways, this chapter's content overlaps and builds on the content in the chapter on technical training. I would recommend that if you are designing or delivering computer training that you read Chapter 12: Participant-Centered Techniques for Technical Training carefully. This chapter will focus on those techniques that are unique for a classroom-based computer-training program compared to other types of technical training.

Many computer trainers consider the training they deliver to be difficult or boring. It's difficult because often the documentation that goes with the software they're teaching is difficult to understand. Frequently it's boring because the training pattern often remains the same: demonstrate, practice, demonstrate, practice, etc.

This situation is not permanent. You can change it right now, beginning today. Most participants have a built-in motivation to learn to use software more effectively. For most, it directly relates to their jobs. It is easy to make a practical connection between the course content and the real world.

First Things First—Room Setup

In a typical computer training room, the computers are in rows facing the front of the room and the instructor. The instructor typically has a computer and faces the participants, though eye contact is limited because the computers and monitors are in the way. This was the typical setup used by American Express in its operations training. It was one of the first recommended changes. Remember that Creative Training Techniques involves participant-centered processes. In profiling over 50,000 adult learners in more than 20 countries using the Personal Learning Insights Profile, we found that, 75 percent preferred learning as a part of a group rather than learning by themselves. This is true even with computer training.

So, we modify the room to make more interaction possible. Here are two diagrams showing a training room set up for 20 participants. The room size is the same. The arrangement is quite different. Notice that in moving from traditional to creative we move the computers to the two side walls and the back wall. In the center of the room, we place a number of 5-foot round tables. When participants engage as a group in dialog with the instructor, they move their seats from the computer to one of the tables. When they use the computers, they move back.

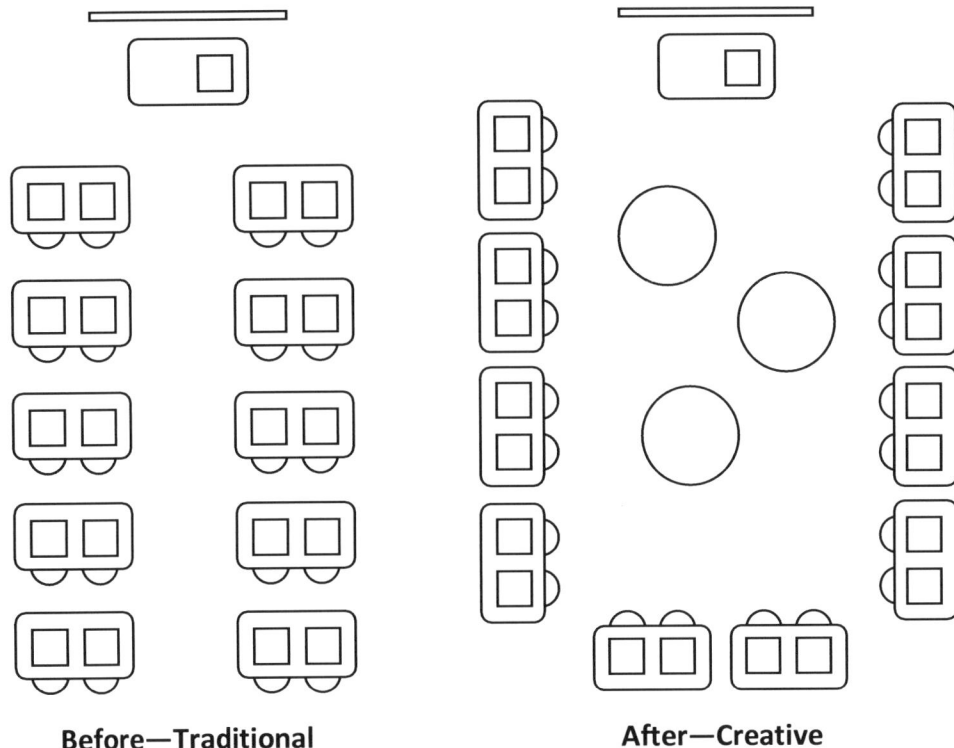

Before—Traditional **After—Creative**

There are a number of advantages to this room arrangement:

- It increases the eye contact between the instructor and the participants.
- It minimizes distractions when new concepts are being explored as a group by moving participants away from their computers.
- It increases the instructor's ability to monitor and coach by providing better sightlines to both participants and their computer screens.
- The instructor can easily walk from computer to computer and check each participant's individual progress.
- It makes it easier to allow participants to work in pairs rather than alone.
- It allows participants to rotate easily from computer to computer for activities that need that movement.

What if the Documentation Is Bad?

Poor documentation is one of the most common complaints that both instructors and participants have about any software package. This hasn't changed since I co-founded a computer consulting company with a partner in 1983. One of the first assignments we had was to redesign documentation and create a training program for a software program that allowed a company's manufacturing software and accounting software to interact with each other seamlessly. The package carried a $650,000 price tag. The client's technical writers had spent six months writing the documentation. On a scale of 1 to10, the beta testers rated it a –2! When we reviewed the documentation with the client, we asked to get it just as if we were a new user. We were handed two boxes. One held the actual documentation. The other held the ring binders for the documentation—all 24 of them! We asked why the documentation was not delivered to the client already assembled. The answer was, "The only way we can make sure they've even looked at it is if we make them assemble it." This was not a good start.

We had only six weeks to make the documentation and training workable. It didn't take long to realize that we could not rewrite 24 separate manuals in a more user-friendly fashion in six weeks. We had to focus on the training itself.

When the training began, we gave each participant only the first of the 24 manuals. All too often, we overwhelm people the first day of a class that already feels overwhelming. Give them what they need right now. Introduce the other manuals as they are needed. Here is the dialog that I used. You might modify it for your own purposes.

Holding the first manual up, I said, "Do you see this? This is the first manual containing the documentation for the software you're about to learn. It is a map to the treasure. The programmers didn't want to provide any documentation. They felt that only the worthy would be able to use their software. If you and I are worthy, we wouldn't need documentation. However, the marketing people said to the programmers that if they didn't provide documentation then no one would buy the software and there would not be any more money to write more lines of elegant code.

"So, the programmers said, 'Fine, but only the worthy will be able to understand the instructions that we write!' So your mission—and my mission—should we choose to accept it, is to find a way over, around, and through the maze they've created so that despite their best efforts to hide the treasure that lies hidden in the software, together we'll find it!"

Was the documentation that bad? In this case, yes! But, most times, not quite that bad. However, by making it seem worse than it is and by putting the instructor and the participant on the same challenging path, the reality isn't as bad as the image we've created.

Here are several ideas that we implement to make documentation more user-friendly:

- We give participants red and green dots (I use ¼-inch file folder dots). They put red dots next to anything they come across that they question or don't understand. Green dots go next to things that are valuable. In small groups, they share the green dot ideas and try to resolve the red dots. Any red dot not resolved goes on a question chart that is always in view on the wall. This allows other groups, as well as the instructor, the opportunity to answer these questions. The green dot ideas are written on keynotes and placed on team charts that we create (at the beginning of each class we create teams of four to six people). Periodically the teams visit the other charts for ideas they can add to their own charts.

- Participants receive tape flags. They color code their manuals with these so that they can quickly retrieve ideas, steps, processes, functions, etc., they want to recall quickly.

- Each section of documentation is assigned to a team of two to three people. The team pores over that section for the top things you need to know (could be top 10, top 20, etc.), the top 10 questions you can answer by knowing this section, etc. Each of the three then becomes responsible for briefing another team of people on this section—and getting their briefing in return. Each person then returns to their original team and debriefs so that the others in the group have the key ideas from two or three other sections of the manual.

Using these processes also ensures that participants leave a class familiar with the resources they have on hand for finding information and getting questions answered later. This has the added benefit of reducing calls to the help desk to answer questions that are covered in the manual. All too many people receive reference materials and never use them in class. Back on the job, they go on a shelf—unused. If we aren't familiar with the documentation, under pressure we'll never use it.

Assessment

How do you know what people know coming in to a class? Dave Arch suggests using physical movement. Place a line of masking tape on the floor with a number "1" at one end and a "10" at the other end. Invite the class to come up and stand anywhere they want along the line. Then, announce various topics, skills, and knowledge covered in the class. Each time you mention something people shift along the line based on their perception of their level of mastery of the subject. This is a quick way to see what level of expertise is in the class. One caution: not everyone has an accurate perception of his or her expertise. Some think too highly of themselves—others not high enough. Use this activity as a starting point.

Here are two other ways to accomplish this assessment—and provide a little more anonymity:

1. Tell participants that you are going to be announcing a number of topics covered in the course. After you name a topic, you'll do a slow count 1–2, 3–4, 5–6, 7–8, 9–10. If participants feel they are at a basic level, they stand up on 1–2. As soon as they have stood up, they sit back down. Know a little, stand on 3–4; comfortable with the topic, stand on 5–6; have mastered the topic, stand on 7–8; can teach the topic, stand on 9–10. People are so busy listening for the topics, quickly assessing where they are in relation to the topic, and standing and sitting that they have no time to look around to see where others are—but you will!

2. For a little more anonymity during the assessment process, another quick assessment tool is to begin by drawing a large tree on an easel pad—turning the easel pad around so that the tree faces the back wall of the room away from the participants. Then the group lines up and goes behind the easel one person at a time. While behind the pad they draw an apple somewhere on the tree. The higher they place their apple on the tree, the more they feel they know about the subject under study in the class. The lower they place their apple on the tree, the more reticent they feel about their knowledge in the class's topic.

When that easel is turned around, the instructor has a sense immediately in terms of what they have to work with in the class. If all the apples are at the top of the tree, the class will undoubtedly be delivered differently than if they are all at the bottom or spread through the foliage of the tree.

Mentoring

Following the assessment, you can build work teams. Sue Ensz shared a great insight into how to create optimum teams in the computer-training environment. Don't put the ones with the most knowledge in a group with those with the least knowledge. Rather, group those with the most knowledge with those with the moderate knowledge and those with slightly above the moderate knowledge level with those who have no knowledge on the subject. This type of grouping will minimize the frustration from all parties.

Screen Curtains

Tape brightly colored bandannas to the top of the computer. This now becomes a "curtain." Participants can "raise the curtain" when ready to do screen work and "lower the curtain" when it's time to do some offline work. This really helps keep participants focused and on-task.

Metaphors

Select a rich metaphor that will give your participants a link to your software application (i.e., a rolodex serving as a metaphor for building a database). This will give them something familiar with which to link the unfamiliar.

Another metaphor that we've used is that of a sieve. In a gravel pit, sieves are used to separate large rocks from gravel. A sieve with smaller holes separates the gravel into sizes. Then gravel is separated from sand.

Here's an activity I adapted from David Meier. It creates an understanding of Boolean logic. Ten volunteers line up in the front of the room. All of those over 30 years of age take one step forward. This represents an "if" statement. Everyone steps back. Next, everyone over 30 and female steps forward. This represents an "if…and" statement (both have to be true for the person to step forward). All step back. Now everyone with at least one year of college or male step forward (this represents an "if…or" statement). The process can be repeated with all the Boolean statements. After the first three, I have the class start making up statements (often the class will come up with things more complex than I would—and never complain that it's too difficult)!

Flow Chart

Put a large flow chart of the system on the wall. The basic chart should be blank except for the heading. Place Velcro® dots in each blank. Create labels for each blank with Velcro on the back. This allows you to provide an overview by placing the labels on the chart, but also gives you the flexibility of removing some or all of the labels and putting them back on the chart as you cover the various parts of the flow chart in the class. Consider giving them a copy of the flow chart with the boxes not filled in. Participants fill in the blanks as the class progresses—giving them a sense of accomplishment each step of the way.

Online Work

Even though you may have one computer for each participant, it is often more effective to have people partner with one another. While one is keyboarding, the partner observes, coaches, etc. Periodically the instructor calls "switch" and the partners switch roles. It can take the pressure off when you are keyboarding what your partner tells you to do—and vice versa!

Offline Work

A person can sit and work at a computer screen for only so long. To maximize the energy in a computer training class, mix up the screen time with offline work away from the computers. Have them do most of this offline work in teams. Here are some activities you might have them do:

- As a team, reproduce the flow chart from memory or create a mobile of the steps to a process.

- As a team, develop 10 questions people can answer if they understand the content we've just covered. These are then passed to another team to review and sign off on and still a third team to actually answer using whatever resources they have on hand.

- As a team, identify the 10 most important ideas, uses, keys to remember, problems that can be solved, etc. These are posted on a chart and compared to those developed by others.

- As a team, use index cards and masking tape to build a mobile that diagrams the steps of the process in diagram form. This can now serve as a job aid when they go back to their job and seek to use the new software.

Self-Paced Projects

When designing application projects for the software, be sure to have them start with the easiest but allow them to progress through other projects (which become increasingly difficult). Using this structure, everyone will remain involved throughout the entire work time (although some will get further than others). Don't worry if everyone doesn't get done with all the projects. Just make sure your "Need to Know" information is in your easier applications with your "Nice to Know" material coming into your more difficult applications.

Consider using some of the design formats I outlined in Chapter 6 on the subject of creating materials, such as start with project 1 and work to project 7 or start with 7 and work to 1—with project 1 and 7 being the easiest. Often giving them a choice gets them jumpstarted.

Arrows

Make double-ended arrows from foam core approximately 12 inches long by 3 inches wide. Color one-half red on both sides, the other half green. Make a small hole in the center and insert a small brass envelope closure through the arrow. Flatten the edges and place a Velcro circle on the brass closure. Place another Velcro circle near the top of each participant monitor. Affix the arrow to the monitor by placing the Velcro circles together. While participants are working individually or in pairs, the green part of the arrow is in the up position if things are fine. If there is a question, the red arrow goes up. As the participants are working, the instructor can circulate. Even while coaching others, the instructor can easily scan the room and see if others need help. This allows participants to indicate a need for help, but also keep working until help is available.

Or for an even quicker impromptu version, have them make a table tent that then rests on top of their monitor. When they tip their table tent up on end, it means that they need the instructor to come over to help. If the table tent is in its normal position, even if they are struggling, they are not desiring help at this time.

Of course, when the instructor does come over, the first question he or she will ask is "Have you asked three before me?"

Ask Three before Me

This sign in your room will encourage participants to ask each other questions before coming to you. This honors the experience and the knowledge that other participants have, reinforces the learning, and makes your computer training more participant centered. The guideline is simple: if there is something you do not understand, ask three other participants for help before you ask the instructor.

Fill in the Form

If your training includes participants learning to fill in online forms, then this technique is for you. Make a PowerPoint of the form. Project the form on a blank piece of chart paper. One participant volunteers to fill in the form. The scribe is not the one on the hot seat. He or she merely fills in the forms based on the input of other group members. You might change scribes periodically. When the form is complete, you simply replace the used chart paper with a new sheet and you're ready to repeat the process.

While this chapter is directed specifically at training to use computers or software, obviously even these ideas can be adapted to technical and other types of training. Remember—modify, adjust, adapt, and then adopt!

Chapter 14:
The Myths and Methods of eLearning

Separating Fact from Fiction and Making the New Technology Work for You

eLearning is a hot topic today—and probably will be for quite some time. Some view it as another fad that will soon fade. Others perceive it as a silver bullet that will solve all problems. Neither of these is quite true. The truth probably lies somewhere between the two of them.

To make eLearning work, we need to understand the potential benefits and the limitations it offers. Here are some of the most common benefits:

- Content can be widely distributed. If you can access a computer, you can access the content.
- Content can be made available 24 hours a day, 7 days per week.
- You save money on travel.
- You do not have to wait for the next class.
- With proper design, it is easily updated.

Here are some of the most common limitations:

- Not everyone likes to—or can—use a computer. As much as 70 percent of the population prefers learning as part of a group, rather than learning by themselves.
- Not everything can be taught online. Dave Arch has a great rule of thumb: If you can test it online, you can teach it online. Can you test someone on swimming ability online? In most cases, the answer would be "no." You can test someone online about the facts of swimming, but not their ability. Therefore, although you could teach someone *about* swimming, you cannot teach someone to swim online.
- A poorly designed classroom course is even worse when converted to an online course.

As I write this chapter, the current data suggests that 85 percent of all online programs developed are abandoned before full implementation and that 65 percent of all those signing up for an online course never complete it. This says a lot—and at the same time says nothing. Just now people are still figuring out how to do online learning effectively. There is a lot of experimentation going on—even if the vendors people choose to work with are not willing to admit it.

There are a number of reasons for this:

- People developing the technology for delivering online learning are not necessarily instructional designers. Too often the only two people involved on a web design team are the subject matter expert and the technologist who knows how to design the website. Poor classroom design transferred online makes for an even worse course.

- There is a tendency for marketers to over promise. Instead of making eLearning a part of the solution, it's being touted as the entire solution.

- When a solution is available 24/7, it's easy to delay signing on. There's always a crisis coming up that must be dealt with now. Soon the online course is buried under the tyranny of the urgent.

- Management many times has even greater difficulty giving uninterrupted time to employees for this type of training since the employee doesn't leave the site for the training but is still at their work station, just not "doing their work" in the eyes of the manager.

- Some people may sign up needing only a part of the content. Once they have those parts, they don't come back—the rest of the course is not needed.

This chapter, unlike most of the others, needs current support to have the greatest value. I suggest that you visit www. CTTNewsletters.com/4thEdition. At this website, we will be constantly refining ideas that apply to this and other parts of this book so that you can stay current with best practices.

Those who are having the greatest success with eLearning are following these guidelines. They ask themselves, "What parts of a course can be delivered online?" rather than trying to transfer all of the contents of a course to an online format. The cognitive objectives (What do I want them to know?) of a course are typically the easiest to transfer. The behavioral (What skills must they be able to do?) and the attitudinal (What attitudes must they have if they are to be successful implementing the learning?) are the most difficult to do in a cost-effective manner online. At this time, we recommend that a client begin by putting only the cognitive pieces of their content online. They would be well-advised at this current time to continue delivering the behavioral and attitudinal pieces in the classroom. Although this isn't quite the silver bullet for which we had hoped, it could cause a four-day class to become a three-day or even a two-day class. An obvious exception to this rule would be those courses that use online learning to teach computer skills. Here behavioral and attitudinal objectives can be trained online since the student is using the very tool on which they are being trained.

eLearning is used *along with* other types of instruction, including classroom instruction, rather than *instead of.*

Research Factoid

> "In a recently released (2002) two-year study comparing a group who learned a computer software product solely online with a group who learned online in a blended environment found that the blended group showed a 30% increase in accuracy of performance over those who learned soley online. In addition, the blended group completed real-world tasks 41% faster than those who learned solely online."
>
> – Thomson Job Input Study: The Next Generation of Corporate Learning, Thomson Learning Company

In transitioning their employees from classroom to online instruction, an effective strategy has been for the organization to begin with synchronous classes (those in which students and teachers are online at the same time) and then move to some asynchronous classes (those in which students and teachers are not online at the same time).

When thinking of blended learning, the most effective companies don't only think of the blending of classroom and online learning. They include both synchronous and asynchronous courses in the overall strategy to allow for varying learning styles. Synchronous classes seem to work better in dealing with deeper processing of cognitive content.

Research Factoid

> "The question is not if we should blend. Rather, the question is what are the ingredients?"
>
> – E-Learning Strategies for Delivering Knowledge in the Digital Age, Marc Rosenberg, McGraw-Hill, 2001

Whenever possible, classroom standards are paralleled in the online course implementation. This includes things like scheduling the time that you will be online for each lesson, even if it's asynchronous, rather than making it available 24/7. If there are multiple modules, participants should complete each module in order or test out of the module, before the next module is made available to them. There is a window of availability for each module so that participants maintain signing on for each module as a firm appointment, rather than delaying until multiple modules must be covered in a much shortened time frame. Those classroom standards also include those proven best practices gathered from generations of working in the classroom as presented in this book (i.e., using the instructor-led and participant-centered instructional model, having an opening and closing, and creatively adapting alternatives to lecture to the online learning environment).

There is an instructional designer involved in the design process. The role of the instructional designer becomes crucial since in an asynchronous class there is no live instructor involved directly in the delivery of the content. In a classroom, it is often the instructor's personality that can help compensate for poor instructional design. In an online asynchronous class, the instructional designer literally becomes the instructor. This person typically serves as a bridge—taking the content from a subject matter expert, reworking it to make it as easy as possible for the student to retain it, and then passing it on to the technologist who will actually put it onto the web. When there is no instructional designer involved, either the subject matter expert or the technologist becomes the instructional designer often without adequate understanding of the best practices involved with such an assignment.

Extensive use is made of eLearning to either prepare participants for classroom segments or to follow up and reinforce what participants have learned in the classroom. This is where eLearning shines and can truly deliver what it promises.

Accountability with and to others is built into the online process. Study groups may be formed, even for asynchronous courses. Learning triads may be developed. As participants develop plans for how they'll use the new knowledge and skills on the job, they have two other people as part of their accountability team. This team is available to help solve problems that may arise. They also hold one another accountable for putting the ideas and skills into practice. One of the most common complaints from eLearning participants is that unlike classroom instruction, it does not include a social component. Through email groups, polling, bulletin boards, chat rooms, and other technological tools, this complaint can be overcome even in an asynchronous environment while increasing the content retention of the participants too.

So, how can you start using this new delivery method? Here are some basic tips and strategies to make online learning work for you. Keep in mind that there are two basic delivery methods, synchronous and asynchronous. With synchronous courses, you have real time delivery. Everyone must be online at the same time (which is what synchronous means—at the same time). Asynchronous courses can be placed online for delivery anytime (asynchronous means *not* at the same time—or at different times.)

Here are some basic strategies that apply to either synchronous or asynchronous classes:

1. **Use incomplete handouts.** Any time people start writing, they start anchoring what they are learning in another way. Writing helps keep people involved and focused. You don't want them writing too much, however. We've all had the experience of having an instructor use a visual that had so much information that we started writing as fast as we could. We were trying to copy the visual before it went away. As a result, we weren't listening to anything that was being said *about* the content of the visual. So in all of the courses we design, both online and classroom, we provide a handout that has much of the content, but with key words left out here and there, along with plenty of note space.

   This is a much better alternative than either no handout or a complete handout. We want to utilize every opportunity we can to create interaction—even between participants and the handout.

Utilizing this incomplete handout method provides structure for the participants, but also uses the Zeigarnik effect. This principle of incompletion is based on the psychological principle that says we want completion. When it is not present, we seek to find ways to make it happen.

This method also helps keep the participant on task as the course progresses while providing them with an opportunity to look away from the screen during this seat work, and then provides them an invaluable job aid to use a resource after they've completed the course.

2. **Utilize lecture alternatives.** As you know from reading Chapter 11 on modifying and customizing training programs, the process includes over 36 alternatives to lecture. When possible, avoid having the student receiving the material merely by reading it. Rather seek to adapt those proven classroom strategies of case studies, debate, video, audio files, etc., to bring variety and greater interactivity (and consequently higher retention) to the learning experience.

3. **Include a social component.** Whether participants are taking the online course at the same time (synchronous) or at different times (asynchronous), it is possible and highly desirable to include a social component. What does this mean? It means that we have to remember that over 75 percent of the people we've surveyed prefer to learn as a part of a group, rather than learning alone. Anything we can do to create that feeling online will enhance people's ability to learn.

   You can use chat rooms, bulletin boards, and email groups (http://www.listbot.com), to ensure a social component is included in your online class—allowing students to interact with the others taking the class even outside the class. You can also take advantage of social media and create a private Facebook fan page, or a private LinkedIn group.

4. **Give access to the instructor even offline.** Of course, with most synchronous courses, an instructor is online with participants. However, having the instructor available offline adds a personal touch both for synchronous and asynchronous participants. Certainly email can (and should) be used, but having an instructor (and even subject matter experts (SMEs) available at set times in a chat room environment greatly increases the satisfaction and success of the students.

   Have you ever tried to contact a company by phone, only to be greeted by a loop of answering machines? Undoubtedly, with each new answering machine, your motivation for using that company's services diminished. The same is true of an online class to which a live instructor is not assigned. The motivation of the students decreases.

   So, even when participants take a program by themselves, seek to provide opportunities when they can connect with an instructor in real time or through email periodically, just as they can go to a chat room at scheduled times and interact with others taking a program on their own.

5. **Prioritize your content.** We covered this in the chapter on transforming programs from leader-based to learner-based. It also applies to both types of online learning. It is no longer possible to teach anyone everything about anything. By organizing around the "Need to Knows," the "Nice to Knows," and the "Where to Goes," we enable participants to feel that to some extent they can get their arms around a subject without being overwhelmed. Using this methodology gives participants a sense of security because they can see the order of the content.

6. **Chunk your content.** Break all of your content into modules of 20 minutes or less. This gives the synchronous learners a chance to then process what they've been learning with others online with them.

   It allows asynchronous learners an opportunity to take a break without feeling they've left something undone. For asynchronous learners by sticking to small units of 20 minutes or less, we can also provide an opportunity for them to answer questions or complete a problem-solving project to help ensure understanding of the content.

7. **Utilize openers, closers, energizers, and review techniques.** Since classroom learning is enhanced using these components, it becomes even more important to build them into our online courses. We are constantly finding new and better ways to make this work based on improvements in technology. Rather than provide ideas that will rapidly become dated, we're referring you to a site that will provide you with ideas for both synchronous and asynchronous classes. Please do visit www. CTTNewsletters.com/4thEdition for some examples and additional resources surrounding this subject.

Here are three bonus strategies that apply to synchronous classes:

1. **Use pre-session activities.** While waiting for everyone to come online, have music playing and an activity (brain teaser, sentence completion, trivia question, etc.) on which they can work. Avoid merely chatting. Have a countdown clock showing how long until the start of the class. This can easily be done with PowerPoint by manually advancing the slides as you build toward the beginning of the class.

2. **Discuss in small groups of three participants each.** In face-to-face classes, we recommend groups of five to seven, but when you eliminate the visual cues by being online, it becomes much more difficult to foster discussion. By using breakout groups during your synchronous classes (either through your software or conference call provider), you will level the playing field between extroverts and introverts and both will participate. Otherwise, extroverts will dominate the synchronous class discussion and introverts will remain passive.

   By appointing a scribe/reporter before going to the discussion groups, you will also have helped facilitate the reporting following the small group discussions. You can rotate the scribe role so that each person in the group has a leadership opportunity.

Web-Based Instructional Design

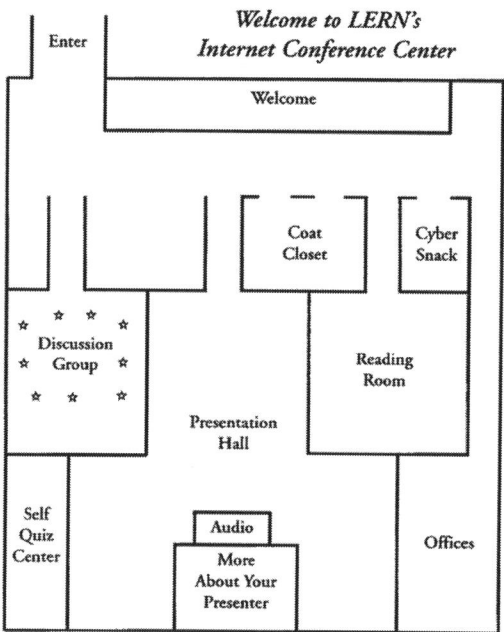

Welcome – where the online course agenda is posted, along with instructions about how to participate.

Presentation Hall – an asynchronous chat room (bulletin board) where instructors provide information and answer questions several times a day. Participants also can make comments here for the instructor to read.

Discussion Group – an asynchronous chat room (bulletin board) where students can talk with other students regarding issues facing them on assignments and answer questions posed by instructors.

Audio – participants can download audio files of presentations made by instructors.

Reading Room – participants can download articles posted by instructors.

Self Quiz Center – participants can take quizzes to see how well they are progressing.

Live Chat Room – at certain times a live chat will be available with the instructors.

Coat Closet – a listing of other presenters with some short bios so others can know who else is participating.

Cyber snack – a cartoon updated weekly for a little break.

Adapted from *Teaching Online* by William A. Draves

Copyright 2002, Dave Arch and Associates. All rights reserved. Used by permission.

3. **Use listening assignments with lectures.** Never lecture without giving a listening assignment (questions they need to be able to answer when the lecture is completed) to the students. You might consider even giving some students one listening assignment and other students another so that afterward you'll have the energy of comparing notes from group to group.

Here are three bonus strategies for asynchronous classes:

1. **Frequently include "submit boxes."** To monitor a student's progress through the process of the class, include frequent stops along the way where the student must submit to a live instructor a response to his/her processing of a given component of the topic. This accountability piece helps the student remain on task and not skip essential processing components within the course.

2. **Encourage personal projects.** Whenever possible, encourage a student to complete a personal project to validate proficiency in addition to any post-testing that you use.

3. **Utilize the "Floor Plan Model" for structuring your course.** On the previous page is an example of a floor plan adapted from the www.lern.org website. This can be the starting point of creating your own.

We recommend this approach to the organization of an asynchronous site since it is a familiar link to your participants' experience in the fact that everyone has been inside a learning center or school of some type.

Using a floor plan also gives the student a sense of physical movement within the courses. At various times within the courses, they will need to go to the "library" to read an article or the "lecture hall" to hear or see a presentation or the "self-testing center" to assess their own competencies.

To see many of the ideas in this chapter come to life, we would also invite you to join us for one of our own online courses. Please visit our website (http://www.CTTNewsletters.com) for the latest in scheduling information.

Chapter 15:
Classroom Management Techniques

How to Let Participant-Centered Techniques Manage Your Classroom and Learning (and Minimize the Impact of Difficult Participants!)

What makes the Creative Training Techniques' instructional model so different from most other classroom delivery processes? One major difference is that we emphasize the power of group dynamics. Our research strongly suggests that more than 75 percent of all learners prefer to learn as a part of a group, rather than by themselves. Learning is a social experience. Yet all too often, we see classrooms where people sit in rows facing the instructor. There is no sense of being part of a group. In fact, we may very well feel alone in a crowd.

If you'd like to test the above thesis, just show up late once to a class. Will the class be sitting there quietly waiting for you? Probably not. In all probability, they will be talking with each other. We are social. Our participants are social. Our instructional model doesn't fight that fact, but rather builds on it.

Instructors normally voice two objections to using the participant-centered process:

1. Involving people adds too much time for the content to be covered. Lecture is faster.
2. If people are allowed to talk to each other, the instructor loses control of the group.

As we've already demonstrated in Chapter 4 on visual aids, when we use the ILPC process, we can reduce the time it takes for participants to master content. This first objection also has as an underlying assumption that covering the content is the goal. When teaching the content becomes the goal, most instructors settle on the fact that by focusing on the "Need to Knows" and giving participants adequate time to process those "Need to Knows," they actually end up teaching more by covering less. In the long run, students will not need to be trained again and again because they didn't "get it" the first time through because way too much content was "dumped" on them. The instructor covered it, but the students did not absorb it.

As for the second objection, the instructor doesn't lose control. Rather responsibility for control passes from the instructor to a group leader. Chaos doesn't reign, learning does. I am fostering an illusion when I believe I am in control just because students are quietly sitting and looking at me during my presentation. They could be mentally sitting on a chaise lounge in Bermuda, and I'd never know it!

The Benefits of the Following Classroom Management Techniques

By using the classroom management techniques that are a part of the ILPC process, you will:

- maximize the involvement of every participant;
- ensure that more vocal participants are heard, but not to the exclusion of your shy participants;
- increase the self-esteem of each participant by providing each with safe leadership opportunities;
- increase each participant's retention of both skills and knowledge by involving more senses in the learning process;
- allow each participant more time to explore and comprehend the key ideas through use of small groups;
- maximize your focus on ensuring each participant's understanding and mastery of skills and knowledge by shifting responsibility for control from you to the participants as a group;
- reduce difficult participant behavior.

Over the years, I've asked participants in my Train-the-Trainer workshops to list the types of difficult participants that they encounter most often. While we have identified 15 different types in my *Dealing with Difficult Participants* book that I co-authored with Dave Arch, there are really five that come up the most often:

1. The know-it-all—or at least they think they do!
2. The Domineering—"I've been here 20 years, and the way I've always seen it work is..."
3. The latecomer
4. The bored
5. The skeptic

Following the strategies in this chapter will eliminate 95 percent or more of the difficult behaviors that most trainers face. And most often your classes will take care of the other 5 percent because you have helped them become responsible for their own learning!

Eight Keys to Classroom Management

The following are eight keys I have found to be very effective in classroom management.

1. Have participants set standards and norms for the class. If a class is longer than a day, I will divide the class into two groups: the Ps (for participants) and the Is (for instructor). Each group is to come up with seven guidelines for either me as the instructor or for them as participants to follow to ensure that everyone gets as much as they can from the class.

After about five minutes, I have each group share their guidelines, and the other group can add or modify based on discussion. I then propose that as the instructor, I'll accept their guidelines if everyone in the class will agree to abide by the participant guidelines. I've yet to see a class that didn't accept this. Then several hours later, I ask each small group to give two scores on a scale of 1 to 10 (10 being perfect): one for me as the instructor in living up to the guidelines and the other for themselves as participants. If the scores aren't 10s, I ask what I need to do to improve as well as what they need to do to improve. Participants will, more often than not, set tougher standards than we would as instructors!

2. Subdivide your class into small groups of five to seven people. If the group is smaller than that, a dominant person can take over; larger than that, and shy people lose airtime.

   Arrange the groups so that each person in the group can see the others. If you have access to round tables, seat them so that they are using no more than two-thirds of the round with the open side of the table to the front of the room. If you don't have access to round tables, push two rectangular tables together and sit two on each side with one or two on the end. Seek to have it so nobody sits with their backs to the instructor. In a lecture hall with rows of seats, I'll have groups form themselves by turning around and getting together with five or six others around them. I once even was faced with just a large conference table for the training. Although not ideal, I was able to use masking tape across the width of the conference table to designate each small group with two people sitting across from each other forming each group and the four participants at the far end of the table being the final group.

3. For each project or activity, have the subgroups choose a group leader. This is a temporary position, not a permanent one. By rotating the group leader, you prevent anyone from claiming ownership of the group.

4. Use variety in choosing these group leaders. One time people might point a finger in the air and on the count of three point to the person they want to be the next leader. Another time, the last leader might choose the next one. Still another time it might be the person in the group with the largest (or smallest) high school, family of origin, number of pets, number of states lived in, etc. Many of these will provoke laughter, which releases positive chemicals into the brain called endorphins. This in turn creates a more positive mood, which is conducive to learning.

   As innocent as these selection processes may appear, they actually give you a method of drawing your more introverted participants out and governing the amount of control and extroverted participant can exercise. When I say, "The person with the most letters in their first name, I know that Bob won't be leading his group that time." When I say, "The person with the most red on will be the new group leader," I know that the introverted person with the red sweater will finally get involved and lead during that round of discussion. I can now control without being heavy handed in my approach. When these classroom management techniques are used exclusively in a classroom, only the scribes ever have opportunity to address the room. Consequently, when I have a negative participant whose poison I don't want spread to the rest of the room, I just need to make sure that the negative person never becomes a scribe for their group.

5. For most activities, have the directions, questions, etc., in print. Have the group leader read the questions, directions, etc., aloud while the group reads along. This ensures that those with undeveloped reading skills still have an opportunity to comprehend the activity. In some cases, you may want only the leader to have the directions. For most activities, it's best for each person to have their own copy for increased comprehension (through reading and hearing), as well as for personal notes, etc. Obviously another alternative is to have the instructions printed on a projected slide or transparency.

6. Have the group leader summarize what the small group discussed with the larger group. In this way, the group leader is reporting the group's thinking, while maintaining the anonymity of individuals within the group. This increases the shy person's sense of safety. The creation of a safe learning environment is essential. These levels of anonymity are key to keeping the training environment safe. Whenever a trainer calls on a participant by name in order to pull that participant into the discussion, I cringe. The training environment has become emotionally unsafe and interactivity will suffer. When I have the randomly selected scribe only report the findings of the group, the scribe is not reporting their own conclusions, but rather only the conclusions of the group. And I don't know what individuals in the group actually suggested those points shared by the group leader or scribe. These layers of anonymity provide a safer environment for honest interactivity.

7. From time to time, change the groups themselves. In a one-day program, establishing groups in the morning and then one more time, say after lunch, is probably enough. In longer programs, we often establish a more permanent "home group" for daily assignments, etc., yet frequently move into other task groups for several hours at a time. Seek to find ways of moving groups that combine some randomness to the selection process. Numbering off is maybe one of the first that might come to mind. However, you might have everyone at the table select a different colored marker. Then designate which table is going to be the "blue table," the "green table," and the "yellow table." You could also have participants select a playing card—indicating then which table is the "diamonds table," the "clubs table," the "hearts table," or the "spades table." The randomness mixed with the movement will help prevent rebellion among participants since it was just the luck of the draw.

Nevertheless, realize that after cards are drawn, numbers are selected, or markers picked, you can designate the table anything you wish. Consequently, if you wish to move a difficult participant to the front of the room, merely notice which colored marker he or she selected and designate one of the front tables with that color. Once again, you've now moved a participant without the need of becoming heavy in the process. I hope your beginning to see that although these techniques feel light, they have the potential of being very tight in your ability to manage the participants.

8. When it's time for questions, either asking or answering them, use your groups. Avoid ever addressing the group at large with that cliché "Are there any questions?" Whenever I use that question, I will typically only hear from the extroverts and most probably from the same extroverts I heard from last time I asked. Does that mean the introverts don't have any questions. Of course not. It merely means I didn't provide a method whereby they could feel comfortable getting their questions heard. Rather say something like, "At your tables, please discuss this question.... You have 90 seconds—Go!" At the end of 90 seconds ask several group leaders to share their group's thinking. If answering questions, have the group take two minutes to come up with two questions they want to ask. At the end of two minutes, announce a time limit for questions and answers of say, 10 to 15 minutes. Have someone keep track of time and announce five-minute intervals—or use a countdown timer that you can project on the screen. Ask a group leader to volunteer a question. Once you've answered, ask the group leader to select the next table to ask a question and so on. You'll have a fast-paced Q&A session, the participants will answer many of the questions for themselves, and you'll have kept control of time.

I once experienced a participant mutiny of sorts. Coming back from lunch, the participants had taken it upon themselves to rearrange the classroom. Of course from what you've read in this chapter, you can be sure that I had seated them around rectangular tables in groups of five to seven participants. They had rearranged all the rectangular tables into a giant horseshoe with participants seated around the outside of the horseshoe. What was I going to do?

I decided that I wouldn't make a big deal about it but rather work with what was in front of me. So we formed our groups of three or four and just had participants push their chairs back from the table to do their discussions before reporting their small group's work to the larger group.

Suddenly, one woman became very loud during the first small-group discussion and launched into a story. It wasn't too long before no one was talking in their small group but were all listening to her. Come to find out, she was the one who had instigated the moving of the tables. It's my theory that she found it frustrating in attempting to control the room as long as they were divided into small groups. In contrast, the horseshoe arrangement of the tables enabled her to gain the attention of the room anytime she wanted.

Of course, that's exactly what I as the instructor didn't want. So the next time I had the groups engage in discussion, I suggested that two of the group members in each group move their chairs to the inside of the U-shaped tables so that they could engage in their discussion—and have something to write on. This they did. When the activity was done, I left them seated there.

Finally, as they did the next activity I said that it was very important that other groups not hear what they were working on. I suggested that they move their tables so that there was some space between them and so that the table members could still see the front of the room. We were now back almost to the room arrangement that we had started with. Notice, though, that I gave a reason for each step I asked them to take. This made it difficult for the woman who had rearranged the room to say anything. What the class was asked to do made sense to them.

Since that day, I have been convinced that the principles for classroom management in this chapter work better than anything I have ever experienced. I challenge you to put them to work for you.

BONUS TIP: When having the small groups discuss, play some quiet background music. This music forms a blanket of noise that makes everyone feel more comfortable to talk in their small group without fear of being heard by other groups. Use music without words or even recognizable tunes to avoid distracting thoughts. Don't play music when individuals are working on a project since many find the music in that context too distracting.

Most people want to learn, most people want to cooperate, most people want to be involved, but sometimes they just don't know how. Using these techniques will help guide them—and at the same time will minimize disruptive behaviors from others that might get in the way.

Chapter 16:
The Virtual Trainer

*Transferring Face-to-Face Classroom Energy Strategies
to the Webinar Environment*

I conducted my first virtual training program in 1986 via satellite. It was for the United States Chamber of Commerce. It was three hours long on the topic of Creative Presentation Techniques, and it was delivered to 10,000 people in 700 locations. By all measures, it was a great success. One key reason it was a success was that I developed and implemented a strategy that allowed me to recreate in a virtual environment what I was able to do in the face-to-face environment so successfully.

I wanted to use small-group discussion in the remote locations and knew that I could not manage them remotely, so I had each remote location appoint a facilitator. I ran a 30-minute pre-session facilitator training session by telephone conference call two days before the actual event. They had in their hands the handout that would be used and the flow outline for the program. It listed what I was going to do and when, and it highlighted what they would be doing and when.

I walked them through these documents, spending extra time and emphasis on what they would be doing to foster interaction and how they would provide feedback to the entire group. They knew that I would have a small group in my studio and that I would model with that group what I wanted them to do in their own groups.

I designed an interactive handout that would have maximum value only if participants filled in as we went along. We took each group and subdivided into groups of five to ensure that everybody would have talking time when it came to the discussions. I followed our 90/20/8 rule, which you learned about in an earlier chapter, to ensure that at least every eight minutes I would have interaction.

Now it's very unlikely that you are ever going to do a webinar for 10,000 people, and to be honest, I'm not sure that delivering a presentation to 10,000 people could ever be considered a training program. The point is, though, if I can apply the techniques and strategies we've been talking about in this book up to now to that size group, we can certainly make it work with the typical webinar of 10, 15, or even 50 people. This chapter will serve as in introduction to all that is needed to be a powerful and positive virtual trainer. If you want to dig deeper, I recommend my daughter, Becky Pike Pluth's excellent book *Webinars with a WOW Factor*.

So let's break it down what we need to do into preparation and the delivery. Special and extra preparations are needed for both participants and the trainer when the webinar is the delivery method for training. This is true because both participants and the trainer initially are unfamiliar with the webinar environment. In the classroom, you know how to raise your hand. In the classroom, we have visual cues that tell us as trainers that participants are tracking with us or that they are not. Not so with the webinar environment. Here are the tips for preparation:

1. Get totally familiar with the tools that are available in your webinar platform. Most commonly available webinar platforms have at the very least text chat, polling, whiteboards, application sharing, and video. Many have voice over IP (VoIP) so that people can hear one another talk and also allow for breakout rooms. Knowing that you have the tools and knowing how to use them are two entirely different things. If possible, attend as a participant a webinar that uses your platform before you serve as an instructor of a webinar.

2. Start small and build from there. Your first webinar should be no longer than an hour, and you should limit the attendance to 12 to 15 people. Build your own skills before you roll out to longer webinars or larger groups.

3. Create a flow for your webinar and design the hour around 90/20/4. Your largest content chunk will be 20 minutes and you will involve everyone every four minutes. Why is this different from 90/20/8? Because in the classroom, we have visual cues; online we do not. We need to make sure that we involve and engage people every four minutes because there are too many distractions that you have no control over.

4. Go over your handout, visuals, content, and flow with your producer. The producer is the person that has been equipped to handle all of the technical details that are needed to make the training flow smoothly. This includes things like making sure that all participants have headsets and microphones so that they can fully participate, making sure that participants know how to download the handout, solving individual technical challenges during the webinar so that you can stay focused on the content delivery, keeping track of questions being sent to you via text chat and cutting and pasting them to the main screen as you answer them, setting up the polls and breakout rooms, and so much more.

5. If you are developing content for delivery multiple times and for larger groups, be sure to include a dry run. This is a complete dress rehearsal with at least six people so that you can check timing, delivery, moving into and out of breakout groups, etc., so that technical concerns do not disrupt your webinar when you roll it out.

6. As you plan your flow, plan for questions and answers, and plan for reflection time/action planning. For a one-hour session, I'm going to plan for five minutes of Q&A at the 40-minute mark. If I have only a one-hour session, I'll allow them to reflect and type their questions in the chat box. The producer puts up a five-minute time and feeds me the most relevant questions. These are the ones that get posted on the main screen and the ones I respond to. At the end of five minutes, I move on. If there are leftover questions, I'll either send a follow-up email with my answers or create a short podcast to provide an audio response.

7. Your ideal breakout size is three people. In the classroom, we say the ideal group is five to seven people. But in the virtual world, we are losing the visual cues. When I go to an audio only breakout, I can readily tell the difference between two other voices and my own. The pauses waiting to see if someone

wants to say something will be shorter than if five people were in the breakout. It is easier to ask and answer questions of one another, make decisions, create a whiteboard response, etc., with just three people.

8. Plan your opener and closer. In a webinar, I'm going to start a soft opener to engage people three to five minutes before the announced start time. At the start time, my producer can either introduce me or let the soft opener go for another minute. After the introduction, I have my opener. For an hour, it's going to be one to two minutes. Often it will be having people respond to a question via text chat. In a one-hour webinar, I'm going to have people take two minutes to action plan just after the Q&A at 40 minutes. Then five minutes before the end, I'm going to give them one more minute to add one more idea. After this, I'll have one question that they text chat the answer to serve as my evaluation. I never say, "Before we close…." Instead I say, "Before we continue…" and ask the question.

9. Use variety. Some people get used to polling, and it's all they do. The same for text chat, etc. You can use the same technique several times; just make sure that it is not several times in a row.

10. Plan for quick energizers to keep energy up and to get people refocused. Here are a few that I've found fool proof:

   a) Fill in the blanks. Put a partial handout on the whiteboard, and in a box to the side, put the hints that complete the blanks. Participants draw a line from the hint in the box to the blank where it is needed.

   b) Conduct a poll. Thirty-five minutes in, I might put a poll like this on the whiteboard:

   > The pace of the webinar is:
   > A. Too fast
   > B. Too slow
   > C. Just about right

   c) Look outside and report back. Participants get up from their computers, go to the nearest window, and come back and text chat something they see. This might be about weather, scenery, etc. This especially helps geographically divergent participants

   d) Stand up, especially in conjunction with action planning. Write down two action ideas on your handout; as soon as you have two, type "up" and stand up for 30 seconds.

   e) Have 30-second text chat discussions to provide quick answers to a question: What is the biggest challenge, mistake, problem, shortcoming, need, etc.?

Now let's turn to delivery. Eighty percent of the effectiveness of a webinar happens because of the right preparation. But delivery is what puts it over the top. Bad classroom training doesn't get better on a webinar. It gets infinitely worse. Here are seven tips for delivery:

1. As a virtual trainer, you need to project as much or more energy than you would in the classroom. The problem is that in the classroom, you can feed off the visual cues you get from your participants to up your energy. This was why I had a small group in the studio I presented from for the Chamber of Commerce. On a webinar, you most often don't have that opportunity. So what do you do? Here's one of best secrets: tape a small photo of someone you care about, someone who energizes you next to your webcam. Focus on the photo, not the camera. This will raise your energy level—at least it does mine. And it helps you focus on the camera so that your eye contact with participants has intensity. Many virtual presenters tend to end up fixated on the whiteboard where their visuals are.

2. Keep a countdown timer running on your smartphone. This enables you to stay on top of the pacing. Have your flow sheet for the webinar right next to it.

3. Be online early. For me, this means 30 minutes before the training starts. I can't count the number of times I've checked all the technology the night before and it worked fine. Then the next morning, when I go online, there is a glitch.

4. Have a backup plan. My producer has several things that they can do to keep the webinar moving if I get kicked off for some reason. I am also log on with two different computers, so if one goes down, I can simply switch to the other.

5. Don't be afraid of silence. If you ask a question and want people to answer verbally, ask it this way: "You have 60 seconds to think of your answer to this question. You can type your answer into the chat box, but don't hit send until the onscreen time hits zero. At the end of your answer, if you'd be willing to talk with me about your response, simply add 'let's talk.'" Generally I'll have at least one or two who will respond positively. My producer can then open their microphone, we have a brief chat, and then move on.

6. Start and end on time. If anything, end a few minutes early. This is almost impossible to do in a one-hour session, and much easier when you are doing sessions of two to three hours (which is normally the maximum time for a single session).

7. Tell people how to choose their group leaders before you send them to breakouts. For example: "In just a minute, you'll be going to your breakouts. When you arrive, you'll find two questions on the whiteboard for your team to answer in two minutes. Your group leader will be the person who most recently played an online game (prior to this session of course!!). Type your answers to the question on the whiteboard. Your two minutes begins now."

Remember that almost everything in this book is adaptable to the virtual environment. It simply takes a little thought. If you want to see how I model these, I have a number of archived webinars at www.trainingmagnetwork.com/calendar. Then simply enter "Bob Pike" in the search box.

Appendix 1
Potpourri

In preparing *Master Trainer Handbook,* I came across a couple of lists that I had written for seminar participants. The content of each list seems relevant to the content of this book but doesn't fit naturally into any one chapter. I offer the following nuggets here for you to mine and use.

27 Factors that Can *Make* or *Break* a Meeting

1. Have a complete agenda.
2. Start and end on time.
3. Keep speakers' introduction brief.
4. Pay attention to small details. Use coffee cups instead of Styrofoam, glasses instead of disposable cups.
5. Provide a pad and pencil for each participant.
6. Use a coffee break alternative. Distribute Popsicles or make sundaes instead!
7. Provide a nonalcoholic alternative at receptions.
8. Be prompt with a post-meeting follow-up.
9. Create opportunities for members to mix.
10. Serve lighter lunches and skip dessert. This helps participants remain alert all afternoon.
11. Allow adequate break time for renewing friendships and informal networking.
12. Make your preparation obvious to everyone. Have a check-in staff that is prepared and knowledgeable.
13. Use a variety in your room setups. For example, for a two-day program, use banquet rounds on day one and herringbone 6 x 30 tables the next day.
14. Check out the audio system beforehand.
15. Make certain that meetings won't be interrupted. Tell the facility management that calls should be held, etc.
16. Know who you should contact if there are problems with the facility—for example, the room is too hot or too cold.
17. Check out the facilities before the meeting begins to see that room setup and audio/video requirements have been met.
18. Make registration simple and easy.

19. If you have a two- or three-day meeting, offer a spouse program. Check out special happenings and points of interest in the city where you are meeting.
20. Make certain that program materials are shipped to a specific person at the meeting site; otherwise, they may be misplaced. Also, clearly mark them as 1 of 3, 2 of 3, etc., to avoid confusion.
21. Send a detailed cover letter along with your signed contract that explains exactly what you expect from the facility staff. Include a few facts about what you *don't* want to have happen.
22. Be available. If you are unable to be at your meeting, confirm with your speaker and facility contact that, should a problem arise, you are only a phone call away.
23. Send copies of facility agreements to all speakers and other necessary meeting staff.
24. If your meeting will last more than one day, arrive a day early. If it is a single-day meeting, arrive at least two hours beforehand.
25. Have your meeting place compatible with your objectives. For example, don't schedule meetings for 16 hours a day in a resort setting or for 4 hours a day where there are no activities available.
26. Have an agreement with your speakers about "selling" during his/her presentation. Nothing turns off an audience more than being subjected to unsolicited commercials.
27. Have your speakers available for informal discussions and functions immediately after presentations and during social hours and meals. Avoid "hit and run" presentations.

Ways to Evaluate Training

1. Ask: How does the training contribute to the organization's goals? Does your training solve performance problems? The problems to be solved must be identified and agreed upon in advance. Management must agree on what constitutes improvement before the training begins.
2. Ask: Does the training achieve learning objectives? In other words, what can the trainees do now or what do they know now that they couldn't do or didn't know before?
3. Ask: Does the training have perceived value? Do the trainees, their managers, and the people who provide the budget feel that the training is practical, relevant, and useful? You must decide whose opinions count and how they are expressed.
4. Identify the tasks the job requires including under what conditions, along with standards. Evaluate pre- and post-participants on their ability to meet those standards.

Appendix 1

5. Evaluate the effectiveness of instructors and others involved in delivering the training.
6. Evaluate the effectiveness and frequency of opportunities to perform the new skills and behaviors back on the job.
7. Evaluate the effectiveness, frequency, and appropriateness of on-the-job feedback and support.
8. Use the experimental approach: Compare trained versus untrained or pre- and post-training participants or some combination of both.
9. Use the critical incident approach: Collect specific incidents or stories that support how the training improved performance.
10. Use the problem-solving approach: Rather than offering generic, one-size-fits-all training, design and deliver training geared to a specific, identified, agreed-upon problem.
11. Evaluate the program's opening: Did it get attention, get agreement of needs, state objectives, and establish learner accountability?
12. Evaluate the learning experiences: Were they real life? Relevant? Involving? Did they provide learners with feedback?
13. Evaluate communication: Was the presenter clear to all learners? Did the nonverbal aspects support the verbal aspects?
14. Evaluate instructor attitudes: Were they inoffensive to all learners? Did they stimulate the interest of all learners?
15. Evaluate training objectives: To what extent did participants achieve the pre-specified objectives?
16. Identify the strongest features of the training program.
17. Identify the weakest features of the training program.
18. Have participants list new ideas they picked up as a result of the program or new behaviors they will practice.
19. Ask supervisors to answer the above question for their participants.

Appendix 2
Do I buy or do I build?

This appendix will provide you with some simple job aids that you can use to help you make buy-or-build decisions when it comes to training programs. These are the same aids we use with our clients in helping them make decisions about the best use of our expertise to help them with instructional design projects or train-the-trainer initiatives.

Buy or Build Checklist

The checklist on the following page will help you decide whether it is better to develop a training program (or anything for that matter) internally or to work with an external resource.

Job Aid: Buy or Build Checklist

Simply adding up the columns of this job aid will not determine the buy or build decision. But it will help to clarify your thoughts before making the final decision.

The first column lists the seven factors to be considered before deciding to make or buy. Space is provided for other factors relevant to your particular situation. The factors listed are not in any priority order. That's your job.

In the second column, rank order the factors by their importance to you and your organization at this time. Rank "1" the factor you consider most important and so forth until you have ranked each factor from most to least important.

In the third column, compare your organization's capability to produce the needed training internally to that of an external resource. Place an "M" next to those factors you believe your company is better suited for than an external resource. Place a "B" where you believe the external resource can do a better job. Place an "O" where you think either one can do the job. Then ask yourself:

- Is the factor you ranked #1 of such overriding importance that it overpowers considering anything else? If so, what letter appears in the third column next to that factor?
- Looking at the top three factors you have ranked in importance, is the same letter next to two of them in the third column?
- Are there a lot of "Os" in the third column? Would this indicate that whichever way you decide, it doesn't make much difference?
- Have you compared your checklist answers with those of others in your organization who also know its internal capabilities and understand what is available externally?

FACTORS	PRIORITY OF FACTOR 1 = most critical 7 = least critical	CAPABILITY M = internal best job B = external best job O = either
Cost		
Budget		
Time		
Expertise/Experience		
Quality		
Audience		
History/Culture		

Copyright © 2000, The Bob Pike Group. All rights reserved.

10 Considerations when Evaluating Off-the-Shelf Programs

This page provides 10 things to look for if you are considering an outside vendor. Never consider one unless their ability to deliver what you need is so superior you need not go elsewhere.

> **10 Considerations when Evaluating Off-the-Shelf Programs**
>
> 1. Up-to-date and relevant content
> 2. Clear learning objectives.
> 3. Interactive.
> 4. Visually stimulating print materials.
> 5. Good audio/visual support materials.
> 6. Easy to follow instructions.
> 7. Reasonably priced.
> 8. Variety of supporting materials.
> 9. Variety of design.
> 10. Ability to personalize/customize.

Choosing the External Resource

The job aid on the following page will help you compare multiple vendors you might be considering for a project. Note that this form allows you to weigh considerations differently. It's important to remember that just because you have five items to consider that all five are not of equal importance in all likelihood. This form allows you to weigh the various factors according to their relative importance.

Job Aid: Choosing the External Resource

This job aid will help you organize the data on the various external resources that have been identified. Like the Buy or Build job aid, this one takes into account your organization's specific situation once you have decided to buy.

Column 1 lists the factors covered previously when considering an external resource.

Column 2 is for weighing each factor relevant to your organization's current situation. These ratings will change as situations change. Rate each factor from "10" for very important to "0" for not important.

Column 3 is for evaluating up to four external resources on all factors. Rate each external resource on each factor from "5" for the highest rating (can satisfy this factor completely) to "0" for the lowest rating (fails to satisfy). Base the rating objectively on the data you have gathered.

Column 4 provides space for a weighted point total for each factor. Multiply the number in Column 2 by the number in Column 3 a, b, c, or d and record the totals in Column 4 a, b, c, or d. To get a cumulative total for each external resource, add the numbers in Column 4.

[1] Factors	[2] Weighing for Factors 10 = high 0 = low	[3] Rating of External Resources 5 = high 0 = low				[4] Point for External Resources Columns 2 x 3 = 4			
		a	b	c	d	a	b	c	d
Objectives/Needs									
Price									
Value									
Time									
Quality									
Expertise/Experience									
References									
Reactions									
					CUMULATIVE POINT TOTALS =				

Firms being considered:

a. _____ b. _____

c. _____ d. _____

Copyright © 2000, The Bob Pike Group. All rights reserved.

Appendix 3

20 Books that Support Bob Pike's Instructor-Led, Participant-Centered Process

As I mentioned in Chapter 1, I seldom in my 45 years have applied research. I have found things that work through experience—and then later either found or was told about research that explained why what I did worked. So, for those who like the research that supports everything in this book—here are the sources I'd recommend:

1. How the Brain Learns, 4th edition, David Sousa, Corwin 2011. Memory and Learning, Chunking, Revisiting

2. The New Science of Learning: How to Learn in Harmony with Your Brain, Doyle, Terry & Zakrasjek, Todd, Stylus 2013. Memory, Movement, Using all the senses, Reflection, Focus and Clarity

3. The Jossey-Bass Reader on the Brain and Learning, Fischer, Kurt, editor, Jossey-Bass, 2007 Memory and Learning, Chunking, Revisiting, Windowpaning, Multiple Intelligences, Music & Learning

4. The Learning Brain: Lessons for Education, Blakemore, Sarah-Jayne and Frith, Uta, Blackwell 2005 Learning and Remembering, Teaching the same thing different ways, Appealing to Multiple Learning Preferences

5. Teaching to the Brain's Natural Learning Systems, Givens, Barbara, ASD, 2002 Reflection, Focus, Memory and Learning

6. Ten Best Teaching Practices: How Brain Research and Learning Styles Define Teaching Competencies, Walker Tileston, Donna E., Corwin, 2011 Learning Environment, Audio-Visual-Kinesthetic, Honoring Experience, Memory and Learning, Collaborative Learning, Real World Application

7. Designing Brain Compatible Learning, Gregory, Gayle & Parry, Terence, Corwin 2006 Graphic Organizers, Windowpaning, Collaborative Learning, Multiple Intelligences

8. Smart Moves: Why Learning is Not All In Your Head, Second Edition, Hannaford, Carla, Ph.D., Great River Books 2005 Movement, Oxygen

9. Tuning the Human Instrument: An Owner's Manual, Halpern, Steven, Spectrum Research, 1978 Music and Learning, Reflection, Discussion, Energizing, Focus and Clarity

10. Soundtracks for Learning: Using Music in the Classroom, Brewer, Chris, Lifesounds Educational Services, 2008 Music and Learning, Reflection, Discussion, Learning Cycles, Music and Memory

11. Human Learning and Memory, Lieberman, David, Cambridge University Press, 2012 Memory and Learning, Experiential Learning, Chunking, Association

12. Unlimited Memory: How to Use Advanced Learning Strategies to Learn Faster, Remember More, and Be More Productive, Horsley, Kevin, TCK Publishing 2014 Concentration, Storytelling, Linking

13. Mind, Brain, & Education: Neuroscience Implications for the Classroom, Sousa, David , Editor, solution Tree Press, 2010 Teaching and Learning, Memory

14. How People Learn: Brain, Mind, Experience, and School—Expanded Edition, Bransford, John D, Brown, Ann L., and Cocking, Rodney R. Editors, National Academy Press, 2000 Learning Environments, Expert versus Novice, Learning and Transfer

15. Mind, Brain, and Education Science, Tokuhama-Espinosa, Tracey, W.W. Norton, 2011 Evidence-based learning, experiential learning, psychology and learning, the science of learning, Memory and Learning

16. The Working Memory Advantage, Alloway, Tracy and Alloway, Russ, Simon and Schuster, 2013, Memory and Learning, Windowpaning, Graphic Organizers, Linking

17. Memory, Mind, and Emotions, Greenwood-Robinson, Maggie, Rodale Press, 2007 Memory and Learning, Memory techniques, Learning and Moving

18. Brain Power: Unlock the Power of Your Mind, Beaumont, J. Graham, Harper and Row 1989, Spatial Learning, Music and Learning, Writing and Memory

19. How Learning Works: Seven Research-based Principles for Smart Teaching, Ambrose, Susan, et al, Jossey-Bass 2010, Honoring experience, Stages of competence, Practice and Feedback

20. Learner-Centered Teaching: Five Key Changes to Practice, 2nd Edition, Weimer, Maryellen, Jossey-Bass 2013, Learning from experience, Learner motivation, Giving choices, not assignments. Collaboration, Reflection

Index

accomplishment, fostering sense of, 28, 45, 139, 165
accountability
    insisting on, 52
    online courses, 222–26
    in small-group environments, 12, 14, 92
acoustics, 71
ACT (Action planning, Celebration, Tie things together) closers, 189–90
action idea lists, 188
action steps, follow up, 34
active learning, 81
activity guide sheets, 130–31
ADA (activity/discussion/application) approach, 90–92
additional ideas checklist, 137
Adventures in Attitudes, 3
advisory committees, 17
AIDA formula for developing presentations, 33–34
American Society for Training and Development (ASTD), 3
anecdotesl, 154–55
Angelo, T. A., 25, 37, 38, 81
applying/using content. *See also* reinforcing/reviewing content
    carry-over activities, 35, 48
    checklists of additional ideas, 137
    planning for, 28–29
    providing opportunities for, 40, 51–52
approval, and motivation, 45
Arch, Dave, 202, 214, 219
Aristotle, 31
arrows, 217
asking, *vs.* telling, value of, 42–43
"Ask It" Basket, 204
"Ask Three before Me" technique, 217
assessments. *See* evaluation strategies; instrumented learning (assessments)
asynchronous online courses, 222, 225–26
attention-getting techniques, 33–34, 56. *See also* energizers; motivation, motivators; openers; visual aids, graphics
audience. *See* participants
audio visual materials. *See* visual aids, graphics
authoritarian instructors, 42–43, 87–88, 94, 227
authority/levels of influence, 21
AWA (Able, Willing, Allowed) process, 11
"awareness" knowledge level, 18

BAR (Break preoccupation, Allow networking, Relate opening to content) openers, 190
behavioral change, as goal, 6, 41, 140, 166
Berger, Mike, 146
Berliner, D. C., 28, 140
biographical sketch, instructor's, in resource materials, 126
Birnbrauer, Bernie, 58
blended learning, 220–21
Bob Pike's Master Trainer Newsletter, xiv
Bob Pike's Performance Solutions Cube, 9–11
books about training, 247–48
brainstorming, example questions, 19
brain teasers, 186, 198
brainwriting, 208–9
breaking things, 203
breakout sessions/groups
    providing opportunities for, 153
    spaces for, 60
    during synchronous classes, 224
    webinars *vs.* classrooms, 234–36
breaks. *See also* energizers; motivation, motivators
    controlled stretching, 191
    instructor availability during, 39, 48
    returning from on time, 44, 90, 104–5, 132, 150, 191
Broade, Mary, 192
Brophy, J. E., 97, 101, 109, 128
buy-in for training
    importance, 8
    tips for achieving, 16–17
Buy or Build Checklist, 244
Buzan, Tony, 27, 144, 208
Buzz Groups, 97, 102

calls to action, 153
calls to action, ending programs with, 144–46
Camtasia program, 61
"Capture the Question" Board, 204
C.A.R.E. (Creator, Advancer, Refiner, Executor) roles, 180
carry-over activities. *See* applying/using content
case studies, effective, 114–15
chalkboards, 63
charts, 133, 225. *See also* visual aids, graphics
children, approach to learning, 4–5
choices, importance of offering, 51, 115
chunking, 142, 171, 224

classroom management techniques (IL-PC). *See also* small groups
   applying to virtual classrooms/webinars, 233
   benefits, 227–28
   and handling difficult participants, 228–29
   managing small groups and group leaders, 229–31
   participant-set standards and guidelines, 228–29
clip art, 76
closers. *See also* applying/using content; reinforcing/revisiting content
   ACT approach, 189–90
   for online courses, 224
   punctuating conclusions, 153–55
   webinars/virtual classes, 235
Coaching Effectiveness Assessment, 179
coaching-related problems, 11
color, in visuals, 75, 199
communications, effective, 161–162. *See also* language; presenting programs/training
competence
   levels of, Howell's paradigm, 7
   of participants, assessing, 18
competition, wholesome, 46–47
computer graphics, PowerPoint, 60–61, 67–70
computer-literacy grid, 21–22, 120–21
computer training
   "Ask Three before Me" technique, 217
   assessing knowledge of participants, 214–15
   "Fill in the Form" technique, 217
   flow charts, 215–216
   handling poor quality documentation, 212–14
   ILPCicizing, 211
   mentoring, 215
   offline and online work, 216
   room setup, 211–12
   self-paced projects, 216
   using double-ended arrows, 217
   using metaphors, 215
   using screen curtains to improve focus, 215
confidence building tools, 25, 57
Confucius, aphorism from, 4, 8, 28
consultants
   evaluating, 245
   using in training programs, 60, 163–66
Consulting Envelopes, 205
content. *See also* presenting programs/training
   applicability/relevance, reinforcing, 27–29, 35, 40, 45, 48, 51–52, 83, 137
   chunking, 171, 224

    lesson development outlines, 27
    presenting, 97–104
    prioritizing for online courses, 224
    varying transitions between, 28
    for webinars, reviewing with producer, 234
conversations, as method of instruction, 101
CPR (Content, Participation, Revisiting) approach, 83, 183–4
Create for Other Teams question-handling technique, 204–5
Creative Training Techniques, 227
credibility, reinforcing, 17, 126, 158
Creek, R., 17
criticism of participants, avoiding, 40, 42
crossword puzzles, 207
cultural differences, approaches to, 50–53
curiosity, arousing, 26, 91, 152, 177, 181
customizing programs, 163–66

data, participants' own, validity of, 5, 19, 29, 43, 82, 151
Dealing with Difficult Participants (Pike and Arch), 18–19
debate
    avoiding as trainer, 87, 94
    as instruction method, 101, 223
DeCecco, J. P., 24
decision makers, identifying, 21
demonstrations, 22, 103
designing/developing programs. *See also* environment, physical; evaluation
  strategies; presenting programs/training'; reinforcing/reviewing content; small
  groups
    audience assessment, 17–18
    brainstorming approaches, 172
    carry-over activities, 29, 35
    choosing an approach, 24–25, 144–145
    choosing and ordering methods, 171
    clarifying aims and goals, 8, 23–24, 82–83, 139–40, 197
    clarifying number of participants, 22
    designing for the senders, 16
    dry runs, rehearsals, 172
    gathering materials, room preparation, 29–30, 67
    handling cultural and generational differences, 50–53
    identifying general and specific needs, 15
    importance, 15
    and learning preferences, 49–50
    lectures. lecturettes, 31–33
    lesson application planning, 28–29
    levels of influence, 20, 21
    levels of language, 19–21

making participants aware of, 89
  mind mapping approach, 168–70
  minimalist sets, 171
  needs assessments, 15–16
  new-twist approach, 145–46
  online courses, 222–24
  openers, 24–26
  outlining lessons, benefits of, 26–27
  past, present, future approach, 145
  pilot programs, 164, 173
  preparing support materials, 123
  presentation development, 33–34
  problem-solving approach,
  researching training topics, 23–24
  time of day, factoring in, 23
  training facilities, 22
  transitions, 26, 28
  webinars/virtual class, 233–37
diagrams, 135
digital video cameras, 60
discussion, debriefing materials, 116
documentation, computer, improving as training exercise, 212–14
dots, colored, 206, 212–14

E–A–T approach (Experience Awareness Theory), 92–93
Ebbinghaus, Hermann, 2, 27
effectiveness grids, 21–22, 116–19, 198
Eggan, Paul, 107
eLearning/online courses
  as adjunct to classroom learning, 220–21
  avoiding lectures, 223
  benefits and limitations, 219–20
  best practices, 220–22
  best uses for, 222
  chunking content, 224
  designing, 222
  handouts, 222–23
  prioritizing content, 224
  providing social components, 223
  rates of course completion, 219
  successful programs, guidelines, 220
electrical outlets/power switches, 71
Ellis, E. S., 13, 27
Elmo, tips for using, 61
The Empathic Communicator (Howell), 7
encouragement. as motivator, 45, 154

energizers
   examples of, 146–52
   for online courses, 224
   for pre-existing training programs, 191–92
   for webinars/virtual classes, 235
Ensz, Sue, 12, 215
environment, physical
   acoustics, 71
   aisles, 71
   chairs and seating arrangements, 70–71, 73
   choosing a room, 70
   electrical outlets/power switches, 71
   importance, 29–30
   lighting, 71
   planning for, 22
   room preparation and setup, 29–31, 67–71, 84–85, 211–12
E–T–A approach (Experience, Theory, Awareness), 92
evaluation strategies, 173–75, 194–95, 240–1
excitement
   building among participants, 6, 205–6
   trainer's, communicating, 47, 157
exhibits, as instructional method, 103
experience, hands-on, and effective learning, 3–5, 28, 65, 203
experience/expertise, sharing and learning from. *See also* small groups
   as motivational tool during technical training, 201
   process model, 107–8
   projects and case studies, 114–16
   role-playing methods, 109–13
   value, 21–22, 107
external resources, choosing, 246
eye contact
   among participants, 84
   during computer training, 211–12
   trainer with participants, 39, 47, 118, 156
   during webinars, 236

familiarity with material, assessing, 18
feedback. *See also* evaluation strategies
   from participants, 46, 59, 159, 162, 173–75, 206, 241
   providing to participants, 58–60, 155, 161, 188, 206
   responding to, 175, 179, 206, 233
   using video for, 60, 167
"Fill in the Form" technique, 217
films. *See* videos/films
flannel graphics/flannel boards, 64–65
flip charts, 31, 63–64

"Floor Plan Model," 225–26
flow charts, 136, 215–16
Fogarty, J. L., 17
follow-up activities. *See also* applying/using content; reinforcing/revisiting content
   after meetings, 239
   follow-up discussion sheets, 131
   planning for, 35
   post-training emails, 234
font sizes, typefaces for visuals, 73
forgetting curve (Ebbinghaus), 2
Four Facts exercise, 130–31
Franklin, Benjamin, 107
Fuller, Buckminster, 1
fun factor. *See also* humor
   communicating at start of training, 26
   and effective learning, 5–6
Funnel Concept, 62

Gage, N. L., 140
gallery walks, 189
games, 202–203
general structure *vs.* specific structure learning preference, 49–50
generational differences, tips for handling, 50–53
Gilmore, A. C., 47
goals, identifying and understanding, 8, 23–24, 82, 140, 163, 197
Good, T. L., 97, 101, 109, 128
graphic organizers, 189
graphics. *See* visual aids, graphics
Green and Red Dots technique for handling questions, 204–5
grids, instructional
   computer literacy grid, 21–22, 120–21
   developing, tips, 121–22
   effectiveness grids, 21–22, 116–19, 198
   Instructional Design Grid, 95–97, 133
   as motivational tool, 185
   value of, 119–22
group discussions, 99
group involvement. *See also* participation; small groups
   activity/discussion/application (ADA) approach, 90–92
   and the distribution of materials, 86
   E-A-T approach (Experience Awareness Theory), 92–93
   E-T-A approach (Experience, Theory, Awareness), 92
   and group management techniques, 89–90
   and retention of information, 81
   and room arrangements, 84–85
   and sharing participant's ideas and concerns, 82–83, 94

    T–E–A approach (Theory Experience Awareness), 93
    trainers' fears about, 81–82
group leaders
    choosing and rotating, 51, 90, 229–30
    reports by, 86, 95, 230
    role and importance, 85–86, 150, 229
group mind-map, 23
groups, small. *See* small groups
guided practice, 84

Halpern, Steven, 2
handouts
    importance, 136–37
    incomplete, benefits of using, 61, 128, 222–23
    for participant completion, 45
    providing, benefits, 123
    for webinars, reviewing with producer, 234
highlighters, 206
HOBS (Help Others Become Successful) analysis, 177–79
Howell, William, 7
"How to Use This Workbook" (resource materials), 127
humor, laughter
    as motivational tool, 149–50, 199–200
    off-color, avoiding, 150
    punctuating conclusions using, 153–4

icebreakers, 123
IL-PC. *See* Instructor-Led, Participant-Centered methodology (ILPC)
improvement, desire for, 9
individual activities, providing opportunities for, 52–53
influence levels, 21
informative *vs.* practical learning, 49–50
Innovate with C.A.R.E. assessment instrument, 180
instructional designers, 222
Instructional Design Grid, 95–97, 133, 185
instructional methods
    buzz groups, 102
    case studies, 114–15
    conversations, 101
    debates, 101
    demonstrations, 103
    exhibits, 103
    grids, 116–22
    group discussion, 99
    laboratory, 103
    lectures, lecturettes, 98, 99

panel discussions, 100
  projects, 104, 114–15
  question and answer, 98
  role-playing, skills practice, 102, 109–13
  symposia, 100
  variety of, 97
instructional systems design. *See* designing/developing programs
Instructor-Led, Participant-Centered methodology (ILPC). *See also* classroom management techniques (IL-PC); closers; energizers; evaluation strategies; motivation, motivators; openers
  applying to computer training, 211–17
  applying to technical training, 199–209
  effectiveness, xiii–xiv
  emphasis on discovery and participation, xiv
  focus on results, 192
  and group involvement, 82
  history and development of, 1–4
  ILPCizing, questions to ask, 195
  implementing, tips and suggestions, 12–13, 94–95, 227
  and the Instructional Design Grid, 95–97, 185
  and learning from shared life experiences, 107–8
  methods of instruction, 97–104
  90/20/8 or /4 rule, 27, 184, 284
  Pike's Laws of Adult Learning, 4–7, 28, 82
  role of the instructor, 87–88
  training as process, 8
  transfer strategies, 193–94
  transforming lecture-based content, 183–84
  using eLearing as adjunct to, 220–21
  what it isn't, 4
instructors/trainers
  accessing, in online courses, 223
  authoritarian, 42–43, 87–88, 94
  being available, 47
  communicating excitement, 47, 95, 157
  competency, demonstrating, 123
  effective presenters *vs.*, 2
  as facilitators, 94
  group management by, 89–90
  importance of preparation, 95
  influence prior to training, 193
  outside consultants, evaluating, 164–66
  purpose, xiv
  role and responsibility, 87–88
  teaching techniques, 168–72
  trainer's, communicating, 157

instrumented learning (assessments)
    Coaching Effectiveness Assessment, 179
    evaluating and choosing, 180–82
    HOBS (Help Others Become Successful) analysis, 177–79
    tests and questionnaires *vs.*, 180
    using properly, 177, 180–82
interest of participants
    assessing, 18
    creating and maintaining, 45
    generating during presentations, 34
interpersonal relations and skills, fostering, 13, 23, 48, 89, 182
interval reinforcement, 27

Jacobsen, L., 139
jargon, avoiding, 19–20, 161, 199
Jarvis, Charles, 154

Kauchak, Don, 107
Keynotes
    creating excitement using, 206
    tips for using, 60–61
key points, covering, 57
keystoning, tips for avoiding, 67–70
KFD (know-feel-do) principle, 32
Kirkpatrick, Don, 194
knowledge assessment, 17–18
Kobialka, Daniel, 2

laboratory, as instructional method, 103
language
    clear, importance of using, 19–20, 31
    gender neutral, 115
    jargon, 19–20, 161, 199
    with participants from multiple disciplines, 20–21
    paternal/simplistic, 20
Larkins, A. G., 47
Laws of Adult Learning (Pike), 4–7, 28, 82
LCD projectors, locating, 68
leaders. *See* group leaders
"learner" interest level, 18
learning
    basic principles, 37
    generating desire to learn, 34
    guided practice, 84
    and having fun, 5–6
    ignorance about, 1

and instructional methods, 97–104
knowing what needs to be learned, 82–83
learning styles and preferences, 49–50
learning through experience and practice, 4–5, 8, 28, 65, 107, 109–10, 203, 305
and levels of competence, 7
maximizing among participants, 228
and participation, 3
and providing a safe environment, 230
and retention of information, 81, 141
role of music, 2
and sharing what is learned, 6–7, 42–43. 107
and time for reflection, 52, 93
and visual information, 55
learning instruments (assessments). *See* instrumented learning (assessments)
lectures, lecturettes
   as a component of presentations, 139
   IL-PCicizing, 31–32, 183–84
   integrating listening assignments with, for online courses, 225
   as method of instruction, 98–99
   outlining, 31
   participant learning *vs.*, 12
   researching, 32–33
   using clear language, 31
lettering, in visuals, 73–74, 76
Lewis, C. S., 6
lighting, 71
linking, 142–143
listening assignments, 225
location for training, identifying early, 22
Lorayne, Harry, 2
Lucas, Jerry, 2

magic tricks, 202
managers
   influence before and after training, 193–94
   obtaining buy-in from, 8, 16–17
"mastery" knowledge level, 18
"Match" games, 206
materials/resources. *See* resource materials workbook
McKinney, C. W., 47
measurements, repetitive nonredundant, 16
meetings, conducting, tips for, 239–240
Mehrabian, Albert, 27, 144, 187
memory. *See also* applying/using content; reinforcing/revisiting content
   chunking, 142
      linking, 142–43

primacy, 142
recency, 142
record and recall, 143
and revisiting/reinforcing content, 143–44, 207
short-term, limits to, 76–78, 141
and standing out, 143
widowpaning concept, 2
The Memory Book (Lorayne and Lucas), 2
mentors/coaches, 13, 215
metaphors, using effectively, 215
methods of instruction. *See* instructional methods
mind map, group, 23
mind mapping
    as program development tool, 168–70
    for reinforcing/revisiting content, 187
    using during technical training, 208–9
models, 65
modules, individual
    in eLearing environments, 221
    rehearsing, 172
motivation, motivators. *ee also* energizers
    basic principles, 37, 51–53
    behaviors to avoid and to foster, 38–43
    and choices, 48–49
    creating a need, 43–44
    examples, 45, 146–52, 191, 199–203
    and interpersonal relations, 13, 23, 48, 89, 182
    and relevance of content, 45
    respecting/praising participants, 45, 47–48
    and self-motivation, 38, 44
    and trainer excitement, 47, 51
MOVE approach, 146
Mucciolo, Tom and Ric, 56
music, as training aid, 2, 95, 232

needs assessments, 15–16, 165
"Need to Know" content, 171, 183–84
networking
    allowing at start of training, 25
    informal, during meetings, 239
    and interpersonal relationships, 13, 23, 48, 89, 182
    providing opportunities for, 51–52, 145, 190
"Never Need to Know" set, 171
Newstrom, John, 192
new-twist approach to presentation design, 145–46
"Nice to Know" content, 171, 183–84

90/20/4 rule, 234
90/20/8 rule, 27, 184
notes pages, in resource materials, 129

objectives, long-range, 47
object lessons, 202
objects, tangible, enhancing presentations using, 65
offline and online work during computer training, 216
off-the-shelf training programs
   Buy or Build Checklist, 244
   evaluating, 245
   selecting/modifying/customizing, 166–67
101 Games for Trainers (Pick), 202
online classes. *See* eLearning/online courses
opaque projectors, 61
openers
   effective, guidelines, 24–26, 155–57
   icebreakers *vs.*, 24
   importance, 190
   for online courses, 224
   for technical training programs, 197–98
   for webinars/virtual classes, 235
optimism, communicating, 51
orientation and previews, at start of presentations, 152
outside resources, when to use, 163–66

panel discussions, 100
PAPER Cycle poster, 62–63
Partial Handouts, 128
participants. *See also* applying/using content; classroom management techniques (IL-PC); environment, physical; presenting programs/training; small groups
   assessing language skills, 19–21
   attention spans, 140
   beneficial competition among, 46–47
   customizing programs for, 129
   desire for practical and personal solutions, 28
   difficult, strategies for handling, 18–19, 228–29
   eliciting new ideas from, 153
   emphasizing discovery and participation, xiv, 31, 52, 81, 88–89, 184–86
   encouraging interactions among, 227
   encouraging questions, 40, 42
   enjoyment of conversations, 83
   evaluating, 194–95, 231
   explaining instructor role to, 88
   handling cultural and generational differences, 50–53
   identifying levels of influence, 21–22

individual motives, valuing, 47–48
interest assessment, 18
knowledge and skills assessments, 17–18, 214–15
learning processes, 3, 49–50, 58–60, 101, 107–8
listening time *vs.* retention time, 144
making choices as source of motivation, 48–49
maximizing involvement and learning by, 228
motivating, energizing, 38–49, 146–2
numbers of, 21–22, 70
obtaining feedback from, 173–75
offering choices to, 115
one-on-one connections with, 48
orienting, previewing program with, 152
passivity/resistance in, overcoming, 39, 227, 229–30
providing a safe environment for learning, 230
providing resource materials to, 123–24
quick *vs.* analytical, 116
returning from breaks, 104–5
sharing individual's questions with the group, 94
treating with respect, 28, 40, 45–46, 82, 95, 152, 217
in webinars, verifying engagement of, 234

past, present, future approach to presentation design, 145
paternal/simplistic language, 19–20
payers, designing training for, 16
Peoples, David A., 55, 153–54
performance problems, addressing through training, 8–11
Performance Solutions Cube, 9–11
personal contact, as motivator, 38–39
personal projects, encouraging during asynchronous training, 226
physical environment. *See* environment, physical
pictures, as visual aids, 61–62
Pike, Bob
  biographical sketch, xiii
  games for trainers books, 202
Pike's Laws of Adult Learning, 4–7, 28, 82
pilot programs, 164, 173
Platform Projector, 61
PLIP (Personal Learning Insights Profile), 177
Pluth, Becky Pike, 233
poetry, reinforcing content using, 154
political advertising, 141
pop quizzes, 198
posters, 62
Post-its, 206
post-training strategies, 8
"potato activity," 91

PowerPoint presentations, 1, 55, 60–61
practical *vs.* informative learning preference, 49–50
praise, importance, 45, 154
preoccupation, distractions, handling, 24–25
Presentations Plus (Peoples), 55
presenting programs/training. *See also* designing/developing programs; motivation, motivators
  answering questions, 153
  building support, 157–58
  communicating effectively, 161–62
  conclusions, strong, 140, 153–55
  definitions, 139
  delivering, make or break tips, 239–40
  effective teaching techniques, 2, 168–72
  eliciting new ideas, 153
  evaluating participants' knowledge and experience, 152
  evaluation effectiveness, 194–95
  explaining program objectives, 152
  generating desire to learn, 34
  generating interest, 34
  identifying actions for follow up, 34, 153
  identifying learning goals, 140
  incorporating outside resources, 163–66
  methods and involvement techniques, 34
  motivators and energizers, 146–2
  off-the-shelf programs, 166–67
  openings, effective, 155–7
  orientation, previewing, 152
  powerful, characteristics, 139
  providing information in bits/chunks, 141
  reviewing resource materials as ice breaker, 123
  revisiting/reinforcing key points, 152–53
  theory and skill sessions, 146, 155
  transitions, overview, 158–59
  using computer graphics, PowerPoint, 60–61
  using videos/films, 57–60
  webinars/virtual class, 235–37
pre-session activities, 224
primacy, 142
"prisoner" interest level, 18
program development. *See* designing/developing programs
projectors, video, 57–60, 67
projects
  completing, being flexible about, 94
  effective, designing, 114–15
  as method of instruction, 104

promises, as motivational tool, 148–49, 200
props, 201–2
provocative statements, 150

questionnaires, tests and assessments *vs.*, 180
questions and answers
    handling effectively, 159–60
    as method of instruction, 98
    as motivational tool, 40, 42, 148, 200
    during presentations, 153, 204–5
    in small group settings, 231
    during webinars, planning for, 234
questions on name tags, 198
quotations, unusual
    as motivational tool, 201–2
    punctuating conclusions using, 154

realism, adding using visual aids, 57
RECAP approach, 146
recency (memory concept), 142
recognizing participant contributions
    as motivational tool, 45–46, 154
    providing privately, 52
record and recall (memory concept), 143
recruitment problems, corrective strategies, 10
reference lists and sheets, 132
reflection, allowing time for, 52, 93
reflective *vs.* participative learning preference, 49–50
reinforcing/revisiting content. *See also* learning; memory; retaining information
    approaches to, 187–89
    eLearning for, 222
    emphasizing applicability/relevance, 25, 27–29, 35, 40, 45, 48, 51–52, 83, 137
    importance, 83, 143, 152–53
    including in design process, 27
    for online courses, 224
    and retention, 207
    revisiting *vs.*, 143–44
    stacking/linking, 207–8
    visual aids for, 56–57, 138, 152, 203, 207
    when using outside consultants, 166
relevance, emphasizing. *See* applying/using content
reliability of assessment tools, verifying, 181
researching training topics, 23–24, 32–33
resource materials workbook
    activity guide sheets, 130–31
    Biographic Sketch, 126

    charts, 133
    checklist of additional ideas, 137
    diagrams, 135
    flow charts, 136
    follow-up discussion sheets, 131
    gathering materials for, 29–30
    "How to Use This Workbook" page, 127
    note pages, 129
    partial handouts, 128
    providing, benefits, 123–24
    reference lists, 132
    reference sheets, 134
    Table of Contents, 124
    Welcome Letter, 125
resources, external, choosing, 246
responsibility, personal, reinforcing, 53
retaining information. *See also* learning; memory
    and chunking, 142, 171
    and group involvement, 81
    and listening time, 144
    and reinforcing content, 207
    research findings, 144
    technical training, 207–10
    visual aids and, 57
Revisiting component (C.P.R. concept), 187–89
Reynolds, J. K., 83–84
role-playing
    as instruction method, 102
    Living Up to Your Potential exercise, 111–2
    quick tips, 113
    role reversal exercise, 112–13
    as skill practice, 109
    written role plays, 110
room preparation/set up. *See also* environment, physical
    arranging, impact on group involvement, 84–85
    for computer training, 211–2
    exit locations, 70
    and group participation, 84–85
    importance, 29–30, 67–68
    set up diagram, 30–31
    size and shape, 70
Rosenberg, Marc, 221
Rosenshine, Barak, 84
Rosenthal, R., 139

Schuck, R. F., 17
screen curtain technique, 215
screens
    computers, and image resolution, 73
    laying out visuals for, 72
    for projected videos, locating within room, 71
    for projected visuals, surface and size, 69
seating arrangements, 70–71, 73
self-discipline, instructors' need for, 87–88
self-esteem of participants, enhancing, 25–26, 228
self-generated data. *See* data, participants' own, validity of
self-interest, 28, 38
self-paced projects, 216
sendees (participants), 16
senders (managers), 16
sharing stories, experiences, 201
short-term memory, limits to, 76–78, 141
shows of hands, 147–48
Silent Messages (Mehrabian), 27
simulators, using effectively, 65
skills practice
    activities during, 155
    guided practice, 84
    role play *vs.*, 109
    using to create excitement during technical training, 207
    videoing for feedback, 58
small groups. *See also* presenting programs/training
    advantages of using, 3, 229
    asking and answering questions using, 40–41, 160, 187, 231
    buzz groups, 102
    changing around during training, 230–31
    developing personal responsibility using, 44, 46
    discussions in, 5, 40
    flip charts, 63
    handling problems within, 88
    and interpersonal relations, 48
    leaders, 51, 85–86, 90, 95, 150, 229
    managing, dynamics within, 89–90
    maximizing learning using, 12, 58–59
    mentoring in, 215
    networking opportunities, 145
    and participating learners, 50
    practicing skills in, 59–60
    promoting involvement using, 85, 148
    rotating roles within, 51
    setting up, considerations, 22–23, 230

scribes, 230
  sharing action ideas in, 94
  synchronous online classes, 224
  turning control over to, 12–14, 22
  using effectively, 51–53, 94, 108, 110–14, 117, 131, 187–91, 228–32
socializer interest level, 18
socializing
  making use of during training, 83
  for online courses, options, 223
speakers, effective, characteristics, 2
specific structure vs. general structure learning preference, 49–50
standing on the line exercise, 199
standing out, being memorable, 143–44
starting/ending on time
  breaks, 44, 90, 104–5, 132, 150, 191
  importance, 89, 94
  webinars, 235–37
statistics, unusual, citing, 150–52, 201–2
stories, sharing, 146–47, 201–2
submit boxes for asynchronous training, 226
support, building during presentations, 157–58
symposia, 100
synchronous online classes, 221–22, 224–26
systems problems, corrective strategies, 10

Table of Contents (for resource materials), 124
tape flags, 206, 213
T–E–A approach (Theory Experience Awareness), 93
teach and learn energizers, 28, 191
teaching techniques, effective, 168–72
team building, 215
technical training
  building excitement during, 205–6
  enhancing memory and retention, 207–10
  generating and answering questions, 204–5
  identifying goals for, 197
  motivators, 199–203
  openers, 197–18
  standing on the line exercise, 199
television receivers, type size minimums, 73
telling, asking vs., 42–43
tests, questionnaires and assessments vs., 180
theory and skill sessions, 146, 155–57
Thomson Job Input Study, 221
time of day, and training schedules, 23
time saving techniques, 55–57

Top 10 Lists, 187
TPR (tools participants, responsibilities) energizer, 191–2
training programs. *See also* environment, physical; instructors/trainers; presenting programs/training; technical training; visual aids, graphics
    creating advisory committee for, 17
    and creating climate for self-motivation, 38
    deciding to buy or build new, 243–44
    effective, program development approach, 168–75
    evaluation strategies, 194–95
    and helping participants feel important, 28
    identifying goals, 8, 23–24, 82–83, 140, 163, 197
    IL-PC, basic characteristics, 13, 192
    importance of organized support materials, 123
    needs assessments, 15–16
    90/20/8 rule, 27
    off-the-shelf, customizing, 166–67
    openers *vs.* icebreakers, 24
    participatory approach, 3
    planning approach, 24–25
    problems during, corrective strategies, 11
    providing choices during, 48–49
    purpose, 2
    researching training topics, 23–24
    and training as a process, 8
    using outside resources, 163–166
Train-the-Trainer workshops, 30–31, 60
Transfer of Training (Newstrom and Broade), 192
transfer strategies, 192
transitions, approaches to, 158–60
triad question approach, 188
Tricks for Trainers (Arch), 202
Tuning the Human Instrument (Halpern), 2
"Two Cents Worth" process, 204
typefaces, font sizes for visuals, 73
Tyson, Lynn, 58

University Associates Annual for Developing Human Resources, 133
upper-case letters, in visuals, 73–74
Use Both Sides of Your Brain (Buzan), 27, 144, 208

"vacationer" interest level, 18
validating assessments before using, 181
value-added questions, 116
variety
    adding, suggestions for, 186
    in group leaders, benefits, 229

Index

   importance of, 26, 34, 51
   in room set ups, 239
   as tool for maintaining interest, 45, 51, 166, 172, 223
   as tool for reinforcing learning, 138, 152, 203, 207
   using in webinars/virtual classes, 235
video projectors, 58
videos/films
   choosing, questions to ask, 57–58
   cost-saving approaches to using, 60
   creating in-house presentations using, 60
   equipment for displaying, 58
   introducing, 58
   minimum font size and screen resolution, 73
   of participants, using during skills practices, 58
visit the wall energizer, 191
visual aids, graphics
   adding realism using, 57
   alternatives to numbering, 76
   attracting attention using, 55–56
   chalkboard and whiteboards, 63
   computer graphics, PowerPoint, 60–61
   and coverage of key points, 57
   display equipment, 58
   effective, characteristics, 66
   emphasizing pictures over words, 74
   flannel graphics/flannel boards, 64–65
   flip charts, 63–64
   to help clarify or avoid misunderstandings, 56–57
   as illustrations of spoken concepts, 56
   models, 65
   as organizing aid, 57
   physical objects, 65
   pictures, 61–62
   positioning information on, 75
   posters, 62
   preparing room and equipment for, 67–70
   projected *vs.* nonprojected, 55
   props, 152
   reasons for using, 55
   reinforcing content using, 56–57, 138, 152, 203, 207
   simulators, 65
   during technical training, 199
   as time and money savers, 57
   tips for pre paring, 72
   using both landscape and portrait modes, 75
   using color, 75

vertical lettering, 76
videos/films, 57–60
for webinars, reviewing with producer, 234
white space, 74
windowpaning concept, 76–78
voice over IP (VoIP), 234

Wang, M. C., 17
web-based instructional design. *See* eLearning/online courses
Webinars Factors (Pluth), 233
webinars/virtual classes
    applying classroom management techniques to, 233
    breakout sessions, 234–5
    delivering, tips for, 233, 235–37
    90/20/4 rule, 27, 234
    openers and closers, 235
    previewing/mastering needed technologies, 234
    producers, reviewing materials with, 234
    rehearsing, 234
    starting small, 234
Welcome Letter (resource materials), 125
"Where to Go" content, 183–84
whiteboards, 63
white space, 74
windowpaning concept, 2, 76–78, 187
WolfVision presentations, 55, 61
words, on visuals, limiting, 72
work groups. *See* small groups
Worthington, L. A., 13, 27

YouTube Channels, private, 60

Made in the USA
San Bernardino, CA
10 May 2019